KAREN BROWN'S

French
Country Inns & Itineraries

OTHER KAREN BROWN TITLES

Austrian Country Inns & Castles

California Country Inns & Itineraries

English Country Bed & Breakfasts

English, Welsh & Scottish Country Hotels & Itineraries

French Country Bed & Breakfasts

French Country Inns & Itineraries

German Country Inns & Itineraries

Irish Country Inns

Italian Country Bed & Breakfasts

Italian Country Inns & Itineraries

Scandinavian Country Inns & Manors

Portuguese Country Inns & Pousadas

Spanish Country Inns & Paradors

Swiss Country Inns & Chalets

KAREN BROWN'S

French Country Inns & Itineraries

Written by

KAREN BROWN

Sketches by Barbara Tapp

Cover Art by Jann Pollard

Karen Brown's Country Inn Series

Editors: Karen Brown, Clare Brown, June Brown, Iris Sandilands
Technical support: William H. Brown III, Aide-de-camp: William H. Brown

Illustrations: Barbara Tapp, Cover painting: Jann Pollard
Maps: Cassell Design

This book is written in cooperation with:
Town and Country - Hillsdale Travel, San Mateo, CA 94401

Distributed by
The Globe Pequot Press, 138 West Main Street, Chester, CT 06412

Library of Congress Cataloging-in-Publication Data

Brown, Karen
    Karen Brown's French country inns & itineraries / written by Karen
Brown : sketches by Barbara Tapp.
       p.   cm. -- (Karen Brown's country inn series)
    Includes indexes.
    ISBN 0-930328-02-7 : $14.95
    1. Hotels, taverns, etc.--France--Guide-books. 2. Castles-
-France--Guide-books. 3. France--Description and travel--1975--
-Guide-books. I. Title. II. Title: French country inns &
itineraries, III. Title: French country inns and itineraries.
IV. Series.
TX907.5.F7B76   1992
647.944401--dc20   91-40774
                                                      CIP

To Rick with Love

Contents

COUNTRYSIDE HOTELS

INDEXES

 *Introduction*

Yes, you can fly to Paris, eat hamburgers, stay in an Americanized hotel and return home safely with stacks of snapshots. If you choose, though, you can travel to France and explore it. You can eat, sleep and drink France, venture off into the country, meet the French and return home with a load of special memories as well as snapshots to recall them.

To tempt you, hundreds of magnificent châteaux, cozy inns and elegant manors owned and managed by some of the warmest and most fascinating people to be found anywhere are tucked away in the French countryside. Many of them, designed and built centuries ago as private residences, are in superb locations, have beautiful surroundings and, fortunately for the traveller, have been turned into hotels. As travellers, we can take full advantage of this opportunity to live France every minute, twenty-four hours a day.

France has much to offer the inventive and adventurous traveller. This book strives to supply enough information to stimulate the interest and imagination of just such people. Beyond the boundaries of Paris, the French provinces are as varied from each other as individual countries and deserve to be visited and explored.

PURPOSE OF THIS GUIDE

This guide is written with two main objectives: to describe the most charming, beguiling lodging throughout France and to "tie" them together with itineraries that include enough details so that travellers can plan their own holiday. The aim is not simply to inform you of the fact that these places exist, but to encourage you to go and see for yourself: explore towns and villages not emphasized on tours and stay at inns that truly reflect the French lifestyle. This book contains all of the necessary ingredients to assist you with your travel arrangements: easy-to-follow itineraries to serve as guidelines, and descriptions of recommended charming hotels throughout France.

Any guide which tries to be all things to all people fails. This guide does not try to give in-depth information on sightseeing - just highlights of some of the most interesting and appealing places. It will be necessary to supplement this guide with detailed reference guides and regional maps. This guide does not try to give a comprehensive, but, rather, a selective listing of hotels in France. On each research trip every attempt is made to investigate as many "new" and promising hotels as possible, and to revisit currently recommended hotels when feedback from readers makes us question if the standards of welcome and accommodation have changed. When a substantial number of new hotels are added to a revised edition, the entire list of recommended hotels is re-evaluated in order to offer a list that reflects only the very best of what France has to offer.

This guide does not try to appeal to everyone. Tastes and preferences vary. This book is definitely prejudiced: the hotels included are ones we have seen and liked. It might be an elegant château dominating a bank of the Loire River or a cozy converted mill tucked into the landscape of the Dordogne Valley. But there is a common denominator from country cottage to stately mansion - they all have charm. Our theory is that where you stay each night matters. Your hotels should add the touch of perfection that makes your holiday very special: the memories you bring home should be of more than just museums, landmarks and palace tours. Such sights are important, but with this guide you can add a romantic element to your trip: travelling the enchanting back roads of France and staying in picturesque hideaways.

2   *Introduction*

CLOTHING

France is a country that stretches some twelve hundred kilometers from Calais in the north to Nice on the Riviera in the south. Expect changes in the weather, regardless of the season and particularly if you are making a grand tour. For winter bring warm coats, sweaters, gloves, snug hats and boots. The rest of the year a layered effect will equip you for any kind of weather: skirts or trousers combined with blouses or shirts which can then be "built upon" with layers of sweaters depending upon the chill of the day. A raincoat is a must, along with a folding umbrella. Sturdy, comfortable walking shoes are recommended not only for roaming the countryside and mountain trails, but also for negotiating cobbled streets. Daytime dress is casual, but in the evening it is appropriate to dress for dinner. Consider yourself a guest in a private home, as that could be the situation.

CREDIT CARDS

Most major cards are accepted widely by stores, restaurants and hotels. However, when a hotel does not accept credit cards the fact that it does not is indicated by "None" in the details under the hotel description. When a hotel does welcome "plastic payment", the type of card is identified by the following abbreviations: AX - American Express, VS - Visa, MC - MasterCard, or simply - All major.

CURRENT

If you are taking any electrical appliances made for use in the United States you will need a transformer plus a Continental two-pin adapter. A voltage of 220 AC current at 50 cycles per second is almost country wide, though in remote areas you may encounter 120V. The voltage is often displayed on the socket.

DRIVING

BELTS: It is mandatory and strictly enforced in France that every passenger wears a seat belt. Children under ten years of age must not sit in the front seat.

CAR RENTAL: All major car rental companies are represented throughout France at airports and in major cities, but it is wise to consult your travel agent on details of car hire. Reservation and prepayment in the United States is not necessarily cheaper but will ensure a guaranteed fixed price. Car companies in collaboration with airlines often offer a variety of rental packages. Be sure to investigate the options available as it might prove financially beneficial to book a car at the same time you purchase your airline ticket. However, taxes and insurance must be paid locally and there are often surcharges for returning the vehicle to a place other than the originating rental location.

DRIVER'S LICENSE: A valid driver's license is accepted in France if a stay does not exceed one year. An International Driver's License, however, is a useful supplement to your travel documents. The minimum driving age is eighteen.

DRUNK DRIVING: It is a very serious offense to drive when you have been drinking. Therefore, as at home, do not drink and drive.

GASOLINE: Prices far exceed those in the United States. There are two grades throughout France: "Essense" (lower octane ratings) and "Super". "Faites le plein, s'il vous plait" translates as "Fill her up, please". At some self-service stations one must pay in advance, before using the pumps. Wonderfully convenient, credit cards such as MasterCard and Visa are now accepted as payment, but company cards such as "Shell" are not.

PARKING: It is illegal to park a car in the same place for more than twenty-four hours. In larger towns it is often customary that on the first fifteen days of a month parking is permitted on the side of the road whose building addresses are odd numbers, and from the sixteenth to the end of the month on the even-numbered side of the road. Parking is prohibited in front of hospitals, police stations and post offices. Blue Zones restrict parking to just one hour and require that you place a disc in your car window on Monday to Saturday from 9:00am to 12:30pm and again from 2:30pm to 7:00pm. Discs can be purchased at police stations and tobacco shops. Grey Zones are metered zones and a fee must be paid between the hours of 9:00am and 7:00pm.

ROADS: The French highway network consists of autoroutes (similar to our freeways), péages (autoroutes on which a toll is charged) and secondary roads (also excellent highways). In recent years the policy concerning drivers who exceed speed limits has changed drastically.   Posted speed limits are now strictly enforced and fines are hefty.   Traffic moves fast on the autoroutes and toll roads with speed limits of 130 kph (81 mph).   On the secondary highways the speed limit is 90 kph (56 mph).   The speed limit within city and town limits is usually 60 kph (38 mph).

Charges on toll roads are assessed according to the distance travelled.   A travel ticket is issued on entry and the toll is paid on leaving the autoroute.   The ticket will outline costs for distance travelled for various types of vehicles.   It is expensive to travel on toll roads, so weigh the advantage of time versus cost carefully.   If you have unlimited time and a limited budget you may prefer the smaller freeways and country roads.   A suggestion would be to use the autoroutes to navigate in and out of, or bypass, large cities and then return to the country roads.   At toll booths French francs are the only acceptable currency and travellers' checks of any kind are not accepted for payment.

ROAD SIGNS: Before starting on the road, prepare by learning international driving signs so that you can obey all the rules of the road and avoid the mistake of heading the wrong way down a small street or parking in a restricted area.   There are several basic sign shapes.   The triangular signs warn that there is danger ahead.   The circular signs indicate compulsory rules and information.   The square signs provide information as to phones, parking, camping, etc.

HOTELS

DESCRIPTIONS: In the second section of this guide you will find a selective listing of hotels that are referenced alphabetically by town.   Every hotel included has been personally visited by myself or a member of our staff.   It is impossible to revisit every hotel on a research trip as there are always new regions and hotels to investigate, but on each journey I try to "check up" on as many as possible.   I also rely on feedback from readers, follow up on any complaints and eliminate hotels that do not maintain their quality of service, accommodation and welcome.

Since the first edition of *French Country Inns & Châteaux* (now titled *French Country Inns & Itineraries)* the accommodation described and recommended has expanded to reflect a wider range of style and type. Places to stay now include private châteaux in addition to château-hotels, hôstelleries, hotels, old mills, country inns and restaurants with rooms. The accommodation varies from luxurious to country-cozy, but it is all charming, quaint and typically French. However, the innkeepers themselves have asked me to stress the difference in services offered between a "hôtel" and a private home. A private châteaux is not a hotel, but rather a residence whose owners offer overnight accommodation and, in some cases, an evening meal ("Table d'Hôte"). The private châteaux recommended in this guide are all very professional and approach their offer of accommodation as a business, not a hobby. They have opened up their homes with a desire to host travellers from all over the world and supplement the never-ending cost of maintaining their properties. The staff is often limited to the hosts themselves and guests should not expect the same services as in a hotel. There is not always room service, in-room phones, night porter or hotel switchboard. Meals other than breakfast, if offered, are on a Table d'Hôte basis, which is usually dining with your hosts and other guests and sharing a set three or four course meal. Because, unlike a restaurant, the homes do not have a large supply of food on hand, if you would like to dine where Table d'Hôte is offered, it is necessary to make arrangements in advance.

Private châteaux and small country inn stays are intended for travellers who want to meet the French, who are willing to conquer their inhibitions and to speak a few French phrases and who prefer antiques and historic charm to a modern plumbing system. People who seek personal experiences and unforgettable accommodation rather than predictable motel-like rooms will appreciate the country inns and château-hotels recommended in this book. The appeal of a little inn with simple furnishings will beckon some, while the glamour of ornate ballrooms dressed with crystal chandeliers and gilt mirrors will appeal to others. I have tried to describe as clearly and accurately as possible what each hotel or private home and setting have to offer so that you can make a choice to suit your own preferences. But although the type of accommodation recommended in this guide ranges from luxurious to country-cozy, it is always memorable, reflecting authentic French taste and style.

RATES AND INFORMATION: Due to the fluctuating exchange rate and the range of prices available at each hotel, giving travellers an accurate idea of cost is difficult. Quoting rates in dollars or ranges proved inaccurate from the moment previous books went to press. With this edition, in the hopes of providing more accurate information, we quote 1992 rates as provided by the hotels. The rates given are for the LEAST expensive to the MOST expensive double room inclusive of tax and breakfast, for two persons. Some hotels only quote rates including breakfast and dinner, and when that is the case we have noted it in the listing, so please read carefully. If you travel off-season and ask for a room without a private bath you will pay a rate lower than we have published. Please ALWAYS CHECK prices and terms with hotels when making bookings.

RESERVATIONS: People often ask, "Do I need a hotel reservation?" The answer really depends on how flexible you want to be, how tight your schedule is, during which season you are travelling, and how disappointed you would be if your first choice were unavailable.

Reservations are confining and lock you into a solid framework. Most hotels will want a deposit to hold your room and frequently refunds are difficult should you change your plans - especially at the last minute. In France a hotel is not required by law to refund a deposit regardless of the cancellation notice given. Although reservations can thus be restrictive, it is also important to realize that major tourist cities can be completely sold out during the peak season of June to September. Hotel space in the cities is especially crowded during annually scheduled events. So unless you don't mind taking your chances on a last-minute cancellation, staying in larger hotels or on the outskirts of a town, it is best to make a reservation. Space in the countryside is a little easier. If you want to plan your travels around a special little inn, reservations should be made as soon as travel dates are firm.

Options for making reservations are detailed below and on the following pages.

Fax: More and more hotels are realizing the ease of making reservations by fax and therefore fax machines are becoming more and more common in hotels throughout Europe. If you have access to a fax, this is the most expedient and efficient way to contact a hotel. If you do not have a fax, many copy and office supply stores will let you use theirs for a fee, both to send and receive. Because you are contacting a machine and not a person, you don't have to worry about what time it is in France. In fact the time difference often works to your advantage: it is possible to fax in the afternoon, and while you sleep (daytime in France) a hotel will often reply and an answer will await you the next morning. We have included fax numbers on the hotel description pages when available.

Letter: If you start early, you can write to the hotels directly for your reservations. There are certainly many benefits to this method in that you can be specific as to your exact preferences. The important point, because of the language difference, is to be brief in your request. Although most hotels can understand a letter written in English, on page 313 we have provided a reservation request letter written in French with an English translation.

Telephone: One of the most satisfactory ways to make a reservation is to call long distance: the cost is minimal if you dial direct and you can have your answer immediately. If space is not available, you can then decide on an alternative or adjust your dates based on availability. Ask your local operator about the best time to call for the lowest rates. Consider the time difference between the United States and France and try to avoid the hectic morning hours when guests are leaving or during the dinner hour when the chef, who is sometimes also the owner/manager, is occupied with the evening meal.

To phone France, dial 011, then 33, France's international code, and then the local number. The telephone numbers appear as they should be dialed in the hotel description section of this book.

Telex: If you have access to a telex machine, this is another efficient way to reach a hotel.   When a hotel has a telex, the number is included under the hotel listings. Be specific as to your arrival and departure dates, number in your party, and what type of room you want and include your telex number for their response.

Travel Agent: A travel agent can be of great assistance - particularly if your own time is valuable.   A knowledgeable agent can handle the details of your holiday and "tie" it all together for you in a neat little package including hotel reservations, airline tickets, boat tickets, train reservations, ferry schedules, opera tickets, etc. To cover their costs, travel agencies often charge for special travel arrangements. Talk with your local agent, discuss your budget and ask exactly what the agency can do for you and what the charges will be.   Although the travel agency in your town might not be familiar with all the little places in this guide, since many are so tiny that they appear in no other major sources, lend them your book - it is written as a guide for travel agents as well as for individual travellers.   (Note for travel agents who read this guide: most of the small inns in this guide pay no commission.)

U.S. Representative: Hotels that are represented by a United States reservations office will appear in listings by representatives at the end of the hotel descriptions section, beginning on page 315.   Contacting a representative is an extremely convenient way to secure a reservation.   However, the majority of representatives charge for their services, often reserve only the more expensive rooms, or quote a higher price to protect themselves against currency fluctuations.   Ask the individual representatives to detail their charges and then decide if the additional cost is worth your time saved.

ITINERARIES

I have divided France into regions: Normandy, Brittany, the Château Country, Dordogne, Le Lot, Gorges du Tarn, Provence, Gorges du Verdon, Côte d'Azur, a Gourmet Itinerary, and Alsace.   For each region I have organized four- to six-day itineraries. The itineraries can easily be joined together, enabling you to extend your journey into another region if you have the time. These itineraries should be used as guidelines; depending on your own preference, you might choose to establish yourself at one inn as opposed to three or four in a specific region. From the numerous hotels recommended on each itinerary it would perhaps be more restful to establish yourself at one, use it as a base, and branch out from there. Checking in and out, packing and unpacking can be time consuming and tiresome.

Covering the highlights of the regions, these itineraries are set up for touring France by car. You should be able to find an itinerary, or section of an itinerary, to fit your exact time frame and suit your own particular interests. You can tailor-make your own holiday by combining segments of itineraries or using two "back to back". We cannot help, however, adding a recommendation: do not rush. Allow sufficient time to settle into a hotel properly and absorb the special ambiance each has to offer.

Please note that although a hotel is suggested for each destination in an itinerary, the hotel is just that - a SUGGESTION. Alternate hotel recommendations are often located in neighboring towns convenient to the itinerary. Review the itinerary maps. Stars indicate locations of alternate hotels and descriptions of each can be found, alphabetically sequenced by town, in the second section of the book.

MAPS

With each itinerary there is a map showing the routing, overnight hotel locations, alternate hotel locations and suggested places of interest along the way. These are an artist's renderings and are not intended to replace a good commercial map. To supplement the routings you will need a set of detailed maps which will indicate all of the highway numbers, autoroutes, alternative little roads, autoroute access points, exact mileages, etc. Our suggestion would be to purchase a comprehensive selection of both city maps and regional maps before your departure.

Before the Paris and Countryside Hotel Descriptions, there is a map outlining the "arrondissements" of Paris and four section maps of France - Maps I, II, III, and IV that detail by numbered circles all the towns in which hotels are recommended. A list of the numbered circles, their corresponding towns and hotels and the pages on which they are described are referenced on a facing page. The numbers flow across the map to aid you in quickly finding alternative hotels in the area should your first choice be unavailable. Which map a town and hotel appear on is cross-referenced in the hotel description section and in the index.

MONEY

The unit of currency is the French franc, abbreviated to F (1F = 100 centimes). It is generally best to cash ordinary travellers' checks at a bank with a "bureau de change" desk - remember to take your passport for identification. There can be quite large variations in the exchange rates and service charges offered by banks even on the same street. "Bureaux de change" are open twenty-four hours at the Paris Charles de Gaulle, Le Bourget and Orly airports, and are normally open from 7:30am to midnight at major railway stations. Some hotels will exchange money as a service to their guests, but they will approximate the exchange in their favor to guard against daily currency fluctuations.

Banks: Banking hours vary, but in most large towns and cities banks are open Monday to Friday, 9:00am to 4:30pm.   Banks close at midday on a day prior to a national holiday and all day on a Monday if a holiday falls on a Tuesday.   In small towns banks are often closed on Mondays instead of on Saturdays.

POST OFFICES

Post offices are open in most towns from 8:00am to 7:00pm Monday to Friday and from 8:00am to midday on Saturdays.   The address of the Paris post office which is open twenty-four hours a day is 52, rue du Louvre, 75001 Paris.   Traditionally we think of post offices as related to mail service.   In France the post offices do of course perform all of the standard expected services, but in addition telephone calls can be efficiently and relatively inexpensively placed at most post offices.   Almost all French public phones are now operated, like those in the United States, either with coins or cards.   The old-style apparatus requiring tokens or "jetons" has been virtually phased out.

RESTAURANTS

French cuisine is incomparable in art and price.   It is not uncommon to pay more for dinner than for a room.   I have not focused on restaurants, as I do not consider myself a worthy judge of French cuisine.   However, if a hotel has a restaurant it is either mentioned in the description or noted in the details following.   Some of France's most charming hotels are actually "restaurants with rooms", principally restaurants that offer rooms to restaurant patrons.   Where hotels are concerned that have restaurants, generally the menu prices are reflective of the room rates, i.e., an expensive hotel will usually have an expensive restaurant.   In this edition, a number of the private châteaux listed offer "Table d'Hôte".   These "hosted guest tables" range from simple, family style meals to elegantly staged dinners.   If a château privé offers meals on a "Table d'Hôte" basis, it will be referenced in the details following the description.   "Table d'Hôte" does not mean "restaurant"; the

owners prepare meals only when arrangements have been made in advance. It is therefore necessary to make dining reservations when confirming accommodations.

There are ways to save both your money and your appetite for a memorable dinner: fruit and croissants for breakfast; bread, cheese and wine for lunch and an occasional pastry in the afternoon are anything but a sacrifice and can be purchased in grocery stores and patisseries along the way. One word of caution, however: stores customarily close from 12:00 midday to 2:00pm every afternoon, and in small towns from 12:00 midday to 4:00pm. On Mondays most stores are closed all day and only a few are open until midday. However, bakeries, fruit stands, cheese shops and butchers open as early as 8:30am and are even open on Sunday mornings.

Almost all restaurants have a tourist menu or menu of the day. These are set meals which usually include specialties of the house and are quite good and reasonable. Sundays, however, only a few restaurants remain open and rarely do they offer a tourist menu, as French families still regard Sunday dinner as a special outing. Restaurants known for their gourmet cuisine often offer a "menu dégustation", so that a sampling of the chef's many artful creations can be enjoyed by one-time guests.

If you want a quick snack, stop at a bar advertising itself as a "brasserie". Here an omelette, a crepe, various salads or a "croque monsieur" (a ham sandwich toasted with cheese) are normally available, tasty and inexpensive.

Many hotels during their high season prefer overnight guests to dine at their restaurant. Also, some hotels were restaurants first and now offer rooms as a convenience for their restaurant patrons. Such "restaurants with rooms" understandably want to reserve rooms for guests of their dining room. To avoid misunderstandings inquire about a hotel's dining policy when making your room reservation.

The French are known for and justifiably proud of their wine. Each region produces its own special wine, a result of the climate and soil conditions which influence the variety and characteristics of the local grapes. The food specialties of each region are selected to complement the local wine. Without writing another book, it would be impossible to detail all the wines available in France. Do, however, sample the wines of a particular region as you travel it. One can select from a region's most famous and expensive labels or, better still, ask the "sommelier" (wine steward) for his suggestion of a good, local wine.

TOURIST INFORMATION

Syndicat d'Initiative is the name for the tourist offices found in all larger towns and resorts in France (their offices are usually indicated by a sign with a large "I"). These tourist offices are pleased to give advice on local events, timetables for local trains, buses and boats, and often have maps and brochures on the region's points of interest. The main tourist office is located at 127, Avenue Champs Elysées, 75008 Paris (near the George V metro stop, open Monday to Sunday from 9:00am to 8:00pm). Telephone: (01) 47.23.61.72, Telex: 611 984, Fax: (01) 47.23.56.91 There are also 45 regional "Accueil de France" offices, (French Welcome), (open every day all year long) that will make reservations at hotels within their area. No reservation can be made by telephone, nor made for more than 8 days in advance.

Information can be obtained before you leave for France by writing the French Government Tourist Office at any one of the following addresses: 610 Fifth Street, New York, New York 10020; 9454 Wilshire Boulevard, Beverly Hills, California 90212; 645 North Michigan Avenue, Chicago, Illinois 60611-2836; or 2305 Cedar Spring Road, Dallas, Texas 75201.   Or information can be obtained by contacting the Information Center at (900) 990-0040 (9:00am to 6:00pm EST Monday through Friday).   Callers will pay 50 cents per minute for the service and will receive additional, detailed information by mail.

TRAINS

France has an excellent train system that serves major towns and cities.   However, it is often necessary to supplement your travel arrangements with either taxi or car rental to reach the small countryside hamlets and isolated inns.   Depending on the number of people in your travel party it can be more economical to travel by train than by private car, but perhaps not as convenient.   Review your travel plans and select the best mode of travel based on your objectives and budget.   If you decide to travel by train, in addition to point-to-point tickets, there are some unlimited travel passes available to you.   Information, reservations and tickets can now only be obtained through your travel agent.

When using the METRO (tube) or buses in Paris, a "carnet" or packet of ten first- or second-class tickets can be purchased at a savings on the individual ticket price. A "billet de tourisme" is a four- or seven-day tourist ticket that allows you unlimited travel on the Métro and the R.E.R. (regional express trains to nearby suburbs).

Normandy

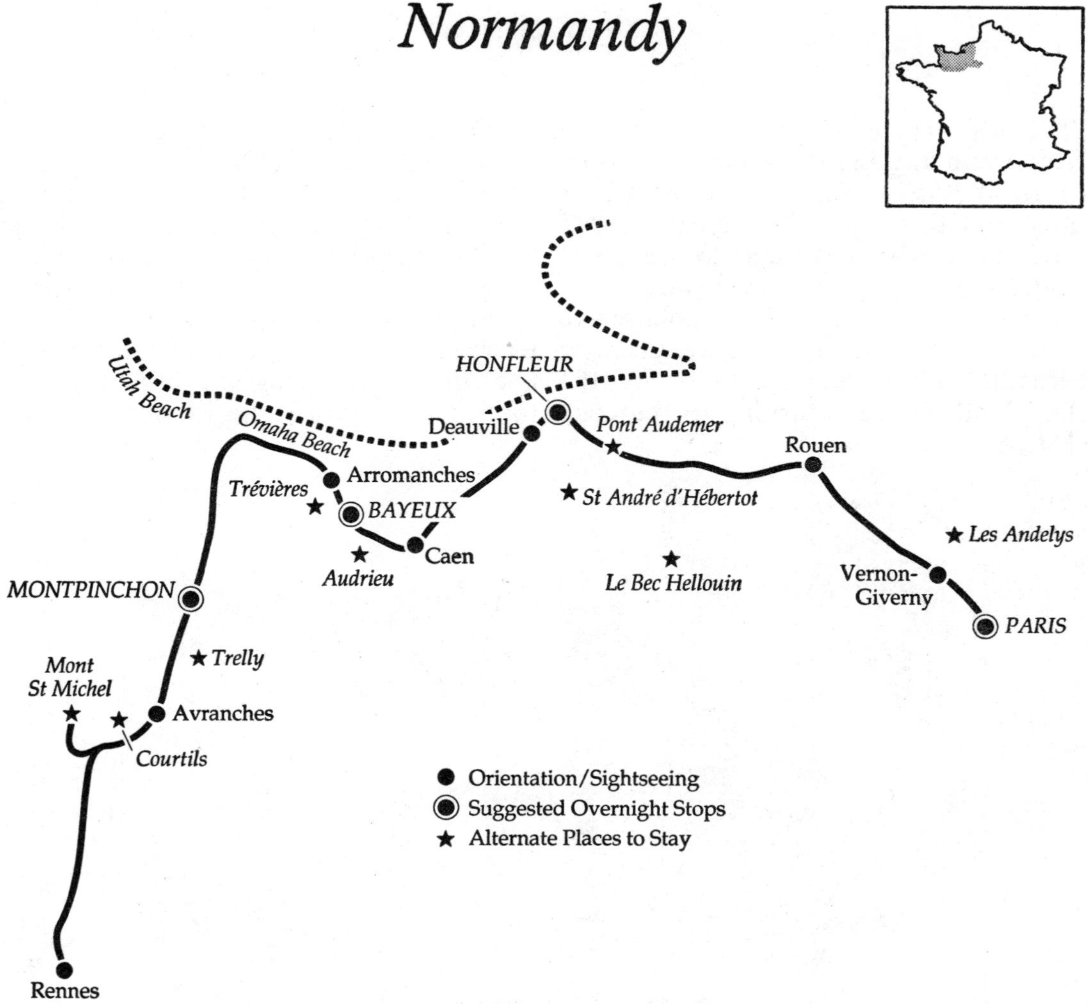

Utah Beach

Omaha Beach

HONFLEUR

Deauville

Pont Audemer

★ St André d'Hébertot

Rouen

Trévières

Arromanches

★

BAYEUX

★ Les Andelys

★

Caen

Audrieu

Le Bec Hellouin

★

Vernon-
Giverny

MONTPINCHON

PARIS

Mont
St Michel

★ Trelly

★

★

Avranches

Courtils

● Orientation/Sightseeing
◎ Suggested Overnight Stops
★ Alternate Places to Stay

Rennes

Normandy

This itinerary takes you to the well-known D-Day beaches where on June 6, 1944 American and British troops landed in a major and dramatic attempt to change the pace of World War II. Decades have passed since then, but pillboxes, although abandoned, remain strategically positioned along the deserted beaches and many vivid memories and tragic losses have yet to be forgotten. Normandy also calls to mind the Vikings and their invasions, as well as William the Conqueror and his. Normandy is also dairies, isolated and beautiful stud farms, mile after mile of rolling green pastures and picturesque resort areas. This itinerary will travel the breadth of Normandy, following the coastline, then progress inland through farmland before returning to the coast to visit the picturesque island of Mont St Michel.

Honfleur

Normandy

Begin your day with what might well prove the highlight of your trip. Follow the Seine north out of Paris to VERNON and GIVERNY, Monet's beautifully restored house, studio, greenhouse and gardens. Here Monet lived and created masterpieces. Walk the gardens and discover the enchantment of the lilypads ... all to understand what inspired the brilliance of the artist. Pack a lunch and take advantage of the fact that for a small fee you can linger and enjoy one of the world's most magnificent spots.

It is not a long drive from Paris to the capital and heart of Normandy, the city of ROUEN, one of the most important tourist centers of northern France. William the Conqueror died here in 1087 and Joan of Arc was burned at the stake in the Place du Vieux Marche in 1431. Although the city was practically destroyed during World War II, it still has many interesting museums and its famous cathedral, so well known to many from Monet's paintings.

Not far from Rouen, deep in the Normandy countryside, is the tanners' town of PONT AUDEMER. It is also the town that the father of William the Conqueror stormed. In spite of World War II destruction, the town managed to salvage a number of old timbered houses which line the rue de la Licorne. Pont Audemer is also the location of a cozy, timbered inn, L'AUBERGE DU VIEUX PUITS, owned by the kind couple, Monsieur and Madame Jacques Foltz. If the hour is approaching midday, you might consider stopping here for lunch.

The next and final destination for today is the picturesque harbor town of HONFLEUR. The narrow, seventeenth-century harbor with its many colorful boats with their flapping sails is lined by numerous, well-preserved old timbered houses. Cafés hug the docks and with the promise of a warm day their tables and umbrellas are set outside, so that customers can enjoy the sun and the picturesque location.   Honfleur is the birthplace of the humorist Alphonse Allais, the musician Erik Satie and the painter Eugene Boudin.   There is a unique wooden church and the house of the King's lieutenant, all that is left of a sixteenth-century château. Wander and explore the streets of this enchanting town.   In addition to having a number of quaint shops and inviting restaurants, Honfleur is still a haven for artists and there are a number of galleries to visit.   For an excellent fish dinner there are numerous restaurants to choose from located on or near the port.

Not more than a mile around the peninsula from Honfleur is a typical Norman timbered farmhouse colored with overflowing flowerboxes at each window, LA FERME ST SIMÉON.   It was purchased not too many years ago by a young couple, the Boelens, who strive to meet your every need.

La Ferme St Siméon
Honfleur

Normandy

La Ferme St Siméon is an excellent hotel and you should consider it "home" for the time you anchor on the Normandy coast. The dining room is cheerful with yellow walls, bright yellow tablecloths and colorful flower arrangements. The cuisine is plentiful and delicious, although expensive. Everything is à la carte. The hotel has recently expanded its accommodation to thirty-nine rooms, every one handsomely decorated with fine antiques. Reservations are a must and should be made long in advance. (Note: A moderately priced alternative would be the Hôtel l'Écrin, located in a residential section of Honfleur.)

With La Ferme St Siméon as your base, be sure to take the time to enjoy Honfleur. It is particularly scenic in the soft light of early morning or in the subtle colors of sunset. There are also other attractive seaside resorts to visit, all within an easy drive of Honfleur. The beachside towns were popular with and inspired many Impressionist artists, especially Monet and Renoir. You might feel as if you have already seen this particular stretch of Normandy coastline if you have spent any time in the Musée d'Orsay in Paris.

TROUVILLE has set the pace on the "Côte de Fleurie" since 1852. A stretch of water divides it from its very close neighbor, DEAUVILLE, perhaps the most elegant resort of them all. Internationally popular, dazzling and luxurious, every variety of entertainment is to be found here. The casinos are a hub of activity and if you visit in the late summer, you will experience the excitement and sophistication of a major summer playground for the rich and famous. For a few weeks each August there is the allure of the race tracks, polo fields, glamorous luncheons and black tie dinners. Celebrities and the wealthy international set come here to cheer their prize thoroughbreds on. Get a relaxed glimpse of these million-dollar babies as they "limber up" with an early morning stretch along Deauville's glorious expanse of sandy beach.

Normandy

Depart from Honfleur to discover the heart of Normandy and to explore the D-Day landing beaches.   Travel through a countryside rich in farmland to CAEN, one of Normandy's largest cities.   Caen is situated on the banks of the Orne, which lost nearly all of its ten thousand buildings in the Allied invasion of 1944.   A large port, it is also the city that William the Conqueror made his seat of government.

Northwest of Caen is BAYEUX, an ancient Roman metropolis that merits an extended visit and serves as a perfect base from which to explore the D-Day beaches.   Once a capital of ancient Gaul, this city was successfully invaded by the Bretons, the Saxons and the Vikings but somehow escaped the Allied invasions which brought with them so much destruction.   As a result, the town still possesses Norman timbered houses, stone mansions and cobblestoned streets.   It is also where the Bayeux tapestry is displayed.   Commissioned in England, this tapestry portrays in fifty-eight dramatic scenes the Battle of Hastings in 1066.   Bayeux is also referred to as a center of lace-making.   In the nineteenth century the craft monopolized the efforts of the village and neighboring towns.   Over five thousand artisans were located here and produced a lace known as bobbin lace.   This kind of lace is made by intertwining and manipulating numerous threads, each from a different bobbin.   Today the five thousand craft centers have been reduced to ten and they are all associated with a center devoted to the preservation of the lace-making heritage of Normandy.   You can visit the Norman Bobbin Lace-Making Center at 5, Place aux Pommes both to view the masters at work and to buy samples of their craft.

Sheltered behind its main gate, the HÔTEL D'ARGOUGES offers accommodation in a quiet country home, just a stroll away from the heart of downtown.   Looking out over a beautiful garden or front courtyard, the bedrooms all have exposed beams and comfortable furniture as well as private shower or bath and phones.

Hôtel d'Argouges
Bayeux

Breakfast can be enjoyed in the privacy of one's room, in the intimate, elegant breakfast salon, or on the back garden terrace overlooking Madame Auregan's vivid flowers. A veritable haven for travellers visiting Bayeux, the Hôtel d'Argouges offers good value in lovely surroundings plus gracious hosts. The Hôtel d'Argouges affords the opportunity to leisurely explore the city and its wealth of attractions. It can be used as a base from which to explore the beaches, or one can depart Bayeux and visit the beaches enroute to the next destination, Montpinchon.

DESTINATION III   MONTPINCHON

After departing Bayeux the main road heading to the northwest intersects with the route that winds along the coast following its curves and the D-day beaches.

The little fishing port of ARROMANCHES LES BAINS, at the center of the British sector, "Gold Beach", was designated to receive the fantastic artificial harbor "Mulberry B" for the disembarkation of ammunitions and supplies. ("Mulberry A" was to be installed on "Omaha Beach", a few miles west at ST LAURENT, VIERVILLE SUR MER and COLLEVILLE, to supply American units.) The Mulberries, designed by British Admiralty engineers, were comprised of massive concrete caissons, floating pier-heads and ten miles of floating pier "roads", towed across the Channel. Landing at nearby Asnelles and Ver sur Mer, the British Fiftieth Division captured Arromanches in the afternoon of June 6, 1944. By the end of August five hundred thousand tons of material had been landed at Mulberry B; half-submerged remnants of the harbor can still be seen. (Mulberry B was destroyed by a freak storm on June 19, 1944.)

Château de la Salle
Montpinchon

Among other displays, the Arromanches Museum shows a film of the 1944 landings which will set the mood for your visit to the beaches. Note: If you are travelling off-season be sure to ask for the headphones with the English commentary.

The traces of war's devastation are a jarring reminder of the fierce and tragic reality of our history. The D-Day beaches stir many emotions. With thoughts, visions and memories, leave the coastline and drive inland across farmland to MONTPINCHON and the CHÂTEAU DE LA SALLE. Once a private estate, this lovely stone mansion is set deep in the Normandy countryside and enjoys the peace and quiet that location has to offer. The Château de la Salle has only ten bedchambers. Each room is large, handsomely decorated and with either bath or shower. The restaurant is intimate with a few heavy wooden tables positioned before a warming fire. The accommodation, the cuisine and the salon warmed by a burning log fire will tempt you to linger at this delightful estate.

DESTINATION IV   MONT ST MICHEL

From Montpinchon travel south in the direction of AVRANCHES. It was here on July 30, 1944 that General Patton began his attack against the German Panzer counter-offensive from Mortain.

From Avranches cross into Brittany to the famous French town of MONT ST MICHEL. One of France's proudest possessions, Mont St Michel is unique, dramatic and definitely a site to visit. The magnificent town is built on a rock two hundred thirty-five feet high and, depending on the tide, is either surrounded by water or by exposed quicksand. Wander up the narrow cobblestoned streets to the crowning twelfth-century abbey and visit the remarkable Gothic and Romanesque complex, culminating in the glories of the "Merveille" (Marvel) - the group of buildings on the north side of the mount. St Michael, the militant archangel, is the appropriate saint for the beaches you have just seen. On the left as you enter under the city gates of Mont St Michel is the entrance to the restaurant of the

HÔTEL MÈRE POULARD.   You will be tempted inside by the smell and cooking display of the famous Mère Poulard omelette.   The preparation of the omelette can be seen from the street and is an attraction in itself.   The eggs are whisked at a tempo and beat set by the chef and then cooked in copper pans over an open fire. You can stay overnight at the Hôtel Mère Poulard, enabling you to experience the town without the midday crowds and tours.   Note: The guest rooms at the Hôtel Mère Poulard are very simple, but there are no deluxe hotels on this tiny island.

From Mont St Michel it is approximately an hour's drive south to the city of RENNES.   From here you can easily return to Paris or, if tempted, journey on into the region of Brittany.   Mont St Michel is also the first destination for the following Brittany itinerary.

Hôtel Mère Poulard
Mont St Michel

Normandy

Brittany

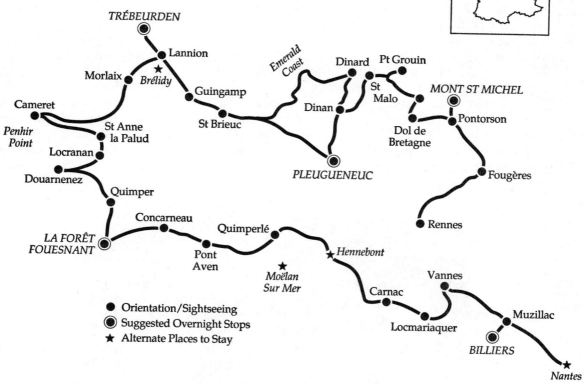

TRÉBEURDEN

Lannion

Morlaix · *Brélidy* · Guingamp

Cameret

Penhir Point · St Anne la Palud

Locranan

Douarnenez

Quimper

Concarneau

LA FORÊT FOUESNANT

Pont Aven

Quimperlé

Moëlan Sur Mer

Emerald Coast

Dinard · Pt Grouin

St Malo

Dinan

MONT ST MICHEL

Pontorson

Dol de Bretagne

St Brieuc

PLEUGUENEUC

Fougères

Rennes

Hennebont

Vannes

Carnac

Muzillac

Locmariaquer

BILLIERS

Nantes

● Orientation/Sightseeing
◉ Suggested Overnight Stops
★ Alternate Places to Stay

Brittany

Brittany is a region of beautiful forests bounded by nearly one thousand miles of coastline. This peninsula, jutting out from the northwest side of France, is culturally different from the rest of the country. The regional language is Breton and traditional costumes are proudly worn by the inhabitants. Crepes or galettes, which are crepes without sugar, filled with ham, eggs or cheese, fish and cider are Brittany's culinary specialties. Most of the houses are fresh white stucco with angled blue-grey roofs. Windmills pop up every so often on the crest of a hill. The people are friendly and their French carries a distinctive accent. This itinerary traces Brittany's coastline from Mont St Michel to Nantes. Each town along the coast is too fascinating to miss. The wooded interior, although not emphasized on this particular itinerary, is also very beautiful and should not be overlooked especially if camping, riding or walking interest you.

Your tour begins at RENNES, the administrative and cultural capital of Brittany. It is a large commercial city but Vieux Rennes, or the old part of town, is composed of quaint narrow streets which are lined by dignified old timbered houses. From Rennes drive north to FOUGÈRES which has a magnificent feudal castle with thirteen large towers isolated on an island.

MONT ST MICHEL crests the coastal skyline approximately sixty-six kilometers from the city of Rennes. The mount has been photographed by millions. This is the militant Archangel Michael's domain. The fantastic two hundred thirty-five foot high church is built on a rock. The distant appearance of the town is that of a child's sand castle, with narrow, cobblestoned streets winding up to the twelfth-century abbey at the top in the center of the town. Mont St Michel is famous for the extreme tide levels which occur every day: at different intervals, according to the type of tide, the city is either completely surrounded by water or by patches of quicksand. Access to the island is across an old causeway that is covered at high tide. Check the tide schedule and then choose a restaurant where you can enjoy a meal or snack and watch the waters surround the island.

The home of Monsieur and Madame Bernard Heyraud is also the HÔTEL MÈRE POULARD, enabling you to stretch out your stay in this island town. The rooms, although not very large, are comfortable though simply furnished. The hotel also has a cheery and bright restaurant which is famous for its Poulard omelette. Please note: Although the restaurant of the hotel is perhaps the best on the island, it does not look out across the water.

Hôtel Mère Poulard
Mont St Michel

DESTINATION II   PLEUGUENEUC

For miles after departing Mont St Michel you will find yourself glancing back at the spectacular citadel until it finally fades on the horizon. From Mont St Michel drive south to PONTORSON and DOL DE BRETAGNE, the capital of the marshland, and then east along the coastline. Heading for St Malo you pass through VIVIER, a large mussel producing area, CANCALE, a picturesque seaside resort, and POINT DU GROUIN where you enjoy a sweeping panorama from CAP FRÉHEL across to Mont St Michel. It is here at Point du Grouin that the beautiful EMERALD COASTLINE begins.

ST MALO, known as the city of Corsairs, was once the lair of pirates. Its setting is beautiful and it has become an important tourist center. The city was destroyed by a Nazi fire in 1944, but the thirteenth- and fourteenth-century ramparts that surround the town have since been restored. It is a wonderful city to explore: the narrow streets at the city center house a number of interesting shops and small restaurants. Linger at lunch time and sample the local crepes (sweet pancakes) filled with butter, sugar, chocolate or jam or the gallettes (wheat crepes) enhanced with cheese, ham, onions or mushrooms and the local, surprisingly potent "cidre". South of St Malo is the walled town of DINAN. Once fortified by the Dukes of Brittany, the town is very old. Dinan is known for its houses built on stilts over the streets and the remnants of its once fortified château. DINARD lies only twenty-two miles north of Dinan. A popular resort, Dinard is a lovely town with many safe and protected beaches. The Emerald Coast between Dinard and Cap Fréhel is impressive, jagged and beautiful.

Château de la Motte Beaumanoir
Pleugueneuc

Not far from this wild coastline is another equally beautiful attraction: the CHÂTEAU DE LA MOTTE BEAUMANOIR. This lovely and spectacular stone manor house is located just four hundred meters south of the town of PLEUGUENEUC which is located on Route 137, forty kilometers west of Rennes. The owners, Charles and Jacqueline Bernard, and their son, Éric, are your warm and gracious hosts.   They moved here from Belgium and it is truly the result of one man's, Charles Bernard's, dream and his personal sense of artistry and labor, that this manor is such an exceptional home and now hotel.   The Bernards accurately describe their home as a dramatic, five-hundred-year-old castle, isolated by vast acres of forest.   On the property they have just completed work on a man-made lake, and stables are available for guests who wish to board their horses.   The Bernards have eight bedrooms, all with private bath, to offer guests.   Handsomely decorated with wall coverings and materials to match the style and period of the castle, six of the rooms face onto the lake and two overlook the grounds at the back. Although the château does not have a formal restaurant, meals will gladly be prepared for guests when requested and served with silver and candlelight in the elegant dining room.

DESTINATION III   TRÉBEURDEN

When you leave Pleugueneuc it is approximately forty-five kilometers to ST BRIEUC, one of the most important industrial centers of the region, located on a bay.   You navigate your way into the town to discover that there are many pretty walks to take, old mansions and majestic townhouses.   Do not miss the fortified cathedral of St Stephen and the fifteenth-century fountain.

The drive continues on to TRÉBEURDEN, one of the northernmost tips of the Breton coastline.   This small town is a very popular and lovely seaside resort set on the hills above the coast, with striking views out to the Grande, Molene and Milliau islands on a clear day.   Yachts anchor off the scattered stretches of sandy beach and shops on the main shopping streets cater to the summer holidaymakers.   Let the season and weather determine your length of stay.

Ti Al-Lannec
Trébeurden

But regardless of whether or not the sun shines, your destination is the charming hotel perched on a point that is convenient to the beaches in warm weather and cozy on a dreary, dark, grey day - the TI AL-LANNEC. The Ti Al-Lannec achieves a feeling of "home away from home", from the smell of croissants baking to the personal touches in the decor. The restaurant is lovely and opens onto glorious views of the coast. The public rooms have been thoughtfully equipped to accommodate the hobbies of the guests and the unpredictable moods of the weather. There are jigsaw puzzles, books and games, in addition to a swing on the lawn and an outdoor, knee-high chess set. Gerard and Danielle Jouanny are responsible for the careful renovation of this once private home and Madame Jouanny's feminine touch is apparent in the sweet choice of prints that decorate the majority of rooms. The bedrooms are all extremely comfortable and invite extended stays. Most of the rooms look out to sea. This is a perfect hotel for families on holiday.

Brittany

When it is time to leave Trébeurden, backtrack to Lannion and head south to take the road which follows the coastline out to the very tip of the peninsula and the lobster port of CAMARET.   In the area there are many scenic peninsulas and the most beautiful of all is PENHIR POINT.   Pass through STE ANNE LA PALUD, one of the most frequented pilgrimage centers in Brittany, to the quaint village LOCRONAN.   Now known for its woodcarvers, it once was called the "city of weavers" when three hundred workers gathered here to weave sails for the British navy.   Located on the square is a group of lovely Renaissance houses. DOUARNENEZ, a lively sardine fishing port, lies to the west of Locronan and QUIMPER, a city famous for its pottery, lies to the south.

From Quimper, it is less than twenty kilometers south to LA FORÊT FOUESNANT and the stately MANOIR DU STANG that offers regal accommodation.   A sixteenth century manor house, Le Manoir du Stang is set behind its own moat and arched gateway and tower and surrounded by well-tended gardens, a small lake, woods and acres of farmland.   The interior is furnished with period pieces in keeping with the mood staged by the handsome facade. Accommodation is offered on a demi-pension basis only and dining is both a gastronomique and visual delight.   Waitresses adorned in costumes of the southern coast of Brittany provide service and lend an air of festivity to the meal.

Manoir du Stang
La Forêt Fouesnant

DESTINATION V   BILLIERS

On the other side of the bay from La Forêt Fouesnant is the attractive city of
CONCARNEAU.   The old port of Concarneau is a walled town which has houses
dating from the fourteenth century.   As with almost all Breton seaside villages,
Concarneau also has its share of white sandy beaches.   From Concarneau continue
on to the peaceful market village of PONT AVEN and then on to the village of
QUIMPERLÉ.   This pretty town is divided by the Laita and Elle rivers.   The
upper town is centered around the church of Our Lady of the Assumption and in
the lower section some interesting old dwellings are grouped around the former
Abbey of Ste Croix.

*Domaine de Rochevilaine
Billiers*

From Quimperlé travel further to the once fortified town of HENNEBONT and then on to the small town of CARNAC, a seaside resort famous for its field of megaliths. Similar to Stonehenge, these huge stones are an important prehistoric find and yet they appear scattered and abandoned in an open field. There are no fences to restrict your exploration nor stands with postcards and mementos. At the far end of the site is a café where you can sample some of the Breton galettes, crepes and cider. A short distance away at LOCMARIAQUER are two additional prehistoric stones: the Merchant's Table and its Great Menhir.

Return to the main road between Vannes and Nantes. At MUZILLAC take the road that leads you to the tip of the Pen-lan peninsula and the small village of BILLIERS. Here on a rocky promontory is a hotel that will leave you with a lasting impression of Brittany - DOMAINE DE ROCHEVILAINE.

The bedrooms of the Domaine de Rochevilaine are found in buildings clustered along the coastal edge. Accommodations are varied in size and decor but they are all attractively furnished. The public rooms are handsome in their appointments and lovely Oriental carpets adorn hardwood floors.

The vast windows in the dining room of the Domaine de Rochevilaine overlook rocky cliffs, and there is a distinct sensation of being shipboard ... all you see from the table is the wild open sea. On sunny days breakfast is enjoyed in the well kept gardens that are protected from salt-water breezes by whitewashed walls.

The Domaine de Rochevilaine is dramatically positioned on Brittany's jagged and rocky coastline. The views from the hotel are stupendous with the sun shining on the glistening sea; or on a stormy day with the wind whipping the waves as they crash against the rocks so near your bedroom window. The setting of this hotel exaggerates Brittany's most spectacular feature - its coastline, and it is a perfect choice for this itinerary's final destination.

Return to the main road and it is a direct route to either VANNES or NANTES. Vannes, the capital city, was constructed around the Cathedral of St Peter and consists largely of ancient houses within thirteenth- and fifteenth-century ramparts. It is a straight line from Vannes to Nantes where your tour of Brittany ends. Nantes was Brittany's capital from the tenth to the fifteenth centuries. It has a beautiful old quarter, Duke's Palace, and Cathedral of St Peter and of St Paul.

Le Mont St Michel

Brittany

Château Country

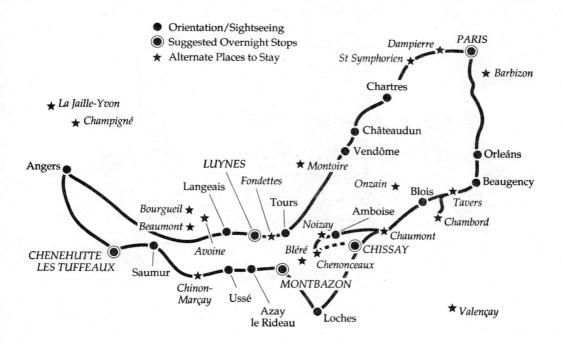

● Orientation/Sightseeing
◉ Suggested Overnight Stops
★ Alternate Places to Stay

PARIS

Dampierre

St Symphorien ★

★ *Barbizon*

Chartres

Châteaudun

Vendôme

Orleáns

★ La Jaille-Yvon

★ *Champigné*

LUYNES

★ *Montoire*

Onzain ★

Beaugency

Angers

Langeais

Fondettes

Blois

Tours

★ *Tavers*

Bourgueil ★

Amboise

★ *Chambord*

Beaumont ★

Noizay

Chaumont

CHENEHUTTE LES TUFFEAUX

Avoine

Bléré ★

CHISSAY

Saumur

Chenonceaux

Chinon-Marçay

Ussé

MONTBAZON

★ *Valençay*

Azay le Rideau

Loches

39

Château Country

A highlight of any holiday in France is a visit to her elegant châteaux nestled along the banks of the Loire. Also known as the "garden of France", the château region conjures up the grandeur and excitement of life at the French Court. This itinerary suggests a route that circles the region and uses a different hotel for each destination. However, the distances are short enough that you can also select just one hotel and use it as a base for exploring the numerous castles.

Château de Chambord

Château Country

An hour southwest of Paris is the city of CHARTRES with its magnificent cathedral. Monopolizing the horizon, the Gothic cathedral is dedicated to Mary, the Holy Mother. Its feminine qualities are best evidenced by its amazing stained-glass windows dappling the church with color and light. The cathedral is considered by many to be the greatest achievement of the Middle Ages, a "stone

Domaine de Beauvois
Luynes

testament" of that period. On most days you find Mr. Malcolm Miller describing the history and design of this marvelous cathedral, his knowledge of Chartres giving an added dimension to any visit. Very British, he is based in Chartres and if you would like to arrange a personal tour, you can write to him care of the cathedral or Chartres' tourist office. From Chartres continue south to TOURS. Located at the junction of the Cher and Loire rivers, Tours has played an important role in history.

Drive west along the north bank of the Loire to the small town of LUYNES and the DOMAINE DE BEAUVOIS.   Here you can go one step beyond just visiting your first château on the Loire; you may stay here for the night.   This fifteenth-century château with its seventeenth-century "improvements" is surrounded by a wooded two-hundred-acre estate and has forty attractive rooms and a heated pool.   Spoil yourself as did the lords and ladies who flocked to the Loire Valley in ages past; enjoy the luxury of the château's accommodation and savor the splendors of its restaurant.   The Domaine de Beauvois offers an enchanting setting.

DESTINATION II   CHENEHUTTE LES TUFFEAUX

Begin your adventures in the Loire Valley by a visit to CHÂTEAU DE LANGEAIS.   Although one of the smaller châteaux in this region, it is beautifully furnished and well worth a visit.   A recent addition to commemorate the royal wedding of Charles VIII and Anne of Brittany that took place on a cold December morning in 1491 is authentically portrayed by a scene staged by wax characters. Built in the fifteenth century, Langeais was completed in a period of four to five years and since then has remained intact.   On a nearby ridge stand the ruins of a tenth-century stone "donjon" or keep, one of Europe's first.   It was a stronghold of the notorious Fulk Nerra ("the Black"), Count of Anjou.

Drive further west to the town of SAUMUR which lies directly on the river's edge. The captivating CHÂTEAU DE SAUMUR is strategically located above the town overlooking the Loire.   The town is very picturesque, set in a region of vineyards famous for their "mousseux" or sparkling wines.

Extending over both banks of the Mayenne on the outskirts of the château region is ANGERS, the former capital of the Dukes of Anjou.   The first castle, built by Fulk

Nerra, was replaced under the thirteenth-century king, Louis IX. During the sixteenth century many of the seventeen massive towers were dismantled, on royal command, to the level of the wall-walk.

LE PRIEURÉ in CHENEHUTTE LES TUFFEAUX is the next destination. This is a dramatic hotel, set high on the hillside, offering a fantastic forty-mile-wide panorama of the Loire Valley. The bedrooms located in the castle proper are very regal in their decor. (However, be aware that there is also a motel-like annex found near the pool.) Enjoy the early evening on the castle terrace overlooking the Loire and make your selections from the enticing menu. The dining room is very elegant and service quite formal.

Le Prieuré
Chenehutte les Tuffeaux

DESTINATION III   MONTBAZON

This morning continue east but this time follow the road along the south bank of the Loire. The first stop is CHINON, one of the oldest castles in France whose fortress straddles the skyline of the town. It is interesting to see the skeleton of the castle, but be prepared to fill in large chunks of the interior with your imagination. The castle is made up of three distinct fortresses: Fort Saint Georges, Château de Milieu, and Château du Coudray, each separated by a deep moat. In 1429, Chinon witnessed the historic encounter between Joan of Arc and Charles the Dauphin. Later that year, inspired by her, he was crowned at Reims as Charles VII, defying the English Henry VI who held Paris as "King of France".

USSÉ is the next destination. The Castle of Ussé, located in the dark forest of Chinon overlooking the Indre, is everything you would expect a castle to be: it has steeples, turrets, towers, chimneys, dormers and enchantment. It is believed to be the castle that inspired Perault to write "Sleeping Beauty".

Domaine de la Tortinière
Montbazon

AZAY LE RIDEAU and its elegant Renaissance château are not far from Ussé. The Château Azay le Rideau is situated on a small island in the Indre and was so beautifully designed and built in 1518 by Gilles Berthelot, a financial adviser of François I, that the King himself took possession. The memory of this ornate château reflecting in the water and framed by wispy trees will linger.

DOMAINE DE LA TORTINIÈRE in Montbazon equals if not surpasses any of the châteaux seen today and serves as an ideally located hotel for touring the region. The château has a fine intricate structure, a lovely pool, grounds designed for romantic strolls, elegant, comfortable bedrooms and a superb restaurant. Each evening a delicious menu is created by the chef in addition to the "à la carte" selection. Mme Denise Olivereau-Capron is your hostess and manages this delightful castle hotel with the help of her three children.

DESTINATION IV   CHISSAY

Southeast of Montbazon is the town of LOCHES, found in the hills along the banks of the Indre, and referred to as the "City of Kings". The ancient castle is the "Acropolis of the Loire"; the buildings around it form what is called "Haute Ville". It was a favorite retreat of King Charles VII and here you will find a copy of the proceedings of Joan of Arc's trial. The king's mistress, Agnes Sorel, was buried in the tower and her portrait is in one of the rooms.

From Loches drive northeast to the lovely CHÂTEAU DE CHAUMONT SUR LOIRE which was built by Charles d'Amboise during the reign of Louis XII. Later the castle was owned by Henry II. After his death, Diane de Poitiers, his mistress, was given the château by his jealous wife, Catherine de Medici, in exchange for the more beautiful Chenonceaux. Surrounded by a spacious park, the castle has a lovely position overlooking the Loire.

Just a few miles to the west of Chaumont sur Loire is another beautiful castle, the CHÂTEAU D'AMBOISE. During the reign of François I court life relished and thrived upon the festivals, masquerades and flourish of the Italian Renaissance. The King finished the wing of the castle begun by Louis XII in an architectural style inspired by the period. He also extended an invitation to Leonardo da Vinci who came to spend his last years at the castle and is buried here. A tour of the castle will also unveil details of its bloody past. The Amboise Conspiracy of 1560 involved a group of Protestant reformers who followed the royal court from Blois to the Château d'Amboise under the pretense of asking the King for permission to practice their religion. However, their plot was betrayed and upon arrival many were hung from the castle battlements, beheaded and quartered or thrown in sacks down to the Loire.

Château de Chenonceaux

A trip to the Loire Valley would lose all significance if the CHÂTEAU DE CHENONCEAUX, only a few miles south of Amboise, were omitted from the itinerary. It gracefully spans the lazy Cher and is known as the "Château of the Six Women": Catherine Briconnet, the builder; Diane de Poitiers, the ever-beautiful; Catherine de Medici, the magnificent; Louise de Lorraine, the inconsolable; Madame Dupin, lover of letters; and Madame Peolouze, lover of antiquity. The château achieved a new dimension with each of its six female occupants. The rooms and bedchambers, elegantly and lavishly furnished, are fun to wander through slowly to avoid missing even the smallest detail.

Chenonceaux merits a leisurely visit and one can linger as the next destination is located, conveniently, just ten kilometers further east. The CHÂTEAU DE CHISSAY is a stunningly beautiful hillside château. Walk through the vaulted stone entry over old cobblestones to reach the inner courtyard and vistas of the Loire Valley. On a twenty-acre estate, with a beautiful pool and elegant restaurant, the Château de Chissay provides a warm and luxurious ambiance and twenty-seven handsome bedrooms.

Château de Chissay
Chissay

DESTINATION V   PARIS

From Chenonceaux retrace a path northeast past Amboise and Chaumont sur Loire and continue on to BLOIS. The castle of Blois is a thirteenth-century château constructed by the royal Orléans family. Highlights of this château are the magnificent François I stairway; Catherine de Medici's bedchamber with its many secret wall panels (used, in the true Medici tradition, to hide jewels, documents and poisons) and the King's bedchamber, where the murder of the Duc de Guise occurred.

The largest of the châteaux, CHAMBORD, is just a short distance further north from Blois. Although almost bare of furniture, it retains its grandeur and enchantment, especially at sunset or shrouded in the morning mist.

The last stretch along the Loire before turning north towards Paris takes you through BEAUGENCY and then ORLÉANS. Beaugency is an ancient town noted for its Notre Dame church. Orléans is famous as the scene of Joan of Arc's greatest triumph, when she raised the English siege in 1429. From Orléans drive back to Paris, the fabulous city that both begins and ends this itinerary.

Azay le Rideau

Dordogne

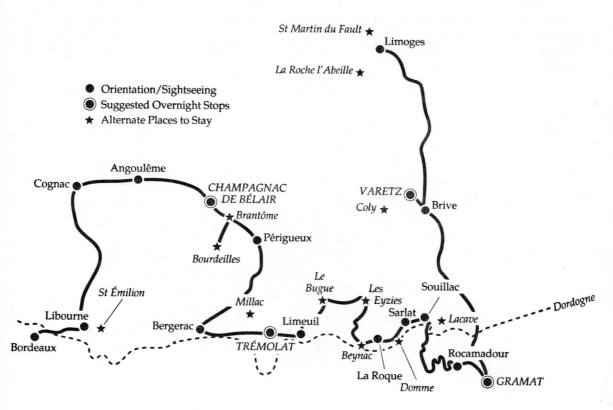

St Martin du Fault ★

● Limoges

La Roche l'Abeille ★

● Orientation/Sightseeing
◉ Suggested Overnight Stops
★ Alternate Places to Stay

Angoulême

Cognac ●

CHAMPAGNAC DE BÉLAIR ◉

★ Brantôme

VARETZ ◉

Coly ★

● Brive

● Périgueux

★ Bourdeilles

Le Bugue ★

Les Eyzies ★

Souillac ●

St Émilion

Millac ★

Sarlat ●

Libourne ●

Bergerac ●

Limeuil ●

★ Lacave

Dordogne

Bordeaux ●

TRÉMOLAT ◉

Beynac ★

La Roque ★

Rocamadour ●

GRAMAT ◉

Domme

49

Dordogne

The Loire Valley is famous. South of the Loire Valley is a lesser known but equally beautiful valley, the Dordogne. Here you will find sleepy country roads, rolling green hills, mountains dressed with vineyards and magnificent châteaux - as one château fades from sight, another seems magically to appear on the horizon. Groves of aspen and birch blaze in the sunlight along the lazy Dordogne as it winds its way through this spendid region of France. This itinerary takes advantage of the Bordeaux wine region and then follows the Dordogne, passing through romantic little villages along the way.

Beynac

Dordogne

The starting point for this itinerary is the beautiful city of BORDEAUX. An important port, the old section is jammed with shops and decorated with ornate fountains and old churches. The name Bordeaux is synonymous with the largest fine wine district on earth: the red wine districts to the north, the Medoc immediately to the south, and all of the country along the north bank of the Dordogne and facing the Medoc across the Gironde. Most of the white wine is grown in the region between the two rivers, an area called "entre deux mers".

This is a region to explore, to visit its marvellous châteaux and their cellars. Leave Bordeaux for LIBOURNE, the center for the wines of ST ÉMILION, POMEROL and FRONSAC. If wine pleases your palate, there are many cellars in the vicinity to sample. Château Videlot lies between Libourne and St Émilion: it is a beautiful house and the owner, Monsieur Jean Pierre Moueix is a true wine connoisseur. The hilltop village of St Émilion is definitely worth a visit and its medieval streets house a number of fine cellars where a selection of regional wines are beautifully displayed and convenient for purchase. It is also in St Émilion, in late September, that the festivities to commemorate the "vendage" or beginning of the harvest are enjoyed in the grandest splendor and tradition. Neighboring the town of St Émilion are two noteworthy châteaux. Château Ausone is the more famous, where you can walk into a ground-floor cellar with a ceiling of vines. Château Cheval Blanc, painted a refreshing cream color, produces some of the most splendid full-bodied red wines. It is generally agreed that Château Petrus, another vineyard, is one of the most outstanding of the Pomerol district.

COGNAC is the name of both a small town and the brandy distilled from grape wine. The Charente Vineyards, now given over exclusively to cognac, originally produced inferior wines sold to seamen from Britain and the Low Countries who ventured here to buy salt. It was only in the seventeenth century that some of these immigrants began "burning" the wine, and once the experiment had been made the word quickly spread. In and around Cognac there are a number of distilleries and warehouses: those of Hennessy and Martell are two of the best known. From Cognac continue east towards ANGOULÊME, founded by the Romans. The upper part of the city is surrounded by ramparts.

LE MOULIN DU ROC awaits you only a short distance from Angoulême. Tucked off a small country road on the outskirts of CHAMPAGNAC DE BÉLAIR is a small seventeenth- and eighteenth-century stone mill, one of France's most splendid little inns. The fourteen rooms, although not large, are each enchanting. Windows throughout the mill overlook the lazy Dronne river, the gardens and the beautiful birch-lined pastures: the waterside setting is peaceful and relaxing. Under dark, heavy beams, the dining room is intimate and the atmosphere is captivating. Madame Gardillou is responsible for the kitchen and the superb cuisine. Monsieur Gardillou serves as a most gracious and charming host. Le Moulin du Roc is a gem.

Le Moulin du Roc
Champagnac de Bélair

From Champagnac de Bélair country roads will direct you to the heart of the Dordogne. Tucked along the banks of the Dronne are the charming villages of BRANTÔME and its neighbor BOURDEILLES. Bounded by the Dronne, Brantôme is a very pretty village with its ancient abbey enhancing the picture. Founded by Charlemagne in 769, the abbey was reconstructed in the eleventh century after it was ransacked by the Normans. The church and adjoining buildings were constructed and modified between the fourteenth and eighteenth centuries. Follow the valley of the Dronne just a few miles further to Bourdeilles. Crowned by its twelfth-century castle, Bourdeilles bridges the river and is a small and picturesque town to explore. Should you wish to lunch in the area there are many outstanding choices. Two suggestions are: in Brantôme, MOULIN DE L'ABBAYE, a converted mill on the water's edge with a gorgeous outlook, and in Bourdeilles, HÔTEL DES GRIFFONS, a delightful restaurant where the chef is flattered when you request regional specialties.

From Brantôme continue on to PÉRIGUEUX, an interesting old city, and then on to BERGERAC, a town directly on the Dordogne and reputedly Cyrano's home. From here the road runs alongside the Dordogne; as it nears TRÉMOLAT the valley becomes more gentle and lush.

LE VIEUX LOGIS ET SES LOGIS DES CHAMPS is an ideal base from which to explore one of France's loveliest regions. The character of Le Vieux Logis matches the beauty of the valley. Opening up on one side to farmland, this charming hotel also has its own little back garden with a small stream and various small bridges. The rooms, recently redone, are perfectly color coordinated down to the smallest detail. In room ten everything is in large red and white checks: the duvets, the pillows, the curtains, and the canopy on the four-poster bed. The restaurant is in the barn where the tables are cleverly positioned within each of the stalls. Take a stroll after dinner and wander through the sleepy tobacco growing village of Trémolat. The large doors of the lofty barns lie open and hang heavy with tobacco. The town's church is one of the oldest in the area and has a lovely stained glass window.

Le Vieux Logis
Trémolat

Linger in this region for as many days as your itinerary allows; use Trémolat as your base and let the river be your guide. Discover the beauty of the Dordogne by driving along the quiet roads and simply happening upon the peaceful riverside villages. However, a few suggestions of what not to overlook follow.

From Trémolat, which is located at the "Cingle de Trémolat" (a loop in the path of the river), it is easy to follow the lazy curves of the beautiful Dordogne. When the sun shines you might want to pick out a picnic spot as you drive through LIMEUIL, a neighboring village of Trémolat at the juncture of two rivers. Limeuil is a pretty hamlet with some picnic tables set on the grassy river banks.

In addition to just driving and absorbing the beauty of the Dordogne, you should stop at LES EYZIES DE TAYAC, known as the prehistoric capital, where the Cro-Magnon skull was unearthed. A national prehistoric museum is installed in the ancient castle of the Barons of Beynac. But most impressive are the caves just outside the town at the GROTTO DE FONT DE GAUME. On the cave walls are incredibly well preserved prehistoric drawings, the colors still so rich that it is hard to comprehend the actual passage of time. The caves are well worth a visit but the hours are limited and the caves a bit damp and dark. To avoid disappointment, please check the opening times with the tourist office.

BEYNAC ET CAZENAC is a beautiful little village on a wide bend of the Dordogne; a castle looming above further enhances its picturesque setting. In the summer months a number of people negotiate the river by boat and Beynac, with its wide grassy banks, proves to be a popular resting spot. Beynac castle can be reached by climbing up the narrow streets or by car along a back road. The furnishings are sparse but the castle is interesting to explore and its dominating position provides some spectacular views of the valley. Beynac also offers one of the loveliest settings for lunch. On the water's edge the HÔTEL BONNET is an excellent choice and it is a memorable treat to dine under vine covered trellises on the riverside terrace. This lovely restaurant-hotel has been operated for generations by the Bonnet family.

LA ROQUE GAGEAC, an extremely colorful medieval town, clings to the hillside above the Dordogne. Be sure to have your cameras ready as the road rounds a bend of the Dordogne on the western approach to town because the town, framed by lacey trees, is a photographer's dream. At La Roque Gageac there is a grassy area along the river bank with a few picnic tables.

It is only a short drive to the medieval hilltop village of DOMME, which, although a bit touristy at the height of the season, guards a position fifteen hundred feet above the river and commands views of the valley that cannot be challenged. Domme also has access to some interesting stalactite and stalagmite grottos.

CHÂTEAU DE MONTFORT, down the river from Domme, is definitely worth a visit. Built by one of the region's most powerful barons, this majestic castle rises out of a rocky ledge. The Château de Montfort, not massive and overpowering, but rather, small and intimate, is a private residence, with its rooms elaborately furnished and renovated.

Also stop in SARLAT, which has an atmospheric old quarter with narrow cobbled streets that wind through a maze of magnificent gourmet shops. On Saturday mornings there is a colorful market in the town square.

DESTINATION III   GRAMAT

Travel east along the Dordogne and then south in order to see the "Mont St Michel of the south", ROCAMADOUR. The road approaching the village is small, twisting and picturesque. Dominated by its church, the town of Rocamadour grips the steep and rugged walls of the Alxon Valley. It is a spectacular sight and has long been a popular pilgrimage spot.

Not far from Rocamadour is GRAMAT, a small village possessing a lovely château hotel. As you travel through, watch for signs directing you to the CHÂTEAU DE ROUMÉGOUSE. Large majestic towers will emerge, peering above the treetops, revealing the château. Monsieur and Madame Lauwaert retired five years ago but the management of the hotel is now in the capable hands of their daughter and her husband, Monsieur and Madame Laine. Elegant furnishings, in keeping with the mood of the castle, are found throughout. The bedroom suites are extremely handsome. The dining room is in Louis XV decor; in summer, dinner is served on the terrace overlooking the valley. The Laines request that overnight guests lunch or dine at the hotel.

*Château de Roumégouse
Gramat*

DESTINATION IV   VARETZ

If time allows, you might want to consider continuing south from the Dordogne to the region of the Lot Valley.   The Lot runs parallel to the Dordogne and is equally as spectacular in its scenic beauty.   An itinerary for the Lot follows this one.   The next destination, however, is suggested for those journeying to Paris or travelling north to tour the castles of the Loire.   (See Château Country itinerary.)

VARETZ is located to the north of the Dordogne just a few miles outside the city of BRIVE. Follow a winding country road up to the magnificent, turreted CHÂTEAU DE CASTEL NOVEL, managed graciously and professionally by the Parveaux family. This is a superb hotel that will surpass all your expectations. The bedrooms are individual in their decor: spend the night in a wooden canopy bed looking out over the back garden or secluded in one of the castle's turrets. The elegant dining room and highly praised menu guarantee a memorable evening. The Château de Castel Novel will prove the highlight of any trip and serves as an ideal place to conclude this itinerary.

Château de Castel Novel
Varetz

LIMOGES, famous for its porcelain, is only ninety-one kilometers north of Varetz. A wonderful exhibition of ancient and modern ceramics from all over the world is at the national Adrien-Dubonche Museum. One can also make arrangements to visit Haviland, one of Limoges' renowned porcelain factories. Limoges is a large city and from here transportation and connections to other destinations in France are easy and frequent.

Le Lot

● Orientation/Sightseeing
◉ Suggested Overnight Stops
★ Alternate Places to Stay

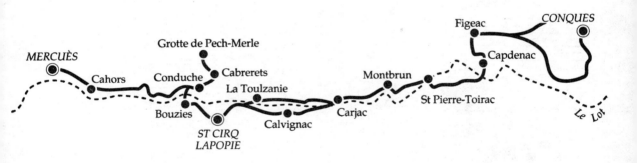

MERCUÈS

Cahors

Grotte de Pech-Merle

Conduche   Cabrerets

La Toulzanie

Bouzies

ST CIRQ
LAPOPIE

Calvignac

Carjac

Montbrun

St Pierre-Toirac

Figeac   CONQUES

Capdenac

Le Lot

Le Lot

This itinerary proposes a section of the Lot Valley that travels perhaps the most stunning fifty-one-kilometer stretch in France. The Lot Valley rivals the Dordogne and yet remains relatively undiscovered and less travelled. The road winds along the curves of the wide, calm river, aggressively cutting into the sides of the chalky canyon walls. At some stretches the route follows the level of the river and at others it straddles the cliff tops. Vistas are dramatic at every turn although the restricting narrow roads will frustrate the eye of any photographer - there is rarely a place to stop.

St Cirq Lapopie

Le Lot

Your adventure begins at CAHORS, a lovely city at the heart of a flourishing wine district.   Of particular interest is the Valentre Bridge with its three impressive towers spanning the Lot.

Just a few miles from the city of CAHORS is the CHÂTEAU DE MERCUÈS perched high on the hills above the Lot in the small village of Mercuès.   For almost twelve centuries the château was a palace of the count-bishops of Cahors, whose names are recorded on plaques in the chapel.   Possession of the Château de Mercuès was taken by the State during the revolution.   However, in this century the chambers of this magnificent castle are being offered as hotel rooms.   Under new ownership, the Château de Mercuès maintains its standards as one of France's finest hotels and the château alone would warrant a visit to this region.

Most of the luxuriously furnished rooms in the château look out through thick castle walls to sweeping vistas of the serene and undeveloped valley.   (Note that a newly constructed wing of rooms has been added.   They are less expensive and principally built to accommodate seminars and conferences.)   The dining room is outstanding.   Elegantly set with china that displays the family crest of the current owners, the tables are positioned in front of windows that frame the valley through majestic thick stone walls.

The valley is planted with vineyards which yield some of the finest grapes in the region.   Under its owners, the Vigouroux family, the Château de Mercuès exports a good deal of its wine.   As a whole, the region is noted for its deep-colored and full-bodied reds, the impressive "black wines" of Cahors which have become more and more widely available in the United States since the mid-1980s.

Château de Mercuès
Mercuès

DESTINATION II   ST CIRQ LAPOPIE

From Cahors the Lot travels under the Valentre Bridge along a route whose beauty remains unchallenged.   The short stretch of river mapped out on this itinerary can be encompassed by car in a day, but try to stretch your stay.   This is a region to be roamed at a lazy pace in order fully to appreciate its character and charms.

Each turn presents a new interest. There are castles, villages whose houses are built into the cliff face, grottos and glorious scenery.

CABRERETS is a pretty village and the nearby GROTTE DE PECH MERLE is a definite attraction. Discovered by two fourteen-year-old boys, the vast caverns of this grotto are painted with prehistoric designs (mammoths, bison, hands, horses) and contain stalagmite columns.

Set your own pace and simply let the river be your guide. Towns and vistas are enchanting. When travelling the road from Cahors, cross the river just before Cabrerets to the village of BOUZIES. Take a moment to look back across the bridge and see the medieval buildings constructed into the walls of the canyon above the small tunnel. Just outside Bouzies, the road climbs and winds to some spectacular vistas of the very picturesque ST CIRQ LAPOPIE. Clinging to sheer canyon walls, this village is a perched cluster of soft ochre and tile-roof buildings. St Cirq Lapopie dominates a strategic position on a wide bend of the Lot and has certainly one of the prettiest settings in the region.

Beyond the ruins of the medieval arched gateway, the HOTEL DE LA PÉLISSARIA, nestled at the foot of St Cirq Lapopie, is an engaging inn whose thick stone walls frame the idyllic scene of the village perched high above a wide band of the meandering Lot River. Fresh and simple in its decor, the inn's white-washed walls contrast handsomely with dark wooden beams and sienna tile floors. This is a delightful place to settle to enjoy some of the valley's most spectacular views. The inn also has a wonderful and intimate restaurant. With just a few tables it is wise to make reservations for dinner when you reserve you room in order to savor the delicious and fresh regional cuisine.

Hotel de la Pélissaria
St Cirq Lapopie

DESTINATION III   CONQUES

As the river guides you further, it presents a number of lovely towns and with each turn reveals another angle and view of the valley. LA TOULZANIE is a small village nestled into a bend of the river, pretty and interesting because of the houses built into the hillside. CALVIGNAC is an ancient village whose fortress clings to a spur on the left bank. On a rocky promontory, the village of MONTBRUN is dressed with the ruins of its fortified castle and looks across to the "SAUT DE LA MOUNINE". Translated roughly as the "Jump of the Monkey", this dramatic cliff face offers incredible views and a legend of romance.

It seems that to punish his daughter for falling in love with the son of an opposing baron, a father ordered her thrown from the cliffs to her death. Dressed in the clothes of a woman, a blind monkey fell to its death instead and the sadness and regret that the father felt for his extreme punishment was erased by joy when he discovered the substitution and that his daughter was still alive. Set on a plateau, the CHÂTEAU DE LARROQUE TOIRAC is open to visitors and makes an impressive silhouette against the chalky cliffs and the town of ST PIERRE TOIRAC.

CONQUES is a bonus to this itinerary but requires that you journey a short distance beyond the Lot. Unfortunately, after FIGEAC the idyllic scenery of the Lot Valley is interrupted by larger towns and traffic, but quiet prevails once again as you detour up a narrow river canyon in the direction of Conques.

Hôtel Ste Foy
Conques

The medieval village of Conques has a dramatic position overlooking the Dourdou Canyon. Tucked a considerable distance off the beaten track, it is a delightful, unspoilt village to explore - especially glorious in the gentle light of evening or in the mist of early day. Conques' pride is a classic eleventh-century abbey. Directly across from the church is a simple but charming hotel, the STE FOY. Some of the shuttered windows of the rooms open onto the quiet cobbled village streets, others open onto the hotel's inner courtyard or look up to the church steeples. Wake in the morning to the melodious church bells that warm the silence of the village and ring out to the surrounding hills. The decor of the Ste Foy is neat and attractive and one can't improve upon its location. Dinner is served family-style on a sheltered courtyard terrace. The menu offers a number of regional specialties and is very reasonable in price. The hotel's finest feature is Madame Garcenot, whose charm, welcoming smile and eagerness to please create the wonderful atmosphere of the Ste Foy. It is easy to settle happily here and Conques serves as a delightful conclusion to this itinerary.

Conques

Le Lot

Gorges du Tarn

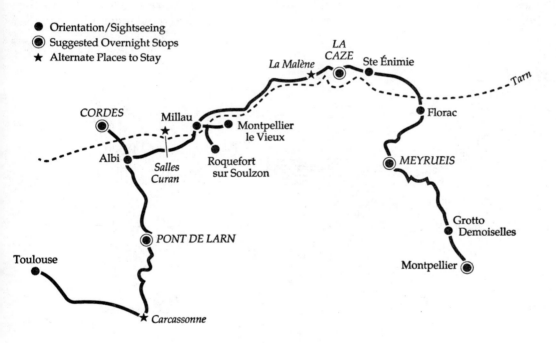

● Orientation/Sightseeing
◉ Suggested Overnight Stops
★ Alternate Places to Stay

LA CAZE

La Malène

Ste Énimie

Tarn

CORDES

Millau

Montpellier le Vieux

Florac

Albi

Salles Curan

Roquefort sur Soulzon

MEYRUEIS

Grotto Demoiselles

PONT DE LARN

Toulouse

Montpellier

★ *Carcassonne*

Gorges du Tarn

This itinerary follows the truly spectacular River Tarn as it winds back and forth along the Tarn Gorge. With each turn the drive becomes more beautiful, never monotonous. The canyon is at its most glorious in early autumn - a perfect time to visit. The French will be back to work or in school again and you will have the autumn beauty to yourself. In autumn the grass carpeting the mountains and hillsides is lush, all shades of green, and the trees blaze gold, red and orange in the sunlight. But whatever time of year, the Gorges du Tarn is incredibly lovely.

Gorges du Tarn

Drive, walk and picnic your way through the Tarn Canyon or, if you prefer to savor the beauty from the water, there is an approximate one hour and fifteen minute boat trip originating in La Malène (the price includes a return taxi trip back to La Malène). This itinerary begins at Montpellier, follows the canyon of the Tarn, includes a visit to the walled city of Carcassonne and concludes in the city of Toulouse.

DESTINATION I   MEYRUEIS

MONTPELLIER, a university town since the seventeenth century, can be considered the "Oxford" and "Cambridge" of France. Capital of the Languedoc, the city's pace is lively and happy - a perfect town for window-shopping or sipping coffee on the Place de la Comedie. A highlight, Montpellier's museum, "Le Musee Fabre", is the home for one of France's most impressive collection of European seventeenth-, eighteenth- and nineteenth-century paintings.

From Montpellier travel approximately fifty kilometers to the famous "GROTTO DES DEMOISELLES"; discovered in 1770, this is one of the most dramatic grottos to visit.

From the grotto it is a lovely drive to MEYRUEIS. Overpowered by the towering Jonte Canyon walls, the picturesque buildings of Meyrueis huddle together along the banks of the Jonte. A farm road's distance from this quaint village is the enchanting CHÂTEAU D'AYRES. Hidden behind a high stone wall, this superb hotel has managed to preserve and protect its special atmosphere, beauty and peacefulness.

The château was built in the twelfth century as a Benedictine monastery. In its colorful past the château has been burned, ravaged and at one time was owned by Nogaret, an ancestor of the Rockefellers, who arrested Pope Boniface VIII at Anagni. The Château d'Ayres came into the possession of the Teyssier du Cros family when the senior Monsieur Teyssier du Cros came to the château to ask for the hand of his wife and recognized the grounds as those where he had played as a child. The Teyssier du Cros family operated the Château d'Ayres for a number of years until they sold it in the late 1970s to an enthusiastic couple, Jean-François and Chantal de Montjou. It is under their care and devotion that the hotel is managed today. Now there are twenty-four beautiful bedchambers instead of the original two, and a superb kitchen where works of art are created daily. The Château d'Ayres, which has a character formed by so many events and personalities, is a lovely and attractive hotel. It will serve as an ideal beginning to an excursion into the Tarn Canyon.

Château d'Ayres
Meyrueis

Gorges du Tarn

From Meyrueis drive northeast to the town of **FLORAC**, the starting point of the canyon. From Florac continue north in the direction of Mende but at the town of Biesset head west. The Ispagnac Basin, located at the entrance to the canyon, is filled with fruit trees, vineyards and strawberries. Here towns are scattered artistically about; châteaux and ruins appear often enough to add enchantment. **STE ÉNIMIE** is a pretty town caught in the bend of the canyon. An old attractive bridge arches across the river and a church wedged into the mountainside piques the curiosity.

Château de la Caze
La Malène

A short distance south of Ste Énimie, majestically positioned above the Tarn is a fairytale castle, the CHÂTEAU DE LA CAZE, converted to a marvellous hotel. You can settle here at the heart of the canyon and pursue your explorations at your own pace and whim. There are many quaint towns to visit: LA MALÈNE, LES VIGNES, LA MUSE (HÔTEL DE LA MUSE has a lovely restaurant with a panoramic view), POINT SUBLIME. Then, at the end of each day, you can return to the Château de la Caze and be royally pampered by Madame Roux.

Although each room at the château is like a king's bedchamber, room number six is the most beautiful of all. It has a large wooden canopied bed and an entire wall of windows overlooking the Tarn and canyon. It was the apartment of Sonbeyrane Alamand, a niece of the Prior François Alamand: she chose the location and had the château built in 1489 to serve as her honeymoon haven. There are paintings on the ceiling of the eight sisters who later inherited the château. These eight sisters, according to legend, were very beautiful and had secret rendezvous each night with their lovers in the castle garden. The restaurant in the château has several house specialties; for dinner you might choose "caneton Château de la Caze" or "les filets de fruit Sonbeyrane".

DESTINATION III   CORDES

When you eventually decide to leave the Tarn Canyon and the Château de la Caze, the scheduled drive will demand an early start. The only disappointment about MILLAU is sadly that it marks the end of the canyon. This agreeable town is known for its leather goods, particularly gloves. MONTPELLIER LE VIEUX is an intriguing rock formation northeast of Millau and southeast is ROQUEFORT SUR SOLZON, the town which is home to the distinctive Roquefort cheese. If this regional specialty appeals, you might enjoy a tour of one of the cheese cellars.

ALBI is about a two-hour drive through farmland from Roquefort. With its cathedral dominating the entire city, Albi, mostly built of brick, is also referred to as "Albi the red". The Toulouse Lautrec Museum is one of its more interesting attractions.

From Albi it is another half-hour drive to the medieval town of CORDES. Perched watching over the Cerou Valley, Cordes has been given the poetic title of "Cordes in the Heavens". It is an enchanting hilltop village, a treasure that will prove a highlight of any itinerary. Known for its leather goods and handwoven fabrics, Cordes offers many "ateliers" or craft shops along its cobblestoned streets.

Hôtel du Grand Écuyer
Cordes

Found at the heart of Cordes is the HÔTEL DU GRAND ÉCUYER which is filled with antiques and charm from the ground entrance to the slanting upper levels. The rooms are impressive with their large old beds, often a fireplace and magnificent views of the velvet green valley below. The hotel has a good restaurant which reflects the expertise of Monsieur Yves Thuriès. His specialty is desserts and they are divine in taste as well as presentation.

It is an undemanding drive south from Cordes to **PONT DE LARN** where, tucked away into the beauty and quiet of the Black Mountains, you will find the spectacular **CHÂTEAU DE MONTLÉDIER.** Here you will develop a taste for the splendor and elegance of a castle hotel.

Château de Montlédier
Pont de Larn

With just nine rooms the Château de Montlédier is intimate in size and atmosphere. The accommodations are magnificent in their furnishings, luxuriously appointed, with commodious, modern bathrooms. Of the nine rooms "Raymond" is the loveliest room of all, with two stunning antique canopied beds and a spacious, modern bathroom. The restaurant, in the cellar, is quite intimate. The cuisine is marvellous and the service impressive; everything is done to perfection and with taste. This is one place where the specialties outnumber the rooms.

Located just a few miles south of Pont de Larn is CARCASSONNE, Europe's largest medieval fortress and a highlight of this itinerary. Carcassonne rises above the vineyards at the foot of the Cevennes and Pyrénées. The massive protecting walls were first raised by the Romans in the first century BC. Never conquered in battle, the mighty city was lost to nature's weathering elements but has been restored. It looks as it did when constructed centuries ago. Stroll through the powerful gates along its winding cobbled streets and wander back into history. The walled city boasts numerous shops, delightful restaurants and wonderful hotels should you wish to linger and possibly overnight. (We recommend two hotels in Carcassonne, one located within the city walls, the other located just below. See hotel descriptions under Carcassonne.)

As you drive on from Carcassonne, glance back at the city with its impressive towers and walls. From Carcassonne continue on to TOULOUSE, known for its pink stone buildings. Located in the midst of a rich agricultural district, Toulouse has become a very important industrial center with electronics and aerospace research as principal interests. Toulouse is also a large artistic center and has many sights worth seeing such as the beautiful Church Basilique St Sermin, picturesque old homes and various museums. In Toulouse your journey ends.

Gorges du Tarn

Carcassonne

Gorges du Tarn

Provence

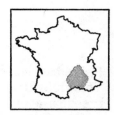

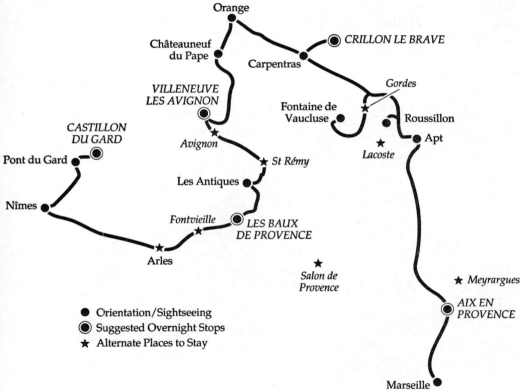

Orange

Châteauneuf
du Pape

Carpentras

CRILLON LE BRAVE

Gordes

Fontaine de
Vaucluse

Roussillon

*VILLENEUVE
LES AVIGNON*

Apt

Avignon

Lacoste

*CASTILLON
DU GARD*

St Rémy

Pont du Gard

Les Antiques

Nîmes

Fontvieille

*LES BAUX
DE PROVENCE*

Arles

*Salon de
Provence*

Meyrargues

*AIX EN
PROVENCE*

- Orientation/Sightseeing
- Suggested Overnight Stops
★ Alternate Places to Stay

Marseille

Provence

Provence, settled by the Romans around 120 BC, is a region of contrasts and colors. This delightful region of the French "Midi" ("the South") is associated with warm breezes, a mild climate and rolling hillsides covered in the grey washes of olive trees.   Some of the world's most popular wines are produced here and complement the regional cuisine.   The romance and beauty of Provence has inspired artists and writers for generations.

Gordes

MARSEILLE is the second largest city in France. Settled as a Phoenician colony, this major Mediterranean port with twenty-five centuries of history is where this tour of Provence begins. Apart from the Roman docks and fortified church of St Victor, there are few monuments within the city to its past. However, you must see La Canebière, a major boulevard which captures the activity, gaiety and pace of Marseille. The old port has a number of museums to draw your interest; the Grobet-Labadie Museum has a beautiful collection of tapestries, furniture, paintings, musical instruments, pottery and sculpture.

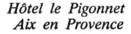

Hôtel le Pigonnet
Aix en Provence

From Marseille drive north to AIX EN PROVENCE, a cheerful city that deserves time to be visited properly. Aix was once the capital of Provence and a great art center under "Good King René" (1470s). There are a number of impressive fountains, hidden squares, charming little back streets lined with shops and majestic avenues. The beckoning cobblestone streets of the old quarter are intriguing to wander at night and the illuminated tree-lined Boulevard Mirabeau is enchanting - a bit reminiscent of Paris with its many sidewalk cafés. From the fountain it is just a fifteen-minute walk to the very professionally run and attractive HÔTEL LE PIGONNET. A road shaded by trees leads you to this hotel away from the noise and traffic of the city. Here you will find an abundance of flowers, cozy sitting rooms, a heated swimming pool, a fine restaurant and pleasant bedrooms.

While in Aix en Provence, with Le Pigonnet as your base and weather permitting, you can stroll down the old streets or join the crowd having coffee in one of the many cafés on the Boulevard Mirabeau. Nineteen seventeenth-century tapestries from Beauvois are on display in the Museum of Tapestries. Another fifteen Flemish tapestries can be found in the Cathedral St Sauveur. Aix is the city where Paul Cezanne studied with Émile Zola and traces of his past can be seen throughout the city.

DESTINATION II   CRILLON LE BRAVE

From Aix en Provence travel north on country roads through groves of olive trees and acres of vineyards to the hilltowns of Provence. Less travelled, the medieval perched villages of this region are delightful and intriguing to explore.

Include the two neighboring towns of ROUSSILLON and GORDES in your explorations. Roussillon is a maze of narrow streets, small shops and restaurants that climb to the town's summit. In various shades of ochres, Roussillon is an enchanting village, especially on a clear day when the sun warms and intensifies the colors. Gordes, perched at one end of the Vaucluse Plateau and dominating the Imergue Valley, is dressed in tones of grey - a wonderful town to explore.

Known for its surrounding fields producing delicious melons, CAVAILLON is another village to include should your schedule permit. From Cavaillon continue north to the amazing FONTAINE DE VAUCLUSE. In the late afternoon as the sun begins its descent, walk around the celebrated natural fountain: at certain times of the year the shooting water is so powerful that it becomes dangerous and the fountain is closed to observers. The most dramatic seasons to visit are either winter or spring.

Hostellerie de Crillon le Brave
Crillon le Brave

North from Gordes travel first to CARPENTRAS and once in Carpentras follow signs toward Mont Ventoux and Bédoin on the D974. About ten kilometers northeast of Carpentras and before reaching the village of Bédoin, take the left turn marked Crillon le Brave. The village is a charming medieval cluster of weathered stone houses. The HOSTELLERIE DE CRILLON LE BRAVE is located at the very top of the village next to the picturesque church. This small hotel of twenty rooms exudes an aura of elegance. Beautiful provençal prints are used throughout in the decor and are a wonderful compliment to the handsome antiques. The hillside location affords magnificent views of the countryside. Either the terrace restaurant or the lower garden and pool are a idyllic spot from which to watch the evening sun bathe the countryside in the soft hues so characteristic of Provence.

DESTINATION III   VILLENEUVE LES AVIGNON

From Bonnieux continue on toward ORANGE. The drive is an easy one and takes approximately an hour and a half. The city has character and the antique theater and commemorative arch, improperly named the "Arc de Triomphe".

Just south of the city of Orange, travel the wine road of some of the world's most treasured labels. The grapes of CHÂTEAUNEUF DU PAPE were first planted to fill the reserve of the Papal city of Avignon. Watch for the signs to the château. Although it has been in ruins since the religious wars, its skeleton still secures a fabulous hilltop position and offers sweeping views of the region. The château would serve as a spectacular picnic spot, so if the weather cooperates, pack some crusty french bread, local cheeses and pâté.

In the fourteenth century AVIGNON was the seat of the Papacy. The Palace of the Popes is grand and dwarfs the rest of the city. Devote the majority of your time to visiting this feudal structure, but if you have time to spare, journey out to the Pont St Benezet (constructed with pedestrians and horsemen in mind) and to the Calvet Museum which has a rich collection of artifacts and paintings from the School of Avignon. Avignon remains one of the most interesting and beautiful of the medieval walled cities of Europe.

Le Prieuré
Villeneuve les Avignon

VILLENEUVE LES AVIGNON is separated from Avignon by the Rhône.   It is a stronghold which has retained several military buildings including the Philippe le Bel Tower (where the caretaker will tell you all the historic facts he feels you lack) and the Fort St André.   If you walk up to the fort you will discover a wonderful view across the Rhône to Avignon and the Popes' Palace.

A highlight of Villeneuve les Avignon is its thirteenth-century priory.   LE PRIEURÉ was constructed by order of Cardinal Arnaud de Via and was purchased and transformed into a first-class hotel in 1943 by Monsieur Mille.   The rooms of Le Prieuré are bursting at the seams with charm.   Be sure to take advantage of the beautiful pool and lovely gardens.

From Avignon it is a very pleasant drive south along a lazy, tree-lined road to ST RÉMY DE PROVENCE.   Of interest is the priory where Van Gogh was nursed, a Romanesque church, Renaissance houses and a busy public square.

L'Oustau Baumanière
Les Baux de Provence

Just a mile or so beyond the outskirts of St Rémy are LES ANTIQUES, the site of the excavations of an ancient Glanum, an arch and a mausoleum.

The next destination for this particular stretch of the itinerary is LES BAUX DE PROVENCE in the hills of the Alpilles just a few miles southeast of St Rémy.   The mineral bauxite derives its name from the town, being first discovered here.   Les Baux de Provence is interesting to explore as it has retained its Provençal charm. The ruins appear to be a continuation of the rocky spur from which they rise.

There are a number of craft shops and inviting creperies tucked away.   From Les Baux you will not only have splendid views of the area but also of a marvelous hotel nestled in its shadow.

L'OUSTAU BAUMANIÈRE is considered one of France's finest hotels.   Set among flowers, trees and gardens, the hotel has a lovely pool, an outstanding restaurant and bedrooms and service that deserve only praise.

DESTINATION V   CASTILLON DU GARD

The distance to be covered after departing from Les Baux is relatively short but the sights to be seen are very interesting.   ARLES is a city abounding in character, a truly lovely city whose growth is governed by the banks and curves of the Rhône. It is a Roman-influenced port city, glorified because of its magnificent Gallo-Roman arenas and theaters.

NÎMES lies approximately thirty-five kilometers west of Arles.   A Gallic capital, it was also popular with the Romans who built its monuments.   Without fail you should see the amphitheater that once held twenty-one thousand spectators, the arenas, Maison Carré, and the magnificent fountain gardens.

Twenty kilometers or so north of Nîmes the spectacular PONT DU GARD aqueduct bridges the River Gard.   Still intact, three tiers of stone arches tower more than one hundred twenty feet across the valley.   Built by Roman engineers about 20 BC as part of a fifty-kilometer-long system bringing water from Uzès to Nîmes, the aqueduct remains one of the world's marvels.

The village of CASTILLON DU GARD sits on a knoll surrounded by grey-green olive trees and stretches of vineyard just a few miles from Pont du Gard. Housed within its medieval walls, the hotel LE VIEUX CASTILLON runs the length of one small street in this village of sienna-tiled, sunwashed houses, so typical of Provence. The style here is one of Mediterranean elegance and leisure. Le Vieux Castillon is a remarkable accomplishment: eight years were spent to renovate a complex of village homes into this luxurious hotel. Care was taken to retain the character of the original buildings and, amazingly, stones were preserved, cleaned and reset within the renovated walls. The restaurant overlooks the pool that is staged magnificently against a backdrop of the town ruins with vistas that sweep out over the countryside. Le Vieux Castillon is a perfect place to conclude any travels.

Le Vieux Castillon
Castillon du Gard

Gorges du Verdon

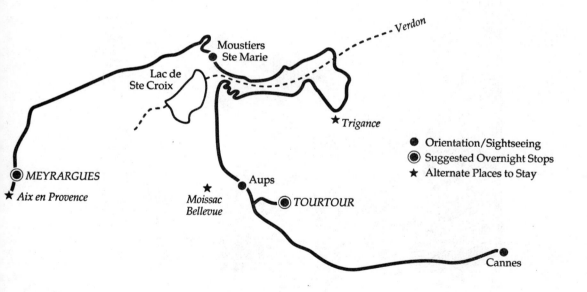

Verdon

Moustiers
Ste Marie

Lac de
Ste Croix

★ Trigance

● Orientation/Sightseeing
◉ Suggested Overnight Stops
★ Alternate Places to Stay

◉ MEYRARGUES
★ Aix en Provence

★
Moissac
Bellevue

Aups

◉ TOURTOUR

Cannes

Gorges du Verdon

The Gorges du Verdon is the French equivalent of the Grand Canyon, but with an even greater variety of colors. The River Verdon has carved through the limestone plateaux and created the magnificent canyons of Haute Provence. The river then plunges into the dramatic trench-like Gorges du Verdon and is enclosed within its steep jagged walls. This area is convenient to visit when travelling from the Côte d'Azur towards central Provence; a few days spent in this region will prove memorable.

Gorges du Verdon

With an early departure from the cosmopolitan city of CANNES, you can take either the coastal route, a bit more demanding in time, or the autoroute through the mountains in the direction of Aix en Provence.   The coastal route sets off in the direction of St Raphaël.   The coastline between La Napoule and St Raphaël is rugged and has been called the "Corniche d'Or" (golden mountain road).   The road is a chain of spectacular views: everywhere the fire-red mountains contrast dramatically with the dark blue sea.   ST RAPHAËL is a small commercial port

Bastide de Tourtour
Tourtour

with a pleasant beach frequented by tourists throughout the year.   Leaving St Raphaël, the road leads towards ST TROPEZ along the Massif des Maures.   En route are dozens of small ports and beaches, but St Tropez, an active port where each fisherman sorts and displays his catch, is easily the most enchanting of all.

Drive inland at Ste Maxime along a scenic mountain road that connects with N7 at LE MUY. Cross the N7 and continue north in the direction of DRAGUIGNAN and watch for signs to TOURTOUR. The drive, along a quiet country road weaving between mountains and through vineyards, is beautiful. On the approach to Tourtour the small road climbs high to a village referred to as the "village in the heavens". The BASTIDE DE TOURTOUR is a dramatically situated hotel on the outskirts of Tourtour. The Provencal-styled rooms all have a private bath and twelve have terraces. Located on one of the highest points in Provence, the hotel provides panoramic views of the region. From the swimming pool area or in the grand restaurant you can relax and watch evening fall on the valley below. The chef prepares divine cuisine - there is an outdoor grill for summer. Although on our last visit we found the Bastide in need of some fresh paint, it is still a very pleasant hotel, one of the best that the region has to offer.

DESTINATION II   MEYRARGUES

It is best to depart early from Tourtour to enable you to take a leisurely tour of the Verdon Canyon. Travelling both roads encircling the ravine, you are able to view every aspect and angle of the impressive canyon.

North of AUPS on D957, the road soon connects with D19, the CORNICHE SUBLIME. Along this two-hour drive, the most startling and magnificent views are exposed. Just past LA COURNERELLE head north towards LA TRIGANCE, a convenient half-way point. The château here is a wonderful place to stop for lunch, if you have not already packed a picnic. The cellar restaurant of CHÂTEAU DE LA TRIGANCE and its delicacies have attracted gourmets from all over France. If you want to extend your stay and perhaps walk the canyon, the Château de la Trigance would prove an ideal place to stay.

Continue now on D955 winding through the valley and at PONT DE SOLEILS pass once again through the jagged mouth of the Verdon Canyon. Every second of the drive is spectacular. The canyon is almost overpowering: its sides plunge down to depths far below where the river forges a path through narrow stretches and then slows and calms in wider sections, pausing to create glistening, dark green pools. A spectacular journey.

Château de Meyrargues
Meyrargues

The road veers away from the edge at points and rolls past beautiful green meadows dotted by a few mountain cabins and hamlets. There are many ideal picnic spots, so many that it will be difficult to choose one. Wildflowers bloom everywhere. It is impossible to describe the beauty of the region. The road gradually returns to the valley, and at the end is the quaint village of MOUSTIERS STE MARIE, famous for its pottery. Considering its size, it is hard to believe, but the workshops of Moustiers Ste Marie fulfil requests from all over the world for their hand-painted faience or pottery.

Leaving the canyon behind, drive towards MEYRARGUES, a small town approximately twenty-five kilometers from Aix en Provence. A tiny road winds up from the little town to the CHÂTEAU DE MEYRARGUES, which dominates the area. Once a stronghold for the mightiest lords of Provence, the château became a hotel in 1952 and is still today majestic and fit for nobility. The building, in the shape of a U, shelters a peaceful terrace where you can enjoy a delicious breakfast and vistas that stretch for miles. All of the rooms are beautiful, some truly exceptional: "Napoleon", with a large canopied bed with red velvet curtains tied to each corner, appears unchanged from the day the titled inhabitants departed. The cuisine is first rate.

From Meyrargues drive south to AIX EN PROVENCE, where you can connect with other transportation or continue on to explore the region of Provence.

Gorges du Verdon

Côte d'Azur

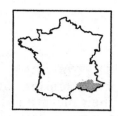

Legend:
- ● Orientation/Sightseeing
- ◉ Suggested Overnight Stops
- ★ Alternate Places to Stay

Grasse

Tourette sur Loup

Vence ★

ST PAUL DE VENCE ◉

La Turbie

Roquebrune

ÈZE VILLAGE ◉

Menton

Nice

MOUGINS ◉

Biot ★

Cagnes ★

BEAULIEU SUR MER ◉

Monte Carlo

Cannes

Antibes

Villefranche

Cap d'Antibes

Cap Ferrat

Côte d'Azur

The Côte d'Azur is known for its continuous stretch of beaches, clear blue water, warm sunshine and the habits of the wealthy international jet-setters who make this their playground. Now filled with millions of tourists, or rather sun-worshippers, the coastal towns are always bustling and guarantee excitement. In the mountains overlooking the Mediterranean are a number of smaller, "perched" towns, removed from the continuous activity of the Riviera and offering a beautiful, yet peaceful, setting.

The French Riviera or the Côte d'Azur is actually the area between Menton and Nice. Even the French say the "Niçoise" are not typically French: they are more gentle and agreeable. This itinerary begins at its capital, NICE, "Queen of the Riviera". Nice is colorful, elegant and always a bustle of activity.

Hôtel Le Hameau
St Paul de Vence

Nice is a large city with an old and a new section: the old quarter is quite picturesque with its flower market and magnificent Baroque churches; the new section is a mecca for tourists with its Promenade des Anglais which runs along the seashore lined with elegant hotels and casinos. Lighted at night, the promenade is a romantic place to stroll.

HÔTEL LE HAMEAU is located just outside the fortified town of ST PAUL DE VENCE. An old farm complex, the whitewashed buildings, tiled roofs aged by years of sun, shuttered windows, arched entryways, heavy doors and exposed beams all create a rustic and attractive setting. Bedrooms are found in four buildings clustered together amidst fruit trees and flower gardens. Le Hameau does not have a restaurant but a delicious country breakfast can be enjoyed in the garden or in the privacy of your room. A lovely new pool overlooking the coastal hills is a wonderful oasis on a hot summer's day. The gracious hosts are responsible for making the hotel a wonderful base from which to tour the riviera.

The fortified town of St Paul de Vence is a picturesque mountain stronghold which once guarded the ancient Var Frontier. Cars are forbidden inside the old town and so it is necessary to go on foot beyond the ramparts to enjoy its feudal atmosphere. The town is a cluster of galleries and tourist shops, cobbled streets and walls from which there are panoramic views of the ever-expanding hilltowns of the Riviera.

Just outside the walled town of St Paul de Vence is the MAEGHT FOUNDATION. This is a private museum that sponsors and hosts numerous collections of works of some of the world's finest contemporary artists.

DESTINATION II   MOUGINS

Just a short distance north of St Paul de Vence is another mountain town, VENCE. Here there are dozens of back streets with interesting shops to discover and little cafés where you can sample regional pastries. Leave Vence in the direction of Grasse along a narrow mountain road that is popular with cyclists who take advantage of the lovely weather and quiet shady roads.

On the way to Grasse you will pass through a few more towns, each consisting of a cluster of medieval buildings and winding, narrow streets that, without exception, encircle a towering church and its steeple. TOURETTES SUR LOUP is just one of the perched towns. After World War II it became active again in the textile market as it had been in the Middle Ages: now it is one of the top "tissage a main" (hand weaving) centers in the world. The workshops and stores are open to the public and fascinating to visit.

Road signs are not necessary: you will know by the sweet fragrance of flowers when you have arrived in the perfume center of GRASSE. No longer a country village, the town is constantly growing but the old section is fun to wander through. A tour of one of the perfume factories - Fragonard or Molinard - is interesting and the views of the valley below are stunning.

Le Moulin de Mougins
Mougins

This region of lavender, roses, carnations, violets, jasmine, olives and oranges is too enchanting to hurry through so continue on to explore the fortified town of MOUGINS, about twelve kilometers south of Grasse. It is characteristic of many of the medieval towns and can be seen only on foot, which luckily preserves the atmosphere that horns and motors all too often obliterate. Located in the center of Mougins is a small courtyard decorated with a fountain and flowers and shaded by trees. Here you will discover a few small cafés where local inhabitants meet to gossip about society, life and politics.

On the outskirts of Mougins in the direction of Cannes is a marvellous inn, LE MOULIN DE MOUGINS. It is actually a sixteenth-century mill that was still producing oil as recently as 1960. Tucked off the busy road to Cannes, the inn is sheltered from the activity of the Riviera by the beauty and calm of its setting. Each of the rooms is charmingly comfortable and the personal attention you will receive during your stay will delight you. The superb cuisine is prepared by the owner himself, Monsieur Roger Vergé. All of his courses are universally known, particularly his "pate de sole en croute sauce grilott" and his "supreme de loup Auguste Escoffier".

DESTINATION III   BEAULIEU SUR MER

From Mougins return to the coast and the cosmopolitan city of CANNES. Located on the Golfe de Napoule, Cannes is the center for many festivals, most famous being the Cannes Film Festival held annually in May. The Boulevard de la Croissette is a wide street bordered by palm trees separating the beach from the elaborate grand hotels and apartment buildings. The Le Suquet quarter at the west end of the popular boulevard appears as if from the past and has a superior view of the colorful port.

Around the bend from Cannes (about twelve kilometers in the direction of Nice) is the small elite town of CAP D'ANTIBES whose sparkling harbor shelters many boats. Their image, reflected in the calm blue water, forms a perfect picture with the old Fort Carré of Antibes on a small peninsula in the background.

A few miles farther along near the coast is a small village, BIOT, where glassware has been made for only just under two decades and yet has already won high acclaim and a valued reputation. A visit to a glass factory to see the assortment of styles and types of glassware available is quite interesting. They vary from the usual types to the Provençal "caleres" or "ponons-bottles" that have two long necks and are used for drinking. The medieval village of small narrow streets, lovely little squares and a maze of galleries and shops is a gem.

Hôtel la Réserve
Beaulieu sur Mer

Driving further you will discover yourself at CAGNES SUR MER, located only a few kilometers south of St Paul de Vence; this is a port town struggling to resemble the other coastal centers. HAUT DE CAGNES, an old section located on the hill, has charm and character. The Château Grimaldi was built by Raynier Grimaldi,

Sovereign of Monaco and a French Admiral in 1309. Also of interest is the house, now the Musée Renoir, where Renoir spent his last days. LE CAGNARD, a hotel-restaurant, is tucked away in the old village and its terrace dining is both atmospheric and excellent.

Continuing for a few kilometers you arrive again at the exciting city of NICE. Travel round the peninsula of Nice on the low road and discover the picturesque ancient port tucked around its sheltered harbor. The old city is colorful and contrasts with the new.

Leaving Nice in the direction of Menton, you not only have a choice between the "high" road and the "low" road, but also of the "middle" road, or you can switch off and on among the three. The roads all run somewhat parallel to each other following the contours of the coast. The Grand Corniche or "high" road was built by Napoleon and passes through two picturesque towns, ROQUEBRUNE and LA TURBIE. The Moyenne Corniche or "middle" road is a lovely, wide, modern road. The Corniche Inferieure or "low" road was built in the eighteenth century by the Prince of Monaco and enables you to visit ST JEAN CAP FERRAT, the wealthy community of BEAULIEU and the small state of MONACO. Take the "low" road out of Nice and you will discover what many have already claimed for their luxurious hideaways - the peninsula of St Jean Cap Ferrat. Drive through this residential district and scout out the villas and the celebrities and then wind down to the coastal village of Beaulieu sur Mer and your luxurious hotel.

To appreciate fully the luxury and grandeur of the Riviera, let yourself be pampered at HÔTEL LA RÉSERVE. Set right on the Mediterranean with a magnificent terrace restaurant, it is one of the Riviera's highlights. The restaurant of Hôtel la Réserve was founded by the Lottier family in 1894 and it is a most elegant "restaurant with rooms".

Its reputation as one of the country's most accredited restaurants is now established and acknowledged by celebrities and royalty. You will be expertly catered to both in the dining room and hotel. The restaurant, with floor to ceiling windows overlooking the salt-water pool and sea, is bordered by an outside terrace where lunch and dinner are served in the balmy summer months. The pool is heated in the winter and is surrounded by a private dock where yachts are moored while guests dine. There are fifty bedrooms (each traditionally furnished) and three apartments (each with a sitting room and a private balcony).

DESTINATION IV   ÈZE VILLAGE

Château de la Chèvre d'Or
Èze Village

Côte d'Azur

As the road leaves Beaulieu sur Mer in the direction of MONACO, it hugs the mountain and tunnels through the cliff-face just above the Mediterranean. MENTON is a bustling but charming port town on the Italian border. Return in the direction of Nice via the "middle" road which affords magnificent views and winds past the medieval village of ROQUEBRUNE and on to the village of ÈZE.

Of all the perched villages, Èze remains a favorite. It is a quaint medieval place with cobblestoned streets overlooking the sea. (Park your car where you can below the village and leave your luggage to be collected by porters.) Walk into this enchanting medieval village and you will discover the fabulous CHÂTEAU DE LA CHÈVRE D'OR.

For more than a thousand years this château has soaked up the sun and looked down upon the beautiful blue water associated with the Côte d'Azur. With restorations, the additions of antiques and touches to decorate the walls, the château came alive once again as the magnificent Château de la Chèvre d'Or. The attractive rooms, attentive service, superb cuisine, glorious views and lovely pool wedged into the hillside make the château a hotel which will be hard to leave and delightful to return to.

Stationed at Èze and the Château de la Chèvre d'Or, you can choose your own time to explore the three corniches and all the port towns. Take advantage of the beautiful beaches and warm blue waters, gamble at the casino in Monaco, enjoy the night life of the cities and sample the many tempting restaurants.

Èze Village is conveniently located just twenty minutes by the Autoroute to the international airport at Nice.

Côte d'Azur

Gourmet Itinerary

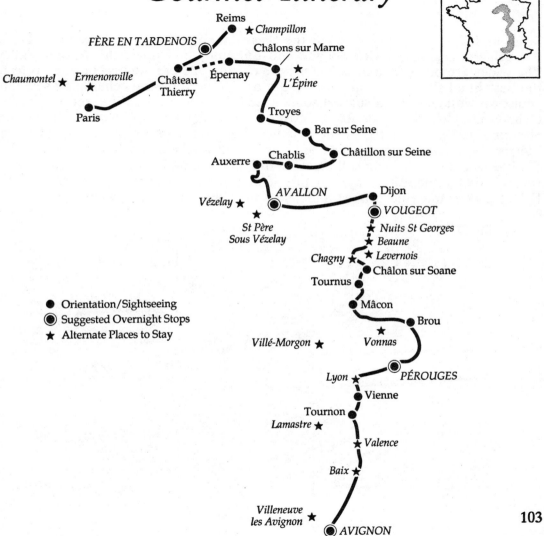

- ● Orientation/Sightseeing
- ◉ Suggested Overnight Stops
- ★ Alternate Places to Stay

Reims
★ Champillon
FÈRE EN TARDENOIS
Châlons sur Marne
Épernay
★ L'Épine
Chaumontel ★   Ermenonville ★
Château
Thierry
Paris
Troyes
Bar sur Seine
Chablis   Châtillon sur Seine
Auxerre
AVALLON   Dijon
Vézelay ★   VOUGEOT
St Père   ★ Nuits St Georges
Sous Vézelay   ★ Beaune
Chagny ★   ★ Levernois
Châlon sur Soane
Tournus
Mâcon
Brou
★
Vonnas
Villé-Morgon ★
Lyon ★   PÉROUGES
Vienne
Tournon
Lamastre ★
★ Valence
Baix ★
Villeneuve
les Avignon ★   AVIGNON

103

Gourmet Itinerary

Wine and dine your way through the "gastronomique" areas of France. Travel through the regions of Champagne and Burgundy and down the Rhône Valley. The wines are plentiful and delicious; the cuisine of Burgundy is considered to be the best in all France. Enjoy the luxury of visiting the wine cellars and selecting your own vintage. I will suggest some specific "caves" of the different proprietors ("vignerons") wherever possible. Most of the châteaux are private residences, but although you might not find their names listed on a tourist pamphlet, if a sign "dégustation" (wine tasting) is posted, you will always be more than welcome. The families are dependent on selling wine and they are delighted to have you sample theirs. Experience their style of life, if only for an afternoon: join them in the fields, pick some ripe grapes and learn how they make the wine.

Leave Paris for the Champagne district. En route is the town of CHÂTEAU THIERRY. Beautifully set on the Marne against a lovely wooded backdrop, Château Thierry has played an important role in many historic battles. The English claimed it as theirs in 1421, then Joan of Arc recaptured it for France. The gates through which she entered the city still stand - Porte St Pierre. Napoleon defended the city against Russian and Prussian troops in 1814.

The Champagne region, whose soil and climate are important factors in making champagne such a delicious wine, is about one hundred sixty-five kilometers northeast of Paris. This region centers around a small range of hills rising from a plain of chalk and divided by the winding Marne. Unlike Burgundy, the quality of champagne is not derived solely from the area but also from the manufacturing process. It is the dose of sugar or "bead" that makes the bubbles, and the smaller the bead, the better the champagne: the quantity of sugar is sometimes increased to cover the poorer qualities of the wine. The essence of champagne is the blending of several different grapes; a branded wine, it is known by the maker and not by the vineyard. There are three distinct zones for the fifty-five thousand acres in Champagne: the "Montagne de Reims", the "Vallée de la Marne" and "Côte des Blancs". Each produces a characteristic essential to the classic champagne blend.

The old cathedral city of REIMS was the traditional coronation city of the French kings; it remains the provincial capital of the Champagne region, situated high on a steep hillside. The views from the medieval ramparts are magnificent. Although Reims is not blanketed with vineyards, it is in the district of the "Montagne de Reims" and its underground chalk tunnels serve as a storage place for bottles of sparkling wine. Take advantage of the many renowned champagne cellars by visiting and sampling their creations. A few of the cellars require letters of introduction and prearranged appointments. However, there are others that conduct tours daily. One of the most famous, Mumm, is located at 34, rue de Champ de Mars and escorts a forty-five-minute tour. There are a number of cellars in the Champ de Mars quarter and at the end of St Nicaise - chalk cellars.

Hôstellerie du Château
Fère en Tardenois

Further details and names of other cellars can be obtained from the tourist office near the railway station; they will be able to supply you with information as to which winery will allow you to visit on that day. Also, before leaving Reims be sure to see the famous Gothic cathedral of Notre Dame, the exceptional twelfth-century monument where most of the French kings were crowned.

Champagne is associated with celebrations and celebrate is exactly what you should do upon arrival at the lovely hotel HÔSTELLERIE DU CHÂTEAU in FÈRE EN TARDENOIS. Tucked away beside the ruins of a castle, the location is peaceful and the views are splendid. The restaurant has an excellent menu (with delicacies such as "turbot au Champagne" and "ecrevisses fine Champagne", and the pastries and fruit tarts are too tempting to resist. There are twenty-three individually decorated and appealing bedrooms with beautiful fabrics covering the walls. The beds are large and comfortable and even the bathrooms are spacious. It is hard to narrow a selection of favorite rooms down to a few; however, Rooms twenty-nine, thirty and twelve are exceptional. The latter two are large, lovely apartments, and twenty-nine is a tower that dates back to 1527. There are windows on two sides wedged between thick walls and overlooking the valley.

DESTINATION II   AVALLON

From Fère en Tardenois head in the direction of ÉPERNAY, which is in the old province of Champagne, now the second of the distinct Champagne zones, the "Vallée de la Marne". Épernay is located thirty-two kilometers south of Reims on the southern banks of the Marne. It is a small town surrounded by vineyards, the best of which are to the south of Épernay and produce the white Chardonnay grape. The cellars to visit here are all familiar labels. With the largest cellars in the world and over thirty kilometers of aging wine, Moët et Chandon is located at 18, Avenue de Champagne. Mercier, at 75, Avenue de Champagne, has in addition to its cellars, twenty kilometers of galleries, a display of wine presses and the largest wine cask in the world (built in 1889 - having a capacity for two hundred thousand bottles of wine). The cellars of De Castellane are found at 57, rue de Verdun. Also interesting to include in a tour of Épernay is a visit to its Museum of Champagne in the ancient Perrier château.

From Épernay drive southeast towards CHÂLONS SUR MARNE, through the third zone, the "Côte des Blancs". Then continue south through the major city of TROYES and from Troyes follow the path of the Seine on to other major champagne towns, BAR SUR SEINE followed by CHÂTILLON SUR SEINE.

From Châtillon sur Seine, it is a lovely drive to the region and town of CHABLIS. For a town whose name is almost a generic term for "white wine", Chablis is a quiet place whose homes are nestled on the banks of the Serein at the base of seven small vineyards. In this serene country town, wine can be tasted from an appropriate "tastevin" (a small shallow silver dish that exposes the qualities and characteristics of the wine). Dauvissat and Servin are particularly good wines to sample at the Chablisien "caves" or cellars.

Château de Lugny
Avallon

From Chablis continue on to AUXERRE and then head south to AVALLON. Outside this lovely city, set back off the road behind its own tall gates is the beautiful CHÂTEAU DE LUGNY that enjoys an idyllic setting. Encircled by a grassy moat the grounds of the château boast endless trails and 800 meters of river frontage with excellent trout fishing. Inside this handsome cream wash building with its wide shuttered windows and weathered tile roof are eleven regal bedrooms. Meals are available at any hour, although, "table d'hôte" dinners are served at a handsome trestle table set before a massive open fireplace hung with lovely old copper. The Château de Lugny affords a wonderful base from which to explore the neighboring villages and savour the neighboring wine country of Burgundy.

Just a few kilometers from Avallon is the walled, hilltop village of **VÉZELAY**. One of France's most picturesque villages, Vézelay is a "must" today just as it was in the Middle Ages when it was considered an important pilgrimage stop. Perched on the hillside overlooking the romantic valley of the Cousin, Vézelay is a wonderful place to spend the afternoon, enjoy a countryside picnic or, if afforded the luxury of time, to linger and spend the early evening in the confines of this medieval village with its splendid views.

Three kilometers southeast of Vézelay, retracing steps in the direction of Avallon, is the small village of **ST PÈRE SOUS VÉZELAY** and the wonderful hotel and gourmet restaurant, **L'ESPÉRANCE**. The Meneaus are your hosts and dining in the care of Marc Meneau is truly a memorable experience.

DESTINATION III   VOUGEOT

The routing from St Père sous Vézelay marks the end of the Champagne and Chablis regions and the beginning of the Burgundy. Within the area titled "Burgundy" there are a number of distinct wines; the region produces a variety of white, red, and rose wines. Burgundies vary: the soil, the grape, the climate, and the individual vineyards which produce them are all responsible for the distinctions. "Burgundy" is a misused term and there are many imitations unjustly claiming the title: this wine can only come from the true Burgundy region where conditions are unique. The "real" Burgundy wine is not plentiful but it is truly great. Leave the isolated region of Chablis and drive towards the heart of Burgundy known as the

Hôtel Dieu
Beaune

CÔTE D'OR which begins at Dijon and ends at Chagny and produces Burgundy's finest wines. Today this "Côte d'Or" or "golden slope" is divided in two: three-quarters of the great red wines are produced in the northern Côte de Nuits; the remainder of the reds and the great white wines are from the southern Côte de Beaune. From Chagny almost to Lyon is an area more generally known for the wines of southern Burgundy which are divided into three districts: Côte de Chalonnaise, Côte de Mâconnais and Côte de Beaujolais.

Retrace your path from St Père sous Vézelay to Avallon and then head for DIJON on the tip of the Côte de Nuits. Very prosperous, Dijon is known for its wine as well as for its mustard. It was the ancient capital of the Dukes of Burgundy, and some of its old streets twist and wind with a character and atmosphere of old.

Traces of history are also glimpsed in the Palace of Charles de Valois whose museum, the Beaux Arts, displays some wonderful old wood carvings and paintings. While in France you will most likely be offered an aperitif called Kir, and it is interesting to note that it originated here in Dijon. Kir is made from a mixture of cassis and wine, Kir Royal is made from champagne and cassis: Dijon produces eighty-five percent of France's cassis. Kir was named for a mayor, Canon Kir, who made the drink of cassis and wine popular. If your travels are in November, visit the superb Gastronomic Fair in Dijon.

South of Dijon is the colorful old city of BEAUNE. Beaune is the wine capital of Burgundy, and some say of the world. Beaune was the residence of the Dukes of Burgundy installed in their fifteenth-century house which now contains a marvelous museum on the history and cultivation of Burgundy wines. Take time also to visit the Hospice and Hôtel Dieu - both hospitals that date from the Middle Ages. Supported by proceeds from an annual sale of their wines, the hospitals contain some lovely tapestries and art. A walk along the town's ramparts affords a leisurely view and tour of Beaune.

Stretching between Dijon and Beaune is a wine route dotted with some of the region's most impressive vineyards. GEVREY CHAMBERTIN'S origin was Clos de Beze and was first produced by the monks of Beze Abbey. The label changed to Chambertin when Bertin purchased the neighboring field and now Charmes Chambertin is the principal wine bottled. The vineyards of CHAMBOLLE MUSSIGNY produce a wine that rivals Chambertin. NUITS ST GEORGES is a small version of Beaune and boasts some highly praised wines. The vineyards of ALOXE CORTON have hung heavy with grapes since the time of Charlemagne. Legend states that Aloxe Corton is known for both its red and white wines because during the time that Charlemagne owned the vineyards, his wife claimed that red wine stained his white beard and so he ordered the production of white wines too. The hillsides of VOUGEOT were first planted by Cistercian monks in the fourteenth century and a stone wall was built to encircle the vineyards and protect them from raiders in the One Hundred Years' War. Now recognized worldwide, an organization called "Chevaliers du Tastevin" chose Vougeot's sixteenth-century château in 1944 as a base from which to publicize Burgundy wines. The château is open to the public, except when the Chevaliers du Tastevin are in session.

Just north of Beaune, at the heart of Burgundy, in Vougeot, the CHÂTEAU DE GILLY has recently opened as a hotel and offers the region handsome accommodation and a wonderful location for exploring the wine route. Once a cisterian abbey the château is surrounded by an expanse of grounds transected by a web of moats and has origins that trace back to the sixth century. Beautifully renovated, the interior of the château is rich in furnishings and comfort. Descend to an underground passageway to the magnificent dining room dressed with deep red fabrics, candlelight, crystal, silver and heavy tapestries. The menu compliments some of the region's finest offerings of wine.

Château de Gilly
Vougeot

POMMARD, MEURSAULT and PULIGNY MONTRACHET are charming and important wine towns which lie between Beaune and Chagny.   These three wine growing communities produce the greatest white Burgundies.   Wine tasting is hosted daily at the Domaine du Château de Meursault.

South from Chagny lie the vineyards of the "Côte de Chalonnaise".   The drive, now bordered with crops as well as vineyards, continues south through the town of CHÂLON and weaves alongside the path of the Saône.   The route passes through the medieval town of TOURNUS with its Romanesque abbey of St Philibert, then on into the region of "Mâconnais" and on to the seventeenth-century town of MÂCON.

Ostellerie du Vieux Pérouges
Pérouges

Between the towns of Tournus and Mâcon, a wine that bears the simple appellation of Mâcon or Mâcon Villages is produced. Some of the communities involved are VIRE, IGE and LA ROCHE LES VINEUSE. Detour south of Mâcon along a steep road that explores little villages and some of the world's most treasured vineyards: POUILLY, FUISSÉ, ST VERAND.

At Mâcon, leave the Saône and drive east. At the town of BROU, with its great monastery and church, begin the drive south. VIEUX PÉROUGES, a medieval village, has cobblestoned streets (explore the character of the village on Place du Tilleul and along rue des Rondes), art and pottery workshops and boutiques.

OSTELLERIE DU VIEUX PÉROUGES and its excellent restaurant are comfortable and attractive, located in one of Pérouges' many old, wood-timbered homes that no longer stand erect, but rather lean out over the narrow streets. The hotel has twenty-eight rooms in two separate buildings; fifteen are furnished with antiques, and the others are more simple, yet still inviting.

DESTINATION V   AVIGNON

Return to the Saône and continue south as the road leads to the metropolitan city of LYON and back to the wine valley. Lyon is the home of the silk industry and has a museum on the history of fabrics. Its restaurants are some of the best in the world, and, depending on your mood, you might want to visit the old Gallo-Roman quarter and have lunch here, or you might prefer to continue south back to the quiet country along the Rhône. Geographically, Lyon is where the Saône valley ends and the Rhône wine valley begins.

Along the course of the Rhône the countryside changes from oak forest to the herbal scrub and olive groves so characteristic of Provence. The wine regions of the Rhône fall into two groups: northern and southern. In the north, the CÔTE DE ROTIE and CONDRIEU are the two principal vineyards, and in the south the wine generally falls under the title of the Côte du Rhône. The first great vineyards lie about forty kilometers south of Lyon across the river from the old Roman town of VIENNE. In the span of just a few short kilometers between Vienne and Valence are the CROZES HERMITAGE, the HERMITAGE, the TAIN, the CORNAS and ST PERAY vineyards whose sun-burnt slopes and granite terrain produce some extremely splendid and full-bodied wines. The town of VALENCE, built on terraces overlooking the Rhône, has a number of Roman monuments and is the location of the famous restaurant PIC, where you might want to have lunch if you did not stop at Lyon.

As the Rhône flows into Provence the best of climate and soil combine to produce ideal conditions and some of the world's finest vineyards: RASTEAU, TAVAL and CHÂTEAUNEUF DU PAPE. The grapes of Châteauneuf du Pape were first

Hôtel d'Europe
Avignon

planted to fill the reserve of the Papal city of Avignon. Travel south along a route that meanders through hillsides terraced by vineyards to a northern gateway of Provence, the beautiful city of AVIGNON.

In the fourteenth century Avignon was the seat of the Papacy. The Palace of the Popes is grand and dwarfs the rest of the city. Avignon remains one of the most interesting and beautiful of the medieval walled cities of Europe. Just inside the Porte de l'Oulle, on the Place Crillon, the HÔTEL D'EUROPE is a converted mansion that is within walking distance of the Rhône and the heart of the city. Handsome furnishings suit the mood and complement the origins of this grand home. Accommodations are spacious and luxurious. Although within the city walls, at least forty percent of the rooms overlook one of the hotel's three courtyards and afford a quiet night's rest. At the front of the building is a peaceful, shaded terrace where one can dine on balmy Provencal nights or inside, the hotel's restaurant, Vieille Fontaine is elegant and formal.

Now, a few pounds heavier and imbued with grander knowledge of wine (or perhaps just with wine imbibed), your "wine and dine" tour comes to an end. Please refer to the Provence Itinerary beginning on page 77 for more detailed information on the region should you wish to extend your stay here.

Gourmet Itinerary

Alsace

★ *Marlenheim*

● Molsheim

● Rosheim

Obernai

Itterswiller ★ ● Barr

Andlau ●

★ *Colroy*

Chartenois ●

Ribeauvillé ●

Riquewihr ●

Kaysersberg ★

Turckheim ●

Colmar ●

Strasbourg ★

● Sélestat

● Orientation/Sightseeing
◉ Suggested Overnight Stops
★ Alternate Places to Stay

Munster Valley

Hohneck ●

Pt Ballon ●

Vieil ●

Route des Crêtes

Cernay ●

◉ *ROUFFACH*

● Quebwiller

● Mulhouse

117

Alsace

The Alsatian region borders Germany and as a result the language has a definite German accent, the people tend to be physically broad and tall, the homes resemble those of the Tyrol and the wine is definitely similar to German in its fruity bouquet (although made in the French manner).   Rooftops ornamented with storks dot the horizon.   Beginning in March, tens of thousands of storks break their journey to the African continent in Alsace.   Then, or any time, Alsace has character: the region is dramatically beautiful and a visit is rewarding.

DESTINATION I   **ROUFFACH**

Depart from MULHOUSE, a fairly large industrial city.   The first few hours in Alsace will be spent following the Route des Crétes which winds along the Vosges and through its valleys.   Strategically located, this road was constructed by the French during World War I to ensure communications between the different valleys.   Thirty thousand German and French soldiers died on the ledges of VIEIL ARMAND during this tragic war.   There are splendid views and many sad memories.

GRAND BALLON, the Vosges' highest peak, deserves a hike.   From its summit the Vosges range, the Black Forest and - on a clear day - the Jura and the Alps can be seen.

HOHNECK is perhaps one of the most celebrated summits of the Vosges.   Again, the panorama is splendid.   From Hohneck this itinerary veers towards the Alsace wine road.   En route you will pass through the Munster Valley where the farmland is fenced by the mountains themselves.

Château d'Isenbourg
Rouffach

Reaching the wine road, N83, drive south to CHÂTEAU D'ISENBOURG in ROUFFACH, an outstanding hotel set on a hillside laced with vineyards.   This is an ideal spot to unpack and settle while you make excursions to the colorful small

Alsatian towns and visit their wine cellars. During the Middle Ages the Château d'Isenbourg was the cherished home of the prince bishops of Strasbourg and more recently it was owned by wealthy wine growers. On the hillside above the town of Rouffach, the château is still surrounded by its own vineyards. You can savor your delicious meal and fine Alsatian wines in the vaulted wine cellars which now serve as a very pleasant restaurant. There are forty bedrooms, a number of which are exceptionally elegant with impressive, handpainted ceilings. The château has a large swimming pool.

The wine road follows the base of the mountains which are dressed with vineyards. In the stretch between Rouffach and Obernai, you will find wine is king, dominating and affecting the character and personality of each town and the lifestyle of the people. In the northern section from Obernai to Marlenheim neither tradition nor culture has suffered in the least; costumes are predominant and festivals and holidays are still adhered to. At intervals buildings group together forming towns, each town a charming stroll. Of these OBERNAI is said to be the prettiest, then RIBEAUVILLÉ, RIQUEWIHR, KAYSERSBERG, TURCKHEIM and EQUISHEIM not far behind. COLMAR is a larger but attractive town on the River Luach. The heart of Colmar, with its old houses, still maintains the charm of a small Alsatian village.

STRASBOURG, on France's border with Germany, is a beautiful city and a convenient point to end your trip. The walls of Strasbourg's Gothic cathedral absorbed much of the city's history. A walk through the old city will take you back to another era. The rue du Bain aux Plantes is bordered by many sixteenth- and seventeenth-century homes of the Alsatian Renaissance; this quarter is where the craftsmen gathered and left their mark in the best preserved section of Strasbourg, referred to as "La Petite France".

Take your time visiting the region, enjoying the wines, the life and culture. Ideally, plan your visit during autumn to coincide with the wine festivals.

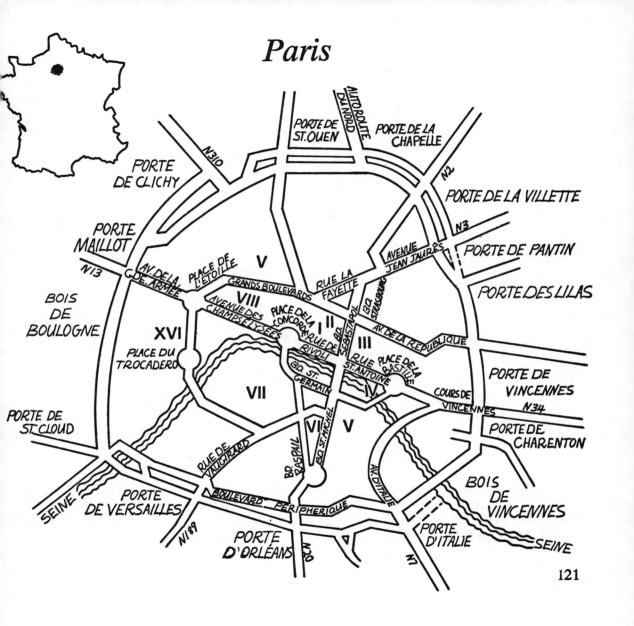

Paris

121

Paris

Paris, beautiful and sophisticated, lives up to her reputation. Sectioned off by "arrondissements", there is not just one interesting area to visit, but many. Each arrondissement has its own character, flavor and style. It is almost as if "Paris" were a name given to a group of clustering villages. Depending on the reason for your trip or the number of times you've been to Paris, each arrondissement will have its own appeal and attraction.

Included are descriptions of selected arrondissements and a few small hotels found within each. The arrondissements chosen are especially interesting and have some charming, almost country hotels to recommend. Included in this edition are a few old favorites and some exciting new discoveries. To avoid disappointment, hotel reservations should be made as far in advance as possible.

First Arrondissement

The FIRST ARRONDISSEMENT is an ideal location for "first-timers" in Paris. As the heart of the city, many of the major tourist attractions are situated here: the Place de la Concorde, Rue de Rivoli, the Madeleine, elegant and expensive shops along the well-known Rue du Faubourg Saint Honore, the Tuileries and the Louvre.

Find a hotel here and you will never have to deal with the Métro or taxi drivers. You can take romantic walks along the Seine or in the Tuileries Gardens. Excitement was born on the Champs Elysees, a wide boulevard that runs from the Place de la Concorde to the Arc de Triomphe at the Place de l'Étoile, officially known as the Place Charles de Gaulle. In the First Arrondissement it is possible to see and experience so many of the different aspects of the city that if you have not spent time in Paris before, this is an ideal place to base.

HÔTEL MAYFAIR   First Arrondissement

On a small street just off the Rue de Rivoli is a well-located hotel combining modern comforts with style. The rooms are pleasing in their decor and service is attentive. The bedrooms are not consistent in size, but all have private bath, direct dial phones and mini-bar. The Mayfair does not have a restaurant, which might prove to be more fortunate than not, for Paris already has numerous restaurants from which to choose. The hotel does have a comfortable salon-bar.

HÔTEL MAYFAIR
Directeur: Monsieur Charles Keyan, 3, rue Rouget de Lisle, 75001 Paris
Tel: (1) 42.60.38.14 Telex: 240037 Fax: (1) 40.15.04.78, Open: All year
53 Rooms - Dbl from 1350F to 1560F, Credit cards: VS, DC, AX
No restaurant, Located: Off the Rue de Rivoli, Métro: Concorde

HÔTEL VENDÔME   First Arrondissement

The Hôtel Vendôme is a small distinguished hotel, located on the Place Vendôme, a neighbor of the famous Ritz Hôtel, designer shops and prestigious financial offices. The varying sizes of the bedrooms are reflected in their prices, but all are attractive and comfortable. On the first floor are a bar and simple restaurant, modern in their decor. The foyer of the hotel is small but is the base for the receptionist and accommodating concierge. Although not as luxurious and polished in its offerings, at the heart of Paris, rates at the Vendôme are reasonable compared to neighboring deluxe hotels.

HÔTEL VENDÔME
Directeur: Mlle Catherine Gigoux, 1, Place Vendôme, 75001 Paris
Tel: (1) 42.60.32.84 Telex: 680403 Fax: (1) 49.27.97.89, Open: All year
46 Rooms - Dbl from 850F to Suites at 1490F, Credit cards: All major
Restaurant, Located: 3 blocks off the Rue de Rivoli, Métro: Tuileries

Third and Fourth Arrondissements

The highlight of the THIRD ARRONDISSEMENT is the picturesque Place des Vosges and the focus of the FOURTH ARRONDISSEMENT are Paris's two picturesque and charming islands, the Île St Louis and the Île de la Cité. The Place des Vosges is a tranquil park, shaded by trees and echoing with the sound of children at play. The Île St Louis is a charming island with many enticing antique, craft shops and neighborhood restaurants. The larger Île de la Cité is home to Paris's "Grande Dame" - the spectacular Notre Dame and the intricate and delicate Sainte Chapelle with its stunning display of stained glass. Crossing bridges in either direction, it is a short walk along the "quai" to the Latin Quarter or a pleasant stroll to the Louvre.

PAVILLON DE LA REINE   Third Arrondissement

Recently opened, this charming hotel offers visitors to Paris a wonderful location on the beautiful square and park, the Place des Vosges. The Pavillon de la Reine, owned and operated by the same management as the very popular Relais Christine, benefits from the same trademarks of tasteful furnishings and, most importantly, the same pride and excellence of service.   Set back off the Place, fronted by its own flowered courtyard, the Pavillon de la Reine was built on the site of an old monastery.   With every modern convenience the hotel offers luxurious comfort and a warm decor of beamed ceilings, antiques, handsome reproductions, beautiful art and paintings.   Accommodations are offered as standard double rooms, two level duplexes and two bedroom suites.   The hotel does not have a restaurant, but a lovely salon, and breakfast is served under the vaulted ceilings of the old cellar.

PAVILLON DE LA REINE
Hôtelier: M. Serge Sudre,   28, Place des Vosges, 75003 Paris
Tel: (1) 42.77.96.40 Telex: 216160 Fax: (1) 42.77.63.06, Open: All year
50 Rooms - Dbl from 1270F, Duplex & suites from 2120F to 3120F, Credit cards: All major
No restaurant, Located: On the Place des Vosges, Métro: St Paul

HÔTEL DE LA BRETONNERIE   Fourth Arrondissement

This is a lovingly cared for hotel whose owners believe in offering good value and quality instead of competitive prices.   Walk the streets of Paris looking at other hotels and you will realize that the Sagots offer excellent value and charming accommodation.   In the basement under vaulted beams, heavy wood tables are matched with high backed chairs and stage a medieval atmosphere for breakfast. The reception is on the first floor and sits opposite an inviting sitting area.   The rooms are found tucked along a maze of corridors, all attractive in their furnishings with lovely modern bathrooms.   Many of the rooms are set under heavy wooden beams, some cozy under low ceilings, ours quite spacious with thirteen foot high ceilings at the back.   Madame Sagot has done a lovely job selecting complementary fabrics, drapes and furnishings for each room.   A few rooms are two level and offer a loft bedroom and sitting room below.   Within walking distance on one side of the Place de Vosges and the Picasso Museum and on the other side of the Pompidou Center and Les Halles, the hotel is set on a quiet street and offers a comfortable and peaceful night's sleep.

HÔTEL DE LA BRETONNERIE
Hôtelier: Monsieur & Madame Pierre Sagot
22, rue Sainte-Croix-de-la-Bretonnerie, 75004 Paris
Tel: (1) 48.87.77.63 Fax: (1) 42.77.26.78, Open: All year
31 Rooms - Dbl from 600F to 1000F, Credit cards: VS, MC
No restaurant, Located: Across the river from Notre Dame, Métro: Hôtel de Ville

HÔTEL DES DEUX-ÎLES & HÔTEL DE LUTÈCE   Fourth Arrondissement

Two neighboring buildings and sister hotels, the des Deux-Îles and De Lutèce are both under the direction of interior decorator Roland Buffat.   On the quiet main street that transects the Île St Louis both hotels enjoy a quiet and charming location.   The Île St Louis has a character all its own and it is a delightful base although limited in its offering of hotels.   Both the des Deux-Îles and the De Lutèce welcome you into charming foyers with log-burning fires, flowers, and antique accents.   The bedrooms, however, recently renovated, have gone up considerably in price, yet are basic and modern in their decor and small.

HÔTEL DES DEUX-ÎLES
Hôtelier: M Buffat, 59, rue St Louis en l'Île, 75004 Paris
Tel: (1) 43.26.13.35 Fax: (1) 43.29.60.25, Open: All year
17 Rooms - Dbl from 670F to 780F, Credit cards: None
No restaurant, Located: On the Île St Louis, Métro: Pont Marie

HÔTEL DE LUTÈCE
Hôtelier: M Buffat, 65, rue St Louis en l'Île, 75004 Paris
Tel: (1) 43.26.23.52 Fax: (1) 43.29.60.25, Open: All year
23 Rooms - Dbl from 640F to 790F, Credit cards: None
No restaurant, Located: On the Île St Louis, Métro: Pont Marie

HÔTEL DU JEU DE PAUME

To find the Hôtel du Jeu de Paume it is easier to locate the imposing deep blue door than the small identifying brass plaque. Behind the large door, a long outdoor corridor with stone tile floor and heavy wooden timbers buffers the hotel from any street noise. Inside the Jeu de Paume is an architectural wonder, whose walls and vaulted ceilings are striped with beams. Dramatic in its furnishing, the decor is an artistic blend of tapestries, chrome, glass and leather set against a backdrop of wood and plaster. The core of the hotel, converted from a seventeenth century Jeu de Paume, is one large room divided up into a series of rooms: the entry, the living room warmed by a lovely fire and the dining room whose tables are overpowered by the stunning end beams and soaring rafters. A few of the guest rooms open on to the central room, while the majority of rooms are located in a side annex and open onto a shared courtyard and garden. The guest rooms, some boasting a tiered duplex layout, are small and minimal in furnishings.

HÔTEL DU JEU DE PAUME
Hôtelier: Mme Elyane Prache, 54, rue St Louis en l'Île, 75004 Paris
Tel: (1) 43.26.14.18 Telex: 205160 Fax: (1) 43.26.14.18 extension 152
32 Rooms - Dbl from 860F to 1160F, Credit cards: All major, Open: All year
No restaurant, Located: On the Île St Louis, Métro: Pont Marie

Fifth, Sixth and Seventh Arrondissements

All three, the FIFTH, SIXTH AND SEVENTH, are the ARRONDISSEMENTS which comprise the ever-popular Latin Quarter. Here you will find activity and companionship abound. There are creperies, sidewalk cafés, food stands, the Sorbonne and its students, antique shops and art galleries, and so many restaurants, all promising "favorites" to be discovered. At night many of the small streets are blocked off and the Latin Quarter takes on a very special ambiance. The left bank of the Latin Quarter is separated from the right bank by the Seine and the Île de la Cité. The grandeur of Notre Dame is overpowering when illuminated at night. Along the "quai" are many secondhand book stalls. Housed in the grand old train station, the recently opened Musée d'Orsay houses an exhibition of Paris's greatest collection of Impressionist art. With the left bank as a base, one can also conveniently tour the Luxembourg Gardens and Les Invalides, and view Paris from the Tour Eifel. The Left Bank and Latin Quarter offer an endless wave of activity, and several charming hotels.

HÔTEL COLBERT   Fifth Arrondissement

Hôtel Colbert is a quiet hotel at the hub of the Latin Quarter. Located on a street of the same name, Rue de l'Hôtel Colbert, it enjoys a secluded location on a small side street. A private courtyard leads to the entrance and adds to the hotel's peaceful setting. Recent renovation has left the bedrooms with a much more spacious feeling and modernized all the baths while retaining character. The top floor now houses two apartments, one a luxurious two-bedroom, two-bath suite connected by a sitting area and the second a two-bedroom, one-bath, both of which afford spectacular views of Notre Dame. Of the forty rooms, ten enjoy glimpses of Notre Dame, and many of the others enjoy the quiet tranquility of the courtyard view. A bar brightly painted just to the left of the reception area is a welcome spot to relax after long Parisian walks.

HÔTEL COLBERT
Hôtelier: M J. Canteloup, 7, rue de l'Hôtel Colbert, 75005 Paris
Tel: (1) 43.25.85.65 Telex: 260690, Fax: (1) 43.25.80.13, Open: All year
40 Rooms - Dbl from 1025F to 1135F, Apt to 2200F, Credit cards: AX, MC, VS
No restaurant, Located: Off Quai de Montebello, Métro: Maubert Mutualite

HÔTEL DES GRANDS HOMMES   Fifth Arrondissement

Facing onto the Place du Panthéon, the Hôtel des Grands Hommes is a haven in Paris. Small and quiet, the lobby has an interior court garden and inviting leather couches and chairs adorning its marble floors. A delicious "café complet" can be savored at small wooden tables paired with tapestry chairs all set under the light stone arches of the house's original cellar. The bedrooms are found up a spiral staircase (or elevator) and are beautiful in their decor of warm colors, fabrics, antiques and exposed beams. The beds are firm and the bathrooms lovely and modern. This is a delightful hotel, a bargain for its price, owned and managed by a very gracious and attentive Madame Brethous. She and her staff are friendly and speak wonderful English, yet they are courteous if you would like to practice your French.

HÔTEL DES GRANDS HOMMES
Hôtelier: Mme Brethous, 17, Place du Panthéon, 75005 Paris
Tel: (1) 46.34.19.60 Telex: 200185 Fax: (1) 43.26.67.32, Open: All year
32 Rooms - Dbl from 720F to 770F, Credit cards: All major, No restaurant
Located: On the Place du Panthéon near the Luxembourg Gardens, Métro: Luxembourg

RESIDENCE DU PANTHÉON   Fifth Arrondissement

This hotel is located next door to the Hôtel des Grands Hommes and is also owned and managed by Madame Brethous. Identical in feeling and decor, both eighteenth-century houses have been attractively converted and the Panthéon's thirty-four bedrooms all profit from Madame's excellent taste and are furnished in period style. Although there is no restaurant, the vaulted basement cellar is now used as a breakfast room or you can enjoy morning coffee and croissants in the privacy of your room.

RESIDENCE DU PANTHÉON
Hôtelier: Mme Brethous, 19, Place du Panthéon, 75005 Paris
Tel: (1) 43.54.32.95 Telex: 206435 Fax: (1) 43.26.64.65, Open: All year
34 Rooms - Dbl from 720F to 770F, Credit cards: All major, No restaurant
Located: On the Place du Panthéon near the Luxembourg Gardens, Métro: Luxembourg

HÔTEL ABBAYE ST GERMAIN   Sixth Arrondissement

Madame Lafortune has achieved a delightful countryside ambiance utilizing tasteful furnishings to accent the charm and character of this restored eighteenth-century residence. Serviced by a lift, the bedrooms, if not large, and four new suites with their own terraces, are pleasantly appointed and each is with private bath and may overlook a tranquil courtyard or bordering garden. Breakfast or refreshments can be enjoyed in the serene setting of a central patio-garden.

HÔTEL ABBAYE ST GERMAIN
Hôtelier: M & Mme Lafortune, 10, rue Cassette, 75006 Paris
Tel: (1) 45.44.38.11, Fax: (1) 45.48.07.86, Open: All year
44 Rooms - Dbl from 840F to 1300F, Suites from 1800F to 1900F, Credit cards: All major
No restaurant, Located: Northwest of the Luxembourg Gardens, Métro: Sèvres-Babylone

LEFT BANK HÔTEL   Sixth Arrondissement

The Left Bank Hôtel is one of Paris's best offerings for travellers. It has a fabulous location on a quiet street just off the Boulevard St. Germain within comfortable walking distance of the Île de la Cité and the colorful, heart of the district with its narrow cobbled streets, many restaurants and shops. The Left Bank Hôtel also offers charming accommodation and very professional service. Monsieur Teil, who is also responsible for the delightful Hôtel Lido on the right bank, has now beautifully restored a second piece of prime real estate. The entry is warm and inviting with its handsome wood panelling, tapestries, paintings and attractive furnishings. Set with tables a small room tucked off the entry serves as an appealing spot for a breakfast of croissants, rolls, juice and coffee which can also be enjoyed in the privacy of one's room. A small elevator conveniently accesses the thirty-one rooms evenly distributed on five levels. Windows of rooms at the back open up to views of the distant Notre Dame and the vantage improves with each floor. Attractive in their decor, often set under exposed beams, the rooms are not overly large, but comfortable with a writing desk, built in armoir, direct dial phones and modern bathrooms. The Left Bank Hôtel is an excellent value, and a personal favorite because of the charming decor and gracious service.

LEFT BANK HÔTEL
Hôtelier: Monsieur Claude Teil, 9, rue de l'Ancienne Comédie, 75006 Paris
Tel: (1) 43.54.01.70 Telex: 200502 Fax: (1) 43.26.17.14, Open: All year
32 Rooms - Dbl from 950F to 1000F, Suite at 1300F, Credit cards: All major
No restaurant, Located: Off the Blvd St Germain, Métro: Odéon

The Relais Christine achieves a countryside ambiance at the heart of Paris's Latin Quarter. A large, flowering courtyard buffers the hotel from any noise and a beautiful wood-panelled lobby ornamented with antiques, Oriental rugs and distinguished portraits is your introduction to this delightful hotel. The Relais Christine is privately owned and now managed by Jean-Jacques Regnault who for many years so successfully directed the Lancaster Hôtel. A converted monastery, the hotel underwent complete restoration and modernization in 1979. Fully air conditioned, there are thirty-five double rooms whose beds easily convert to twin beds. There are two-level and single-level accommodations, all individual in their decor - ranging from attractive contemporary to a dramatic Louis XIII. A few of the bedrooms overlook a small back street, but the majority open onto the garden or front courtyard. The Relais also has sixteen beautiful suites, of which four on the ground floor open directly onto a sheltered garden. The Relais Christine is an outstanding hotel and the only property on the left bank to offer secure, underground parking.

RELAIS CHRISTINE
Hôtelier: Jean-Jacques Regnault, 3, rue Christine, 75006 Paris
Tel: (1) 43.26.71.80 Telex: 202606 Fax: (1) 43.26.89.38, Open: All year
51 Rooms - Dbl from 1460F to 1960F, Suites to 2660F, Credit cards: All major
No restaurant, Located: A few blocks up from the Pont Neuf, Métro: Odéon

LE RELAIS SAINT GERMAIN

Look for the rich green door standing proud under windows hung with geraniums and you will discover an enchanting left bank hotel. Recently converted to a hotel, the walls between two adjoining buildings were knocked down to accommodate ten guest rooms. There are just two rooms that share the landing of each floor, all facing onto the Carrefour de l'Odéon, a quiet plaza. The rooms are narrow, intimate and set under heavy beams. The prints chosen for the furnishings, spreads and drapes coordinate beautifully and are individual to each room. Accommodations, although not spacious, are extremely commodious with excellent lighting, modern bathrooms, direct dial phones, mini-bar and television. Of the ten rooms, one is an apartment that is accessed by its own private stairway. Prices are at the top end but then so are the style and accommodation.

LE RELAIS SAINT GERMAIN
Hôtelier: Gilbert Laipsker, 9, Carrefour de l'Odéon, 75006 Paris
Tel: (1) 43.29.12.05 Telex: 201889, Fax: (1) 46.33.45.30, Open: All year
10 Rooms - Dbl from 1320F, Apt to 1760F, Credit cards: All major
No restaurant, Located: Off the Blvd Saint Germain, Métro: Odéon

HÔTEL DUC DE SAINT SIMON

Seventh Arrondissement

Hôtel Duc de Saint Simon is a quaint hotel where all the personnel speak English due to the many British and American guests. The bedrooms are cheerful and sweet in their decor. Some have private balconies and others overlook the small courtyard and garden in the back. The largest and double rooms with twin beds are four and eleven and the suites are more spacious as well with a bedroom and sitting area. The hallways are spotlessly clean, hung with nice prints, and the delightful foyer is welcoming and brightened by geraniums. I was pleased to discover that both day and night you are away from the noises of the city.

Paris Hotel Descriptions   133

HÔTEL DUC DE SAINT SIMON
Hôtelier: M G. Lindquist, Directeur: Mme G. Lalisse, 14, rue de St Simon, 75007 Paris
Tel: (1) 45.48.35.66 Telex: 203277 Fax: (1) 45.48.68.25, Open: All year
34 Rooms - Dbl from 1100F to 1600F, Suites to 2000F, Credit cards: None
No restaurant, Located: Off the Blvd St Germain, Métro: Rue du Bac

Eighth Arrondissement

Crowned by the Arc de Triomphe and graced by the Champs Elysees, the EIGHTH ARRONDISSEMENT is a bustle of activity. There are shops, pavement cafes, nightclubs, cinemas and opportunities for endless people-watching.

HÔTEL LIDO   Eighth Arrondissement

Bright, overflowing windowboxes hung heavy with red geraniums caught my eye and tempted me down a small side street just off the Place de Madeleine to the Hôtel Lido. My small detour was greatly rewarded. The Hôtel Lido is a "gem". Tapestries warm the heavy stone walls and Oriental rugs adorn the tile floors.

Copper pieces are set about and wooden antiques dominate the furnishings in the entry lobby, an intimate sitting area and cozy bar. Downstairs breakfast is served under the cellar's stone arches. Comfortable but not large, rooms are charmingly decorated with reproduction antiques, handsome fabrics and set under heavy beams. An excellent value for Paris, the Lido now has a sister hotel on Paris's "Rive Gauche", an equally lovely hotel, the Left Bank Hôtel.

HÔTEL LIDO
Hôtelier: Monsieur & Madame Teil, 4, Passage de la Madeleine, 75008 Paris
Tel: (1) 42.66.27.37 Telex: 281039 Fax: (1) 42.66.61.23, Open: All year
32 Rooms - Dbl from 800F to 850F, Credit cards: AX, VS, DC
No restaurant, Located: Off the Place de Madeleine, Métro: Madeleine

HÔTEL SAN REGIS   Eighth Arrondissement

Small, traditional and intimate, the San Regis was once a fashionable townhouse. With exclusive boutiques and embassies as its sophisticated neighbors, the hotel maintains an air of simple yet authentic elegance. It is easy to pass this marvellous hotel by: a small sign is the only thing that advertises its presence. Beyond the small foyer is a comfortable lounge area and small dining room, where one can enjoy a quiet drink and/or an often-welcome light meal (soups, salads, sandwiches). The bedrooms are large and handsomely furnished, and the bathrooms are very modern and thoughtfully stocked. Huge double doors buffer sounds from other rooms. The rooms that front the Rue Jean Goujon are favored with a view across to the tip of the imposing Eiffel Tower, but rooms on the courtyard are sheltered from any street noise and quieter.

HÔTEL SAN REGIS
Hôtelier: M Maurice George, 12, rue Jean Goujon, 75008 Paris
Tel: (1) 43.59.41.90 Telex: 643637 Fax: (1) 45.61.05.48, Open: All year
44 Rooms - Dbl from 2030F to 2560F, Suites to 4760F, Credit cards: All major
Restaurant, Located: Between the Seine and the Champs Elysees, Métro: Franklin Roosevelt

For those who appreciate discreetly elegant small hotels, the Hotel de Vigny is appealing.   The lounge has the understated, yet expensive look of a private club with comfortable chairs, the finest fabrics, paneled walls, handsome oil paintings, and a fireplace.   A small writing desk where guests register is the only subtle indication that this is not a private home.   Not just the decor, but the location is also excellent: just a couple of blocks north of the Champs Elysees.

HÔTEL DE VIGNY
Hôtelier: Christian Falcucci, 9-11 rue Balzac, 75008 Paris
Tel: (1) 40.75.04.39 Fax: (1) 40.75.05.81, Open: All year
37 Rooms - Dbl 2080F to 5180F, Credit cards: All major
Restaurant, pool, Located: Near the Champs Elysees, Métro: George V - Etoile

Sixteenth Arrondissement

The SIXTEENTH ARRONDISSEMENT is Paris's elite residential district.   It is a quiet area, characterized by stately elegant apartment buildings, lovely shopping streets and corner markets.   The Rue de la Pompe and the Avenue Victor Hugo are two well-known avenues lined with beautiful and expensive shops.   The Sixteenth Arrondissement is bordered on one side by the Bois de Boulogne, a large scenic park where people stroll with their dogs, cycle, run, play soccer and unwind.

Tucked amongst the elegant designer boutiques of the Avenue Victor Hugo, the Hôtel Alexander is highly spoken of by many who return time after time. The rooms are stylishly decorated and extremely comfortable and the entrance and sitting area are attractive. The hotel is popular with American travellers, and English is spoken by all the employees. Hôtel Alexander is a lovely hotel that offers consistently comfortable accommodation and a friendly welcome.

HÔTEL ALEXANDER
Hôtelier: M. Del Prete, 103, Avenue Victor Hugo, 75116 Paris
Tel: (1) 45.53.64.65 Telex: 610373 Fax: (1) 45.53.12.51, Open: All year
60 Rooms - Dbl from 1300F to 1870F, Credit cards: AX, DC, VS
No restaurant, Located: Near Place Victor Hugo, Métro: Victor Hugo

L'HÔTEL MAJESTIC   Sixteenth Arrondissement

Just off the Champs Elysees a few blocks from the Arc de Triomphe is a lovely hotel that feels more like a private residence than commercial property. L'Hôtel Majestic is a pleasingly attractive hotel located in a quiet, residential district of Paris. Under the direction of Madame Baverez, the thirty bedrooms and three suites are extremely handsome in their decor and although not inexpensive, priced reasonably for Paris. Lovely antiques, oriental carpets and elegant fabrics feature in the decor of each guest room. Comparable rooms, perhaps not even as spacious or attractive, would cost considerably more in some of Paris's better known hotels. There is no restaurant but breakfast is beautifully offered and there are a number of attractive public rooms for guests to enjoy. Personalized service and attention to needs of the guest seem to take precedence and are a proud trademark of L'Hôtel Majestic.

L'HÔTEL MAJESTIC
Hôtelier: Madame Baverez, 29, rue Dumont d'Urville, 75116 Paris
Tel: (1) 45.00.83.70 Telex: 640034 Fax: (1) 45.00.29.48, Open: All year
30 Rooms - Dbl from 1000F to 1300F, Apt to 1800F, Credit cards: All major
No restaurant, Located: Near the Champs Elysees, Métro: Kléber

THE ST JAMES'S CLUB   Sixteenth Arrondissement

The exclusive St James's Club with properties in London, Antigua and Los Angeles has recently selected the prestigious residential district, the sixteenth, for its Paris location. Temporary membership is available when reserving accommodations. An imposing arched entry frames the elegant stone manor that is set back behind a lovely large fountain and circular drive. A proper British taxi (for guests' use) and a cherry red phone booth are present on the grounds and claim the heritage of the club. The interior of the club is quite grand in its spaciousness and furnishings. The famous interior decorator, Putnam, has established a fresh, clean, albeit somewhat modern, theme to the decor. The bedrooms are equipped with every imaginable comfort from exterior blinds that open and close at the touch of a switch found within reach of the bed to a coffee table that rises to accommodate a morning breakfast tray. The traditional roof of this mansion has been replaced with a glass dome to benefit the four top suites. A wide central corridor is a maze of ivy-covered lattice work that sections off individual garden patios for each suite. As every British club should, this has a handsome, richly decorated library bar and the basement sports a billiard table, sauna and exercise room. The dining room is elegant, with soft rose drapes and an abundance of crystal and china.

THE ST JAMES'S CLUB
Directeur: Kenneth Boone, 5, Place Chancelier Adenauer, 75116 Paris
Tel: (1) 47.04.29.29 Telex: 643850 Fax: (1) 45.53.00.61, Open: All year
48 Rooms - Dbl from 1350F to 3500F, Open: All year, Credit cards: All major
Restaurant, Located: Near Avenue Foch, Métro: Porte Dauphine

Countryside
Hotel Descriptions

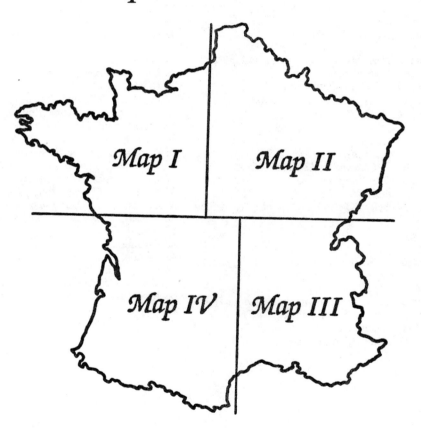

MAP I

NORMANDY:

BRITTANY:

LOIRE VALLEY:

Map I

St André d'Hebértot

Honfleur

Trévières

ROUEN

Pont
Audemer

Bayeux

Montpinchon

CAEN

Les Andelys

Trébeurden

Audrieu

Croutts

Le Bec
Hellouin

Gacé

Brélidy

Trelly

Clécy le Vey

Mont St Michel

ST BRIEUC

Courtils

La Forêt Fouesnant

Pleugueneuc

RENNES

Neuvy en Champagne ·

LE MANS

Noyen sur Sarthe

Chaumont sur Loire

La Jaille-Yvon

Montoire

Tavers

Hennebont

Joué lès Tours

Champigné

Luynes

Onzain

Chambord

Moëlan sur Mer

Chenehutte les Tuffeaux

Fondettes

Noizay

Billiers

NANTES

Bourgueil

Chissay

Beaumont

Chenonceaux

Les Sorinières

Avoine

Artannes

Bléré

Chinon

Marçay

Montbazon

Valençay

TOURS

Map I Showing Hotel Locations

MAP II

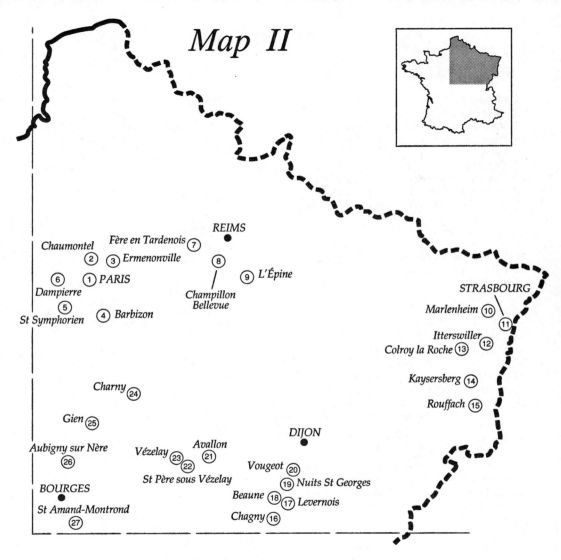

Map II

Chaumontel

Fère en Tardenois ⑦

REIMS ●

② ③ Ermenonville

⑧

⑥ ① *PARIS*

⑨ *L'Épine*

Dampierre

Champillon
Bellevue

STRASBOURG

Marlenheim ⑩

⑤

⑪

St Symphorien

④ *Barbizon*

Itterswiller ⑫

Colroy la Roche ⑬

Kaysersberg ⑭

Charny ㉔

Rouffach ⑮

Gien ㉕

DIJON ●

Aubigny sur Nère

Avallon

㉖

Vézelay ㉓ ㉑

Vougeot ⑳

㉒

⑲ *Nuits St Georges*

St Père sous Vézelay

BOURGES ●

Beaune ⑱ ⑰ *Levernois*

St Amand-Montrond

Chagny ⑯

㉗

Map II Showing Hotel Locations   **143**

MAP III

Map III

Marcigny
①
②
Villié-Morgon
③ Vonnas
④ Pérouges
⑤
LYON
GENÉVE
⑥
Talloires
Lamastre ⑧
⑦ Valence
⑨ Baix
⑩ La Malène
Château Arnoux
Èze Village
⑪ Meyrueis
⑤
Beaulieu
sur Mer
㉟
Crillon le Brave ⑰
②⑤
㉞
Castillon du Gard ⑫ ⑬ Villeneuve les Avignon
Trigance
Vence
Avignon ⑭ ⑯ Gordes
㉘
㉝
NÎMES
St Rémy ⑱
Moissac-Bellevue
㉖
㉙ Mougins
㉗
Tourtour
Arles ㉑
㉔
CANNES
Biot
Fontvieille
en Provence
⑳
㉓ Meyrargues
Aix en Provence
㉚
Cagnes
sur Mer
㉛
㉜ St Paul
de Vence
⑲
Les Baux
de Provence
㉒
Salon
de Provence
⑮ Lacoste

Map III Showing Hotel Locations

MAP IV

Map IV

Chantelle ㉕

㉔ St Martin du Fault

● LIMOGES

Champagnac de Bélair ㉒   ㉓ La Roche l'Abeille   CLERMONT-
Brantôme ㉑   FERRAND ●
Bourdeilles ⑳

                                    Coly   ⑩ Varetz
                                     ⑪   ㉖ Pléaux
St Émilion   Le Bugue
⑲   ⑯ ⑫ Les Eyzies de Tayac
             Millac ⑱ ⑰   ⑬ Vezac
● BORDEAUX   ⑭ Domme
             Trémolat   Beynac ⑮   AURILLAC ●

                        ⑨ ⑧ Gramat
                    Lacave   ⑤ Conques
             Mercuès ⑦   ⑥
                      St Cirq Lapopie

                    Cordes ④
                                    ③
BIARRITZ   Salles Curan
㉗ Segos
㉙ ㉘ Lac de Brindos
㉚   Sare   TOULOUSE ●
St Jean   ② Pont de Larn
de Luz   ● PAU

                        Carcassonne ①

                PERPIGNAN ●

Map IV Showing Hotel Locations   147

Aix is an intriguing city to explore.   The beckoning cobbled streets of the old quarter are lovely to wander and at night the illuminated tree-lined Boulevard Mirabeau is enchanting - a bit reminiscent of Paris with its many pavement cafes. I have returned to Aix a number of times in search of a special inn in the heart of the old section, but without any success.   However, it is just a fifteen-minute walk in the opposite direction to the very professionally, family run and attractive Hôtel le Pigonnet.   A tree-lined road leads you to this hotel away from the noise and traffic of the center.   Set in its own two and a half acre garden the Hôtel le Pigonnet is surrounded by an abundance of flowers and towered over by ancient chestnut trees.   It was from the garden that Paul Cezanne painted the Mountain of Sainte Victoire.   Most inviting on a hot summer day in Provence, the hotel also has a lovely large pool.   Inside, cozy sitting rooms and a large airy restaurant that looks out onto the expanse of back gardens tempt guests to linger.   The hotel's fifty bedrooms are pleasantly decorated and commodious and all are with private bathroom.   Le Pigonnet is not a "country inn" but a lovely hotel with first class accommodation and service that maintains a country ambiance and setting within the city of Aix en Provence.   *Directions: Take the "centre ville" exit off the autoroute and turn north in the direction of the center of town.   At the third light turn left.   Le Pigonnet is fifty meters on the left.*

HÔTEL LE PIGONNET
Hôtelier: Famille Swellen
5, Avenue du Pigonnet, 13090 Aix en Provence
Tel: 42.59.02.90 Telex: 410629 Fax: 42.59.47.77
50 Rooms - Dbl from 700F to 1500F
Open: All year
Credit cards: All major
Restaurant, pool, garden, free enclosed parking
Region: Provence

Located on the outskirts of Les Andelys, the Hôtel de la Chaîne d'Or looks up to the castle ruins and backs onto the Seine.   Just an hour or so to the north of Paris, Les Andelys is convenient to Charles de Gaulle Airport, Roissy and just a few kilometers from Giverny, Monet's home: a visit to Monet's home and the gardens that inspired his genius will prove a highlight of your trip.   This hotel is managed by the owners, the Foucault family, who strive to excel in service and attention to detail.   They take great pride in welcoming guests and overseeing the restaurant. Each year Monique redecorates a few bedrooms - soon all the accommodation will achieve her desired standard and atmosphere.   The bedrooms, six with private bath, all enjoy views of the Seine and the constant, entertaining parade of barges. Jean Claude was a baker in Paris before purchasing La Chaîne d'Or and reason alone to overnight here would be to sample his breakfast croissants.   The restaurant's windows overlook the Seine and across to a small island with an abandoned manor.   It is an intimate and a delightful place for lunch or dinner: the service is relaxed and comfortable and the menu offers an appealing selection of items.   The Foucaults ask that overnight guests dine at the hotel.   *Directions: Take the D313 out of Vernon, a very scenic route, twenty-six kilometers northwest to Les Andelys.   La Chaîne d'Or is located in the old town, along the river's edge.*

HÔTEL DE LA CHAÎNE D'OR
Hôteliers: Jean Claude & Monique Foucault
27, rue Grande, 27700 Les Andelys
Tel: 32.54.00.31
12 Rooms - Dbl from 480F to 680F, Apts to 980F
Closed: January
Credit cards: VS, MC
Restaurant, overlooking Seine
Region: Normandy

Transected by the sweeping Rhône, Arles is a beautiful city, rich with Roman and medieval monuments. Just fifty kilometers to the sea when following the path of the Rhône, Arles has long guarded a strategic location. It is also convenient to all of Provence and an ideal base for exploring the region. The Hôtel d'Arlatan is tucked off one of the small streets in the center of Arles near the Place du Forum within easy walking distance of all the city's major sights. In the twelfth, fifteenth and seventeenth centuries the Hôtel d'Arlatan belonged to the Counts of Arlatan de Beaumont and served as their private home. It is now the pride of Monsieur and Madame Yves Desjardin who offer you an ideal retreat with charming accommodation and service. This is a quaint hotel, ornamented with antiques and pretty fabrics. Many of the hotel bedrooms overlook a quiet, inner courtyard or garden. Although the hotel does not have a restaurant, a delightful breakfast can be enjoyed in the inviting salon or on the patio. For those travelling by car it is also wonderful to note that the hotel can offer secure parking in their private garage. *Directions: Arles is located thirty-six kilometers south of Avignon travelling on the N570. At Place Lamartin enter through the ramparts on Rue 4 Septembre which becomes the Rue du Sauvage.*

HÔTEL D'ARLATAN
Hôtelier: M & Mme Yves Desjardin
26, rue du Sauvage, 13200 Arles
Tel: 90.93.56.66 Telex: 441203 Fax: 90.49.68.45
46 Rooms - Dbl from 520F to 780F
Open: All year
Credit cards: All major
No restaurant
Patio, garden
Region: Provence

In the middle of the seventeenth century a Carmelite convent was erected in Arles by Mother Madeleine St Joseph.   It was a residence for nuns until 1770 when the order was expelled in the midst of the French Revolution.   The convent then became State property until it was purchased and transformed into a hotel in 1929. In this beautiful old convent, the Hôtel Jules César (a member of Relais et Châteaux) has earned a rating of four stars under the directorship of Monsieur Michel Albagnac.   The hotel is situated next to and shares a courtyard with the Chapelle de la Charite, which belongs to the hotel and dates from the seventeenth century.   The restaurant, "Lou Marques", is air conditioned and lovely and known for its classic and Provencal cooking.   On warm mornings, breakfast is served on the terrace restaurant, "Le Restaurant du Cloitre", in front of the chapel. Monsieur Albagnac has supervised over the years the renovation and refurbishing of the hotel's fifty-five bedrooms.   The majority of rooms are large, air conditioned and spacious: room seventy-two, with windows opening onto the garden, is the choice room - an elegant large room with two double beds.   The management has just informed us that a swimming pool is now available for guest use - a welcome addition for those hot summer days in Provence. *Directions: Arles is located thirty-six kilometers south of Avignon travelling on the N570.   The Jules César is located on the Blvd des Lices, a main artery that bands the ramparts on the south.*

HÔTEL JULES CÉSAR
Hôtelier: Michel Albagnac
Blvd des Lices, BP 116, 13631 Arles Cedex
Tel: 90.93.43.20 Telex: 400239 Fax: 90.93.33.47
55 Rooms - Dbl from 820F to 1800F
Open: 21 December to November
Credit cards: All major
Restaurant, interior garden, pool, garage
Region: Provence

We happened upon this lovely eleventh-century château a month before it was due to open its doors as a hotel. I have since returned and am pleased to write that the gardens of the château are more beautiful than remembered, and that the Hoffmans have accomplished all that they had hoped to and offer unique accommodation in a very private setting. The Château d'Artannes is the former residence of the archbishops of the city of Tours and is still attached to an old, neighboring church. Although now sealed, a private passageway once linked the two buildings. Set in its own garden and park, the home is entered through beautiful old wooden doors at the base of the central turret. Well worn stone stairs curve up to the seven bedrooms, some of which are furnished in museum quality furniture and tapestries. No two rooms are alike and yet all have private bath or shower and direct dial phones. The living room, dining room and library are all panelled in polished dark wood and display an abundance of hunting trophies, paintings, animal skins, comfortable furniture and other authentic artifacts from previous centuries. French doors in the main salon open out to the peaceful back garden, inviting one to slow one's pace and drink in the historical surroundings. A stay can be booked on a bed and breakfast or full pension (all meals) basis. *Directions: To locate Artannes, travel south from Tours ten kilometers on N10 and then approximately the same distance west from Montbazon along the D17.*

CHÂTEAU D'ARTANNES
Hôtelier: M & Mme Hoffmann
Artannes, 37260 Monts
Tel: 47.65.70.60 Fax: 47.65.72.36
10 Apartments - Dbl from 1500F to 2500F
Open: All year
Credit cards: All major
Restaurant (by reservation only), sauna, jacuzzi
Region: Loire Valley

A breathtakingly lovely Renaissance castle, the Château de la Verrerie offers the comfort and refinement of an English country home coupled with incomparable French flair for artful decoration and fine cuisine. Each guest bedroom is spacious and unique, with its own color scheme and special charm. A fine example of a room is one done in shades of rose, complemented by a grey marble fireplace, authentic antique furniture and collectibles. The adjoining spacious bath comes complete with claw-footed bathtub. A writing desk placed near the window overlooks the well manicured lawns and gardens which extend to nearby woods. The highest level of comfort and good taste is found throughout the Château de la Verrerie. An inviting guest sitting room combines warmth and elegance to the perfect degree, offering plenty of comfortable seating, good lighting, and reading materials in several languages. In addition to the relaxed, esthetically beautiful setting, one can also tour the historic chapel and Renaissance gallery and enjoy gourmet lunches and dinners served in the nearby "Auberge d'Helene". The restaurant is found in a cozy and atmospheric eighteenth century cottage and features regional dishes and fine wines. *Directions: From Bourges travel north on the D940 thirty-four kilometers. At La Chapelle d'Angillon travel northeast on the D926 six kilometers to Le Grand Rond. La Verrerie is located four kilometers north by following the D39 and the D89.*

CHÂTEAU DE LA VERRERIE
Hôteliers: Comte & Comtesse Antoine de Vogüé
Oizon, 18700 Aubigny-sur-Nère
Tel: 48.58.06.91 Fax: 48.58.21.25
11 Rooms - Dbl from 1000F to 2200F
Open: 15 March through 15 November
Credit cards: VS, DC
Restaurant, grounds, lake, riding, tennis
Region: Berry - Center of France

The Château d'Audrieu affords the countryside traveller luxurious accommodation within the walls of a beautiful eighteenth-century château. This large, somewhat austere, grey stone manor dominates its own expanse of manicured gardens. On the grounds a lovely pool proves a welcome treat on warm summer days. Always a family home, the furnishings throughout the Château d'Audrieu are original to the house and dramatic in that they are authentic of the period. All twenty-eight bedrooms, seven of which are commodious suites, are furnished in elegant antiques and have private bathrooms. Although a château demands constant upkeep, the accommodations are beautifully maintained and the family takes pride in refurbishing one or two rooms each year. Bridging the two wings of the château are richly appointed drawing rooms, which offer a lovely retreat for house guests to spend a quiet afternoon. There are three intimate dining rooms where service is elegant and formal. *Directions: Turn off N13, the road that travels between Caen and Bayeux, onto D158B, and head south on a small country road, in the direction of Tilly sur Seulles. Travel three kilometers to the Château.*

CHÂTEAU D'AUDRIEU
Hôtelier: M & Mme Livry-Level
Audrieu
14250 Tilly sur Seulles
Tel: 31.80.21.52 Telex: 171777 Fax: 31.80.24.73
21 Rooms - Dbl from 710F to 1370F
7 Apts from 1730F to 1960F
Open: March to January
* Restaurant closed Wednesdays*
Credit cards: VS
Restaurant, pool, park
Region: Normandy

I wanted to abort my travels, unpack bags and settle in at the beautiful Château de Vault de Lugny. I arrived on a warm spring afternoon and the obvious contentment of guests who were lounging at tables on the front lawn was enviable. Voices were subdued and did not break the lovely quiet of the setting - perhaps because the individual desires of each guest were well tended to. It was early afternoon, yet, I noticed one guest lounging over a late breakfast, a few guests sleeping with books neglected on their laps and a foursome playing a game of cards under the shade of a large central tree. The Château de Vault de Lugny is a handsome cream wash building with its white shuttered windows and weathered tile roof and is set back off the road behind its own tall gates. Encircled by a grassy moat the grounds of the château boast endless trails and 800 meters of river frontage with excellent trout fishing. There are eleven rooms in the château, all with lovely modern bathrooms. Lavish and regal in their decor, the suites have proven most popular with American guests, but although smaller, I found the standard rooms also charming and a better value. Meals are available at any hour, although "table d'hôte" fashioned dinners are served at a handsome trestle table set before a massive open fireplace hung with lovely old copper. *Directions: Travelling the A6 between Paris and Beaune, take the Avallon exit and follow the direction of Vézelay west to Pontaubert, turn right after the church.*

CHÂTEAU DE VAULT DE LUGNY
Hôtelier: Elisabeth Matherat-Audan
89200 Avallon
Tel: 86.34.07.86 Fax: 86.34.16.36
11 Rooms - Dbl from 700F to 2200F
Open: 23 March to 11 November
Credit cards: AX, VS, MC
Restaurant, Table d'Hôte, Tennis
Region: Burgundy

Le Moulin des Ruats is a charming, wood-shingled cottage set on the river's edge, in the shade of the surrounding lush greenery.   Located on a scenic stretch of road as it winds along the banks of the Cousin, between the town of Avallon and the hilltop, medieval village of Vézelay, the setting of this renovated mill is quite peaceful.   Madame Bobin and Monsieur Tourgueneff are the new owners of this riverside inn.   In the afternoons Madame Bobin is present in the lobby to welcome guests and at mealtimes either in the restaurant or on the terrace to offer menu suggestions.   When the weather cooperates, breakfast is quite memorable when enjoyed under a canopy of trees on the edge of the rushing Cousin river.   The setting is quite peaceful and affords a good night's rest.   The accommodations are not luxurious: they are decorated in simple prints, and are almost motel-like in their furnishings, but are moderate in price.   Not all of the hotel's twenty bedrooms have private baths, but the rooms are quiet and clean.   Le Moulin des Ruats is an inviting hotel and Avallon, a reasonable drive from Paris, would serve as an ideal overnight destination en route to the Burgundy wine region.   Be sure not to venture too far, however, without first visiting the neighboring village of Vézelay with its acclaimed Romanesque basilica.   *Directions: At Avallon take the direction Vézelay (N957).   At the first village, Pontaubert, turn left on the Route de la Vallée du Cousin. Le Moulin des Ruats is the second hotel in the valley.*

LE MOULIN DES RUATS
Hôtelier: Mme Michele Bobin & M Pierre Tourgueneff
Vallée du Cousin, 89200 Avallon
Tel: 86.34.07.14 Fax: 86.31.65.47
26 Rooms - Dbl from 380F to 700F, 1 Suite - 980F
Open: 15 December to 15 November
Credit cards: MC, VS, DC
Riverside setting, restaurant
Region: Burgundy

Nestled along the river's edge with a terrace banked by flowers in the lovely valley of the Cousin, Le Moulin des Templiers offers a peaceful night's rest at an inexpensive price.   The rooms are all very simple in their decor, very few with private bath, small and sparse in furnishings, but fresh, clean and carefully tended to by a charming Madame Hilmoine.   Sound the horn in the snug reception area and she will appear to offer a smile and a welcome.   The setting here is idyllic. The bedrooms, although not overlooking the rushing Cousin, open up to the sounds of the cascading river, and a small farmyard of roosters, chickens, goats and one lone, lazy boar.   If you are blessed with warm sunshine, enjoy either afternoon drinks or breakfast of fresh bread, jam and hot coffee at white wrought-iron tables set along the water's edge.   With a number of outstanding restaurants as neighbors (Marc Menau's L'Esperance at St Pere Sous Vézelay is located just a few miles away in the direction of Vézelay) it is a welcome fact that Le Moulin des Templiers does not have a restaurant where one feels obligated to dine.   This is a dear little hotel, quite inexpensive in price and convenient to exploring Vézelay and a perfect overnight en route to Burgundy.   *Directions: Located between Avallon and Vézelay on the Route de la Vallée du Cousin.   At Avallon take the direction Vézelay (N957).   At the first village, Pontaubert, turn left on the Route de la Vallée du Cousin.   Le Moulin des Templiers is the third hotel in the valley.*

LE MOULIN DES TEMPLIERS
Hôtelier: Mme Francoise Hilmoine
Vallée du Cousin, Pontaubert, 89200 Avallon
Tel: 86.34.10.80
14 Rooms - Dbl from 304F to 384F
Open: 15 March to 2 November
Credit cards: None
No restaurant
Region: Burgundy

Hôtel d'Europe is a classically beautiful sixteenth-century mansion, formerly the home of the Marquis of Gravezon. Just inside the Porte de l'Oulle, on the Place Crillon, the mansion was converted into a hotel in 1799 as it was within walking distance of the River Rhône, a prime location to attract travellers who in that period voyaged predominantly by boat. The present owner, Monsieur Daire, purchased the hotel in the early eighties and has completely modernized the hotel with the comfort of his guests as his primary concern, while using handsome furnishings that suit the mood and complement the origins of this grand home. The walls of the marble entry hall, once an open courtyard, and the walls of the upper levels are now hung with magnificent tapestries. The bedrooms of the hotel are all different in character and size and furnished in traditional pieces and antiques. Many of the rooms are quite spacious and extremely comfortable for extended stays. Although within the city walls of Avignon, at least forty percent of the rooms overlook one of the hotel's three courtyards and afford a quiet night's rest. The hotel has a fine restaurant, La Vieille Fontaine. One can dine in its elegant formality or under the trees in the courtyard on balmy Provencal nights.

Directions: On the A7 from the south take the Avignon "Sud" (south) exit direction Avignon. Follow the ramparts around to the left until the entrance of L'Oulle in front of the Pont (bridge) de Villeneuve les Avignon. Turn inside the ramparts. Place Crillon is on the left.

HÔTEL D'EUROPE
Hôtelier: René Daire
12, Place Crillon, 84000 Avignon
Tel: 90.82.66.92 Telex: 431965 Fax: 90.85.43.66
47 Rooms - Dbl from 625F to 1250F, Suites to 1900F
Open: All year
Credit cards: All major
Restaurant (closed off season)
Region: Provence

The Château de la Poitevinière dates back over two hundred years and its neighbors are numerous other, elegant and lavish châteaux that remain as evidence of the decadent lifestyle and grandeur of the French Court. Château de la Poitevinière is situated six kilometers to the north of the medieval village of Chinon. It was a private home until 1985 when it was purchased by American friends who have impressively restored the house and incorporated every imaginable modern day convenience. The Château is furnished with antiques and art that maintain the integrity and ambiance of an eighteenth-century French château. There are five spacious bedrooms, each with luxurious private bath, that open on to glorious views over the lovely twelve walled acres of park and gardens. Breakfast is a delicious presentation of croissants, homemade muffins, yoghurt and fresh fruit and is served in the sunny dining room. La Poitevinière's chatelains, either Dianne and Mark Barnes or Nancy and Charles Loewenberg, are present to provide a warm welcome, a glass of wine and knowledgeable guidance as to what to see and where to eat in the area. This is one of few country houses where one can experience France but, with American hosts, never worry about language.

Directions: From Chinon or Tours take the D751 to the D16; north six kilometers to the D118. La Poitevinière is noted by a small sign that directs you down a tree-lined drive on the right.

CHÂTEAU DE LA POITEVINIÈRE
Hôteliers: D. & M. Barnes, N. & C. Loewenberg
Huismes, 37420 Avoine
Tel: (USA) (415) 922-1496 (France) 47.95.58.40
Fax: (USA) (415) 928-2863 (France) 47.95.43.43
5 Rooms - Dbl from 850F
Open: 10 April to 10 November
Credit cards: None
No restaurant, lovely grounds, bikes available
Region: Loire Valley

The Hôtel La Cardinale is an impressive estate that dominates a position on the banks of the Rhône River. This is an elegant, country residence, ivy-clad and ornamented with heavy shutters. The hotel, dating back to the seventeenth century, is handsomely appointed with traditional pieces and luxurious furnishings. Five bedrooms are found in the main house, La Cardinale, while two kilometers away additional accommodation is available in a second building, Sa Résidence. Surrounded by its own beautiful park, Sa Résidence, under the same outstanding management, has five guestrooms and five apartments, all exceptionally furnished and inviting. The home is set in a captivating garden and has a lovely swimming pool, definitely a welcome treat on a hot summer afternoon. Guests staying at Sa Résidence return to La Cardinale to experience the gourmet delights of its romantic restaurant, where fine French cuisine is served with great reliability, creativity and style. La Cardinale et Sa Résidence is a splendid hotel, located in the Rhône Valley, halfway between Burgundy to the north and Provence to the south. *Directions: From the A7 exit at Loriol, turn west. At Le Pouzin take the RN86 south in the direction of Cruas Leteil. Two kilometers on the right is La Résidence, two kilometers further is La Cardinal.*

LA CARDINALE ET SA RÉSIDENCE
Hôteliers: Messieurs P. Brunel & J. Carteau
Quai du Rhône
07210 Baix
Tel: 75.85.80.40 Telex: 346143 Fax: 75.85.82.07
La Cardinale: 5 Rooms, Sa Résidence: 10 Rooms
*   Dbl from 940F to 1100F, Suites to 1700F*
Open: 15 March to 31 December
Credit cards: AX, VS, MC
Restaurant, pool
Region: Rhône Valley

The cobblestoned town of Barbizon has attracted artists for many years and the nineteenth-century, timbered Hôstellerie du Bas-Bréau has also had its share of famous guests.   Robert Louis Stevenson wrote in "Forest Notes" about this hotel and because of this, it is often called "Stevenson's House".   Famous painters who treasured this corner of the Forest of Fontainebleau include Millet, Corot, Sisley and Monet.   Some accommodation is in the main timbered house but most is in a two-story building in the back garden.   Each room is different in decor and has a bath.   The restaurant is superb, drawing dinner guests from as far away as Paris. With unusually attractive flower arrangements on each table, the atmosphere of the dining room is elegant and romantic.   Political leaders from Italy, West Germany, Great Britain, Ireland, Greece, Luxembourg, Denmark and the Netherlands recently selected the hotel as a conference location - you will understand their choice when you dine at Hôstellerie du Bas-Bréau where the menu features homegrown vegetables and herbs and specialties such as wild boar.   The house wine list is incredible. *Directions: From Paris take the A6 south in the direction of Fontainebleau. Exit at Barbizon. From the south on A6 exit at Fontainebleau. At the Obélisque in Fontainebleau take the N7 in the direction of Paris and travel eight kilometers to Barbizon.*

HÔSTELLERIE DU BAS-BRÉAU
Hôtelier: M Fava, Directeur: M. Nalchiodi
22, rue Grande, 77630 Barbizon
Tel: (1) 60.66.40.05 Telex: 690953 Fax: (1) 60.69.22.89
20 Rooms - Dbl from 1870F, Apt to 2970F
Closed: 3 January to 2 February
Credit cards: AX
Park, tennis, pool, excellent restaurant
On edge of Fontainebleau Forest
Region: Île de France

L'Auberge de la Benvengudo is tucked farther along the road from La Cabro d'Or as it winds through the valley travelling away from Les Baux de Provence.   When I first visited L'Auberge de la Benvengudo, the Beaupied family offered rooms in their home to overnight guests.   In response to the number of returning guests as well as those who were guided here by their praise, the Beaupieds have expanded their private home into a proper hotel complex.   Sheltered behind a mass of garden, buildings extend out from, and beautifully copy the design of, the original home.   It will take time for the ivy to cover the stucco walls as it does on the main home, but the Provencal sun has already warmed and mellowed the red tile roofs. Green shuttered windows open onto the surrounding rocky hillsides, low green shrubbery and the large swimming pool, tennis court and gardens of the property. Heavy, dark colors (very Mediterranean in flavor) are used to decorate the bedrooms.   Accommodations are comfortable, basic, some quite spacious, all with modern bathrooms.   For those on a longer stay, one might want to reserve a room equipped with a kitchenette.   Although the Beaupieds have changed their policy and no longer request that guests dine at the auberge, the restaurant is lovely and convenient and the menu is tempting in its selection.   *Directions: From Avignon take the N7 south twenty-three kilometers to Plan d'Orgon and then turn west on N99 and travel fourteen kilometers to St Rémy.   At St Rémy travel south nine and a half kilometers along a scenic stretch of the D5 to Les Baux de Provence.*

L'AUBERGE DE LA BENVENGUDO
Hôtelier: M & Mme Daniel Beaupied
Dans le Vallon, 13520 Les Baux de Provence
Tel: 90.54.32.54 Fax: 90.54.42.58
18 Rooms - Dbl from 550F to 690F, Apt to 850F
Closed: 10 November to 1 February
Restaurant (dinner only), Closed Sun., tennis, pool
Region: Provence

Set in the shadow of the enchanting village of Les Baux de Provence, La Cabro d'Or is under the same ownership as L'Oustau Baumanière. Compared to its sister hotel, however, La Cabro d'Or does not boast the same grandeur of clientele - a fact which might actually serve as an attraction to others. Its restaurant is lovely and praised highly for its cuisine but it does not receive the same status of gourmet excellence nor does it demand the same prices. Spaciously set in an expanse of beautiful grounds, bathed in the warm air of Provence, the accommodation is very attractive and comfortable and half the price of that offered at L'Oustau Baumanière. The hotel's twenty-two bedrooms are located in two-story buildings whose green shuttered windows open onto a central courtyard and garden. Also found on the large expanse of grounds are a lovely large swimming pool and tennis courts. La Cabro d'Or is a delightful hotel and children will enjoy feeding the swans and ducks with crumbs from the morning croissants. *Directions: From Avignon take the N7 south twenty-three kilometers to Plan d'Orgon and then turn west on N99 and travel fourteen kilometers to St Rémy. At St Rémy travel south nine and a half kilometers along a scenic stretch of the D5 to Les Baux de Provence.*

LA CABRO D'OR
Hôtelier: M Charial
Dans le Vallon, 13520 Les Baux de Provence
Tel: 90.54.33.21 Telex: 401810
22 Rooms - Dbl from 770F to 1020F
Closed: mid-November to 21 December
  Restaurant closed Mondays in low season
Credit cards: All major
Restaurant, pool, tennis courts
Region: Provence

L'Oustau Baumanière is a fine hotel with an atmosphere and furnishings rich in antiques and tradition.   Guests enjoy magnificent bedrooms, a beautiful pool and lovely hotel grounds.   Raymond Thuillier, now in his eighties, achieved a level of gourmet excellence in the fifties and sixties by which other restauranteurs set their standards.   He is still ever-present at the hotel, but it is his grandson, Jean Andre Charial, who, with the help of chef Alain Burnel, supervises the kitchen.   The restaurant serves exceptional cuisine accented with the flavors of Provence. Offering such specialties as "Lobster with Ratotouille" or "Herb-stuffed Rabbit", it is often referred to as the finest restaurant in the region.   On a warm afternoon or balmy evening dine on the terrace overlooking the pool - less formal and a refreshing setting.   Products regional to Provence are beautifully packaged and can be purchased in a gift shop opposite the parking area.   The hotel is located not in the hilltop village of Les Baux de Provence but on a country road that winds through the valley beneath it.   *Directions: From Avignon take the N7 south twenty-three kilometers to Plan d'Orgon and then turn west on N99 and travel fourteen kilometers to St Rémy. At St Rémy travel south nine and a half kilometers along a scenic stretch of the D5 to Les Baux de Provence.*

L'OUSTAU BAUMANIÈRE
Hôtelier: M Thuillier
Dans le Vallon
13520 Les Baux de Provence
Tel: 90.54.33.07 Telex: 420203 Fax: 90.54.40.46
25 Rooms - Dbl from 1130F to 1580F
Closed: mid-January to March
  Restaurant closed Wednesday off season
Credit cards: AX, VS
Restaurant, pool, tennis
Region: Provence

Monsieur and Madame Auregan are your charming and helpful hosts at this lovingly restored eighteenth-century townhome in Bayeux, a picturesque city known for its outstanding tapestry museum.   A large courtyard and stone, semi-circular staircase lead up to the front entry of their hotel, the Hôtel d'Argouges, and to a warm welcome.   Off the entry hall, French doors in the beautiful and gracious salon-library lead out to the quiet back garden and terrace.   Sheltered behind its main gate, the Hôtel d'Argouges manages to retain the feeling of a quiet country home while its address is, in actuality, downtown Bayeux.   Looking out over the beautiful garden or front courtyard, the bedrooms all have exposed beams and comfortable furniture as well as private shower or bath and phones.   There are also two charming suites which have a small extra room for children.   Next door the Auregans have begun renovating another very old home and some of the bedrooms are found there.   Breakfast can be enjoyed in the privacy of one's room, in the intimate, elegant breakfast salon, or on the back garden terrace overlooking Madame Auregan's vivid flowers.   A veritable haven for travellers visiting Bayeux, the Hôtel d'Argouges offers good value in lovely surroundings plus gracious hosts who have great pride in their metier.   *Directions: Coming from either Cherbourg or Caen follow directions to "Centre Ville" and you will find yourself on Rue St Patrice.*

HÔTEL D'ARGOUGES
Hôtelier: Marie-Claire & Daniel Auregan
21, rue St Patrice
14400 Bayeux
Tel: 31.92.88.86 Telex: 772402 Fax: 31.92.69.16
25 Rooms - Dbl from 310F to 600F
Open: All year
Credit cards: All major
No restaurant, garden
Region: Normandy

Hotel Descriptions

Le Castel was Monsieur Ville d'Avray's summer retreat as a child. His family would come here to escape the Paris heat. With family portraits hung in their dining room and "wellies" left neatly by the back door, caked with mud that hints at the labors of their afternoon outing, there is still much evidence and warmth of family members that return. An eighteenth century private mansion on a three acre park the setting of Le Castel is ideal, just a ten minute walk to the center of town. Bayeux, a beautiful and charming town, is especially well known for its tapestry that was commissioned during William the Conqueror's reign. They have one double bedded room and bath, one twin bedded room tucked under the eaves looking out to the steeples of the 900 year old cathedral, and a lovely twin bedded room with shower. They also have for longer stays an end wing apartment with a double bedded room, one twin bedded room, a living room, kitchen and bathroom. The decor is not luxurious but comfortable, quiet and thoughtfully decorated with family treasures and knick knacks. The Ville d'Avrays are a charming couple, very outgoing, very gracious and extremely fond of their American and British guests. *Directions: Rue de la Cambette is a small one way road off the "pérephérique" (the road that circles Bayeux). Take the "pérephérique" to the south from N13, turn right on rue de la Cambette opposite the turn off to St. Lo.*

LE CASTEL
Hôtelier: M & Mm de Ville d'Avray
7, rue de la Cambette, 14400 Bayeux
Tel: 31.92.05.86 Fax: 31.92.55.64
4 Rooms - Dbl from 320F to 510F
  1 Apt with Kitchen - 820F/day, 3470F/week
Open: April to November
Credit cards: All major
No restaurant
Region: Normandy

La Réserve is described by the management as a "restaurant avec chambres". It is certainly one of the most luxurious "restaurant with rooms" in France, and La Réserve is one of France's most accredited restaurants. You will be expertly catered to both in the dining room and in the hotel. One may dine in a very elegant restaurant with floor to ceiling windows overlooking the salt-water pool and ocean. This elegant room is bordered by an outside terrace which is used for lunch and dinner in the balmy summer months. There are also two small dining rooms in each wing that can be reserved for private functions: one opens onto the terrace and would make an ideal setting for any special occasion. The swimming pool (heated during the winter months) is filled with sea water and surrounded by a private dock where guests moor for lunch in summer. To accompany your meal, the wine cellar features an excellent selection of local wines and those of Bordeaux and Burgundy. Guests not only return year after year to La Réserve, but request the same rooms. There are fifty traditionally furnished bedrooms plus three apartments, each with a sitting room and private balcony. *Directions: Located halfway between Nice and Monte Carlo (eight kilometers) right on the Mediterranean Sea. The N98 goes right through Beaulieu sur Mer and at one point becomes the Blvd Général-Leclerc.*

HÔTEL LA RÉSERVE
Hôtelier: Michel Chardigny
5, Blvd Général-Leclerc
06310 Beaulieu sur Mer
Tel: 93.01.00.01 Telex: 470301 Fax: 93.01.28.99
50 Rooms, 3 Apt - Dbl from 1180F to 4780F
Open: 23 December to 18 November
Credit cards: All major
Restaurant, pool, waterfront setting
Region: Riviera

Dating from the fifteenth century, the Château Hôtel de Danzay is very regal with large, high-ceilinged stone rooms, massive walls hung with muted tapestries and enormous, open hearth fireplaces.   Stone steps leading up to the guest bedrooms are well worn by generations of passage and customarily lit by candles in the evening.   All of the comfortable bedchambers have modern private baths and are furnished with large antique pieces, fitting to the grand scale of this castle.   The bedrooms are all luxurious, but the public areas are more austere: they do not invite one to sit for a cozy chat, but rather to marvel at what life in the fifteenth century must have been like.   Almost historical in tone, the entry hall and grand salon are furnished with sparse heavy antiques, with candelabras casting light on the high stone walls and a few carpets warming the expanse of tile floors.   Monsieur and Madame Sarfati purchased the château over a decade ago and after extensive renovation, opened it to guests in 1981.   The Château Hôtel de Danzay offers modern comforts contained within the stone walls of an elegant fifteenth-century residence.   It is located just north from Chinon. *Directions: Take D749 five kilometers north of Chinon and then watch for signs at the town of Bourgeuil that will direct you, west, to the château.*

CHÂTEAU HÔTEL DE DANZAY
Hôtelier: M & Mme J. Sarfati
37420 Beaumont en Vèron, Chinon
Tel: 47.58.46.86
10 Rooms - Dbl from 770F, Apt to 1620F
Closed: 1 November to 1 April
Credit cards: All major
Dinner offered for overnight guests, pool
Region: Loire Valley

In the heart of the lovely, medieval town of Beaune, Le Cep offers a gracious welcome, charming and comfortable bedrooms decorated with elegance and taste, and very attentive service. The forty-six bedrooms, individual in decor, vary in size but are all handsome: highly polished wooden antique furnishings are accented by the beautiful, softly colored fabrics used for the curtains, bedspreads and upholstery. In the bar and public areas heavy beamed ceilings, old gilt-framed portraits and fresh flower arrangements add character to the comfort and elegance. The former wine cellar, a cozy room with a low, arched stone ceiling, is used as a breakfast room when the weather does not permit service in the pretty stone outdoor courtyard. Dinner in Le Cep's dining room, with fresh flowers, peach toned curtains, soft hued tapestry chairs, fine silver, china and glassware, is a treat. The Bernards are relatively new owners and carry on the tradition of Le Cep's reputation of caring and professional managements. Feedback from guests who have stayed since the Bernard's acquisition is further assurance that the tradition of excellence has been maintained. An ideal base for touring the gourmet wine region of the Côte d'Or, Le Cep combines elegance and warmth in perfect proportions. *Directions: Beaune is located at the heart of Burgundy, forty-five kilometers south of Dijon. Circle the town on the road that follows the ramparts. Turn right into the center of town on Rue Maufoux. Le Cep is on the right hand side of the road.*

HÔTEL LE CEP
Hôtelier: M & Mme Bernard
27, rue Maufoux, 21200 Beaune
Tel: 80.22.35.48 Fax: 80.22.76.80
46 Rooms - Dbl from 950F to 1500F
Open: 15 March to 30 November
Credit cards: All major
New restaurant
Region: Burgundy

Although it is sometimes a bit noisy, there are advantages to staying in a town which is both the capital and at the heart of the Côte d'Or wine region. With Beaune as a base, one can easily venture out to explore and sample some of the world's finest wines. Beaune has an architecturally unique town hall and an interesting wine museum. The famous Hospices de Beaune, founded in 1443, is known the world over because every third Sunday in November, the region's premium wines are auctioned at a public sale. Built in 1660, the Hôtel de la Poste the hotel was owned and operated by the local Chevillot family since 1904. It was recently purchased by Stratigos Baboz who has since renovated more than ninety percent of the rooms. The restaurant has maintained its standard of excellence and some of France's finest Burgundies are a perfect accompaniment to the hotel's outstanding menu selections. The restaurant serves both lunch and dinner. This elegant hotel has twenty-five rooms, four of which are luxury suites, all available on a demi-pension basis. To stay at the Hôtel de la Poste is to enjoy the ambiance of a French residence in the attentive care of its owners. *Directions: Beaune is located at the heart of Burgundy, forty-five kilometers south of Dijon. Circle the town on the road that follows the ramparts. When the road takes on the name of Blvd Clemenceau, look for La Poste on the outside edge.*

HÔTEL DE LA POSTE
Hôtelier: M Stratigos Baboz
1, Blvd Clemenceau, 21200 Beaune
Tel: 80.22.08.11 Telex: 350982 Fax: 80.24.19.71
25 Rooms - Dbl from 760F, Apt to 1700F
Open: 1 April to 19 November
Credit cards: All major
Restaurant
Region: Burgundy

L'Auberge de l'Abbaye is a very pretty, Norman, half-timbered inn in an equally charming village. Le Bec Hellouin is a cluster of half-timbered and thatched buildings set around a medieval abbey, nestled along a trickling stream, a peaceful setting removed from the main road (D39). When we entered the cozy, low ceilinged restaurant of the eighteenth-century L'Auberge de l'Abbaye we were greeted by the sight and aroma of a large, freshly baked apple tart. We were told by the welcoming owner, Madame Sergent, that her restaurant is renowned all over the world for apple tarts. Grand Marnier, a specialty of the region, is also featured here, with large bottles present on each table. Madame Sergent has owned the inn for a quarter of a century and her taste and feminine touches are apparent throughout. Lace curtains at the windows, polished copper and faience ornamenting the walls, and pretty fabrics enhance the decor of the inn. The stairway leading to the inn's ten bedrooms is flanked by former exterior walls whose heavy old half timbering add character to this charming auberge. The bedrooms are simple, yet pretty in their furnishings and all have private bath or shower and either overlook an interior courtyard or a shaded town square. Inside and out this inn is truly what one imagines a simple, country French inn should be. *Directions: Located forty-two kilometers southwest of Rouen. Take the N138 from Rouen in the direction of Alençon to Maison Brulée. Just before Brionne turn right to Le Bec Hellouin.*

L'AUBERGE DE L'ABBAYE
Hôtelier: Sergent Family
27800 Le Bec Hellouin
Tel: 32.44.86.02
10 Rooms - Dbl from 420F to 520F
Open: 28 February to 7 January
Credit cards: VS, MC
Restaurant
Region: Normandy

Map: I

...ublication of the first edition of this guide, I was directed to the ...d have since returned for repeated visits.   Serenely located on a ...rdogne, in the shadow of the impressive Château de Beynac, the ...d a "gem".   The bedrooms are simple in decor, but the restaurant ...ndoors with large windows looking onto a river panorama or on the vine-cove... terrace, encourages one to linger for hours. The Dordogne meanders through the Perigord, a region whose products have attracted the recognition of true gourmets.   Turkeys, ducks, geese, foie gras, crepes, a variety of truffles, plentiful vegetables and fruits (particularly strawberries and raspberries) are all found in abundance.   Chef Monzie was trained in Perigord and his excellent cuisine reflects the regional specialties.   With the vineyard regions of Bordeaux, Bergerac and Cahors nearby, the Restaurant Bonnet is able to offer you a fine selection of wines to accompany your meal.   Generations of the Bonnet family have managed this inn for almost a century and today Mademoiselle R. Bonnet is in residence to act as gracious host.   Stay here for a minimum of three nights and take advantage of the fantastic pension rates.   This is a reasonably priced, simple, but delightful, inn with an incomparable riverside setting. *Directions: Located approximately sixty-five kilometers south of Périgueux, take the D710 and D47 south from Périgueux to Sarlat.   At Sarlat travel ten kilometers on the D703 west to Beynac.*

HÔTEL BONNET
Hôtelier: Mlle Renée Bonnet
24220 Beynac et Cazenac
Tel: 53.29.50.01
22 Rooms - Dbl from 270F to 335F
Open: 15 April to 15 October
Credit cards: VS, MC
Terrace restaurant, riverfront setting
Region: Dordogne

Domaine de Rochevilaine is dramatically located on Brittany's jagged and rocky coastline and its setting typifies the most spectacular quality of Brittany. The views from the hotel are stupendous, especially when the sun shines on the glistening sea or when the wind howls as the waves crash against the rocks. The vast windows of the dining room overlook a rocky promontory and there is a distinct sensation of being shipboard - all you see from your dining table is the open sea. Beautiful Oriental carpets adorn hardwood floors and on sunny days breakfast is enjoyed in the well kept gardens that are protected from the open sea breezes by whitewashed walls. Bedrooms are handsomely furnished and beautifully appointed. The hotel also has a dramatic salt-water pool built into the rocky promontory below the hotel. *Directions: The Domaine de Rochevilaine is at Pointe de Pen Lan, five kilometers from Muzillac on the D5. Muzillac is located twenty-five kilometers to the southeast of Vannes on the road that travels between Vannes and Nantes.*

DOMAINE DE ROCHEVILAINE
Hôtelier: Madame Maya Guillerand
Pointe de Pen Lan
Billiers, 56190 Muzillac
Tel: 97.41.61.61 Telex: 950570 Fax: 97.41.44.85
28 Rooms - Dbl from 500F to 1150F,
  Suites to 2100F
Open: 20 February to 5 January
Credit cards: All major
Restaurant with ocean views
Salt-water pool
Region: Brittany

The village streets of the picturesque Biot are narrow, a bit difficult to negotiate, and parking is limited, but the effort will be rewarded once you reach the Place des Arcades and the inviting Hôtel Galerie des Arcades.   Cafe tables monopolize the sidewalk in front of the arched doorways of this little inn.   The indoor café-bar is always a bustle with local chatter and usually a member of the Brothier family is found here tending the bar.   Very friendly, the Brothiers welcome numerous artists, photographers and models as their guests.   The inn focuses around the three rooms that Monsieur Brothier opened as a gallery and provincial restaurant more than thirty years ago.   Rooms on the upper floors were renovated and offered to overnight guests a decade later.   Steep, old tile stairways climb to a maze of rooms that are like an extension of the gallery as they are hung with an array of abstract, original art.   The bedrooms are moderate in price and those with private terraces that look out over the rooftops of Biot are a real bargain.   Many of the rooms are equipped with private bath, shower, washbasin and toilet.   Full of character, the decor is a bit bohemian in flavor and arrangement, with heavy armoirs and often four-poster beds.   Sitting at tables that face onto the square it is easy to transcend time and envision the likes of Van Gogh and Gauguin frequenting the Café des Arcades. *Directions: Biot is a small village located fifteen kilometers southwest of Nice.   Take the N98 from Nice and at La Brague turn northwest on the D4 to Biot.*

HÔTEL GALERIE DES ARCADES
Hôtelier: André Brothier
16, Place des Arcades, 06410 Biot
Tel: 93.65.01.04
12 Rooms - Dbl from 350F to 450F
Open: January to 20 November
Credit cards: AX
Café-Restaurant
Region: Riviera

We truly felt that we'd discovered a special little inn when we happened upon the Hôtel le Cheval Blanc. Facing the Place de l'Église (now a pedestrian zone), Le Cheval Blanc is easy to spot with its lovely timbered facade and wrought iron sign of a white horse. Dating from the seventeenth century, this was once an annex for the neighboring church. Now filled in, an old stone archway that once opened onto a passageway to the stables stands as evidence of its earlier history. After the revolution, the building was converted to a café-bar and remained a popular, local spot for almost two centuries. It was just a few years ago that Michel and Micheline Blériot converted the café into one of the most charming, most reasonably priced inns in the Loire Valley. The restaurant's decor is endearing in its simplicity; a pretty wallpaper covers the walls, and wooden chairs and tables dressed with crisp white linen are set beneath dark beams. An inner courtyard latticed with vines and set with white outdoor tables is a delightful spot for breakfast. The bedrooms are unbelievably attractive, particularly when one considers the bargain rates. Each room has its own private bath or shower and overlooks either the central courtyard or a quiet back street. Bléré is a convenient base from which to explore the castles of the Loire Valley and Le Cheval Blanc is a reasonably priced, delightful inn. *Directions: Bléré is a small town on the N76 twenty-seven kilometers east of Tours and eight kilometers west of Chenonceaux.*

LE CHEVAL BLANC
Hôteliers: Michel & Micheline Blériot
5, Pl. Charles Bidault, Pl. de l'Église, 37150 Bléré
Tel: 47.30.30.14 Fax: 47.23.52.80
13 Rooms - Dbl from 310F to 420F
Open: All year, closed Sun & Mon (except Jul & Aug)
Credit cards: VS, DC
Restaurant, garage
Region: Loire Valley

When searching for a luncheon spot for my first tour group to France I was thrilled to discover the enchanting village of Bourdeilles.   Tucked ten kilometers farther up a quiet valley from the larger town of Brantôme, the setting of Bourdeilles is idyllic.   In this old village, crowned by a castle, the Hôstellerie les Griffons clings to a narrow bridge.   The hotel met and surpassed my every wish and expectation. Madame Denise Deborde manages the hotel, supervises the restaurant and personally pampers her guests.   Her command of the English language is limited, but she and her husband always sport a welcoming smile.   Bedrooms dressed in pretty fabrics and tucked under old beams are charming and many overlook the quietly flowing river.   The restaurant is intimate and inviting with windows opening up to the soothing sound of cascading water.   Tables are set on the terrace on warm summer nights - the outdoor setting is romantic and perfect for enjoying wonderful Perigord specialties.   The food is excellent: beautifully presented and very reasonably priced.   Monsieur Deborde heads off each week to the market and purchases only the freshest ingredients.   The Hôstellerie les Griffons is a delightful inn and an excellent value on the northern boundaries of the Dordogne.
Directions: Bourdeilles is located twenty-four kilometers northwest of Périgueux. From Périgueux take the N939 north to Brantôme and then travel ten kilometers west on the D78 to Bourdeilles.

HÔSTELLERIE LES GRIFFONS
Hôtelier: Mme Denise Deborde
Bourdeilles, 24310 Brantôme
Tel: 53.03.75.61
10 Rooms - Dbl from 450F to 560F
Open: April to 15 October
Credit cards: All major
Restaurant, charming town
Region: Dordogne

This storybook château is actually located in the small town of Port Boulet on the road between Chinon and Bourgueil.   Travelling south from Bourgueil on D749, turn right immediately after the bridge over the railroad tracks where a sign is posted for the château.   Built by the same family who went on to build the well known châteaux Azay-le-Rideaux and Chenonceaux, the Château des Réaux could be out of a fairytale with its twin, red-checked towers and pretty setting.   Inside, Madame Goupil de Bouillé establishes a friendly atmosphere and is present to genuinely welcome all her guests.   Climb the well-worn turret stairs to the salon where aperitifs are served round a table amidst elegance and comfort.   Madame's feminine touch is evident throughout and she has managed to make every room an inviting haven of antiques, paintings, polished silver and authentic memorabilia. Many friendships are made and congenial hours spent in the comfy salons and at the large oval dining table where all the guests may share a meal.   The twelve bedrooms in the château and five in a neighboring annex all have private baths and are charmingly decorated with antiques set off by delicate floral print bedspreads, curtains and wallpapers.   We look forward to returning to the Château des Réaux, a historical monument that radiates warmth, hospitality and beauty. *Directions: From Chinon travel twelve kilometers north on the N749 to Port Boulet.   After crossing La Loire, turn left on a small road that leads to the Réaux.*

CHÂTEAU DES RÉAUX
Hôtelier: Jean-Luc & Florence Goupil de Bouillé
Le Port Boulet, 37140 Bourgueil
Tel: 47.95.14.40 Fax: 47.95.18.34
17 Rooms - Dbl from 500F to 1000F
Open: All year
Credit cards: None
Family style dining, reservations required
Region: Loire Valley

Twelve years ago the Laxtons took an early retirement and began their search for a country home in the Dordogne River Valley. They wanted a home where they could host their many friends, met through their travels, from all over the world. Le Chatenet, whose history dates to the seventeenth century, has cream stone walls and a sienna tiled roof and sits on a hillside outside the village of Brantôme. The Laxtons fell in love with this Perigordian manor home, although in a state of disrepair, and dedicated their time and money to restoring it. Designers by profession, their combined efforts have resulted in a magnificent home. Local conversation focused on Le Chatenet when it was learned that they had renovated ten rooms and, more impressively, had installed a full bathroom for each one. It was then that Regis Bulot of Le Moulin de l'Abbaye suggested that the Laxtons rent out rooms to accommodate his overflow of dinner guests since he had too few rooms. Once one experiences the comforts and luxury of Le Chatenet and the warm, open hospitality and kindness of Philippe and Magdeleine, one returns and shares the glorious discovery with friends. As a result, the Laxtons' home is now a full time inn, although they describe Le Chatenet as "private but opened to friends and friends of friends". *Directions: Brantôme is located twenty-seven kilometers northwest of Périgueux on the N939. From Brantôme take D78 in the direction of Bourdeilles. Le Chatenet is located 1500 meters outside Brantôme on the right.*

LE CHATENET
Hôteliers: M. & M. Philippe Laxton
24310 Brantôme
Tel: 53.05.81.08 Fax: 53.05.85.52
10 Rooms - Dbl from 460F to 810F
Open: All year
Credit cards: MC, VS
No restaurant, pool, tennis court
Region: Dordogne

With its beautiful Benedictine abbey, lovely grey-stone homes, peaceful expanses of green, narrow streets crossed by or following the course of the River Dronne, and a unique elbow bridge, Brantôme receives many tourists.   Enhancing the charms of this village is the Hôstellerie Le Moulin de l'Abbaye.   From its quiet setting straddling the Dronne the inn looks across the span of water to the town.   The romantic bedrooms are beautifully appointed.   The majority of bedrooms are located in the mill and open onto river views, while an additional few are tucked away in an annex across the street.   Currently many of the restaurant guests enjoy the hospitality and luxurious accommodation of the Laxtons and their neighboring inn, Le Chatenet.   Regis Bulot takes great pride in supervising his renowned kitchen and, whether served on the outdoor terrace or in the elegant dining room, the cuisine is superb (and expensive), having received only accolades and a coveted three stars from Michelin.   Both dining locations profit from this idyllic riverside setting.   This is a charming inn, an enchanting village and a wonderful base for exploring the beautiful region of Perigord.   *Directions: Brantôme is located twenty-seven kilometers northwest of Périgueux on the N939.   Le Moulin de l'Abbaye is located on the outskirts of town on the road to Bourdeilles.*

HÔSTELLERIE LE MOULIN DE L'ABBAYE
Hôtelier: Regis Bulot
Directeur: M & Mme Dessum
1, Route de Bourdeilles, 24310 Brantôme
Tel: 53.05.80.22 Telex: 560570 Fax: 53.05.75.27
17 Rooms - Dbl from 750F to 1200F
Open: 2 May to end of October
Credit cards: AX, VS, dc
Restaurant, lovely riverside setting
Region: Dordogne

The Château de Brélidy is located in central Brittany, in an area surrounded by quiet woods and fishing streams. Monsieur and Madame Yoncourt-Pemezec and their son are the gracious, English speaking hosts who solicitously attend to their guests' every need. They run a professional château hotel offering luxurious accommodation and a warm welcome to tourists and business travelers alike. The fourteen bedrooms are located in a beautifully reconstructed sixteenth century wing of the castle, and although decorated in period style furniture and tapestry-style fabrics, are modern and spotless. They all have private baths and direct dial phones. Guests are invited to relax in the castle's salon where tapestry chairs, a huge open fireplace, vases of fresh flowers and objets d'art create a refined setting. A stay here is as comfortable as it is atmospheric, for, although the castle dates from the sixteenth century, the Yoncourt-Pemezec family has worked hard to restore it to its current polished state of perfection. For travellers with smaller pocketbooks, the Yoncourt-Pemezecs also offer modest bed and breakfast accommodation in four small attic rooms that each have private bath and toilet and are homey, comfortable and spotlessly clean. *Directions: Located approximately forty kilometers northwest of St Brieuc, from St Brieuc take the N12 in the direction of Brest to the D767 and exit for Lannion-Bégard. At Bégard take the D15 in the direction of Pontrieux, eleven kilometers to Brélidy. Directions to the château are well marked once you arrive in the village.*

CHÂTEAU DE BRÉLIDY
Hôtelier: Yoncourt-Pemezec Family
Brélidy, 22140 Bégard
Tel: 96.95.69.38 Fax: 96.95.18.03
14 Rooms - Dbl from 425F to 980F
Open: 22 March to 4 November
Credit cards: VS
Table d'Hôte: 160F per person without wine
Region: Brittany

Paul and Jenny Dyer came to the Dordogne Valley from Eng
country setting in which to raise their two daughters. Th
wonderful, seventeenth-century farmhouse, abandoned and in a
spent their time and savings to literally rebuild and restore it. In
the Auberge du Noyer, named for the large walnut tree that fronts
inviting inn. Guests have only glowing reports and praise for the
the food and the hospitality of the hosts. The auberge's intimate   ...n has
a large, open fireplace and orange and brown tablecloths which blend warmly with
the stone walls and sienna tile floors. There is a veranda to front the home and
extend the seating area for morning breakfasts, or dinner on a balmy night. A
lovely swimming pool sits on a hill behind the farmhouse. The inn has ten
bedrooms all decorated beautifully in Laura Ashley prints and all with private bath
or shower. Open later in the season than most hotels in the region, guests return
when the weather turns a bit cooler to sit before the large fire, read or don
Wellingtons and walk the countryside lanes. The atmosphere at the Auberge du
Noyer is very relaxed and comfortable. Reservations accepted on a demi-pension
basis. *Directions: Le Bugue is located forty-one kilometers south of Périgueux on the D710.*
From Le Bugue travel west on the D703 five kilometers in the direction of Sainte Alvère to the
Auberge du Noyer.

AUBERGE DU NOYER
Hôteliers: Paul & Jenny Dyer
Le Reclaud de Bouny Bas, 24260 Le Bugue
Tel: 53.07.11.73 Fax: 53.54.57.44
10 Rooms - 720F: Dinner, bed & breakfast for two
Open: Palm Sunday to November
Credit cards: MC, VS
Restaurant, pool
Region: Dordogne

atmosphere of the Middle Ages prevails in the narrow, winding, cobblestoned streets leading to the Château Grimaldi, built by Raynier Grimaldi, the ruler of Monaco, in 1309. As the streets become narrower, you pass under buildings which form an archway and then arrive at Le Cagnard, which has been in operation for forty years. Monsieur and Madame Barel make guests feel welcome and at home. Dinner on the terrace, set under a full moon, or indoors with the atmosphere of a medieval castle and candlelight flickering against age-old walls, is a romantic experience and the presentation of the cuisine is exceptional. Chef Johnay creates a feast of rich delicacies and ensures that specialties such as "foie gras frais de canard" and "carre d'agneau" are professionally and artfully served to tempt the palate. The lift is charming, biblical paintings changing with each floor, and I found some marvelous rooms and views. Rooms two to twelve have a medieval flavor to their decor. *Directions: From Nice travel southwest on the N98 ten kilometers to Cros de Cagnes. Turn north on the D36 to Cagnes sur Mer and follow directions to Haut de Cagnes. The hôtel is found by turning right just after the private parking. Management cautions that it is a very narrow street.*

LE CAGNARD
Hôtelier: M & Mme Barel
Rue Pontis Long, Haut de Cagnes
06800 Cagnes sur Mer
Tel: 93.20.73.21 Telex: 462223 Fax: 93.22.06.39
26 Rooms - Dbl from 620F to 1420F
Open: All year
Credit cards: AX, MC, DC
Terrace restaurant
Region: Riviera

Domaine d'Auriac is a lovely ivy-clad manor on the outskirts of Carcassonne. To locate the hotel, travel two and a half kilometers southeast from the walled city on the D118 and D104. The twenty-three bedrooms of the Domaine d'Auriac are elegant and quiet and provide a relaxing environment. The rooms are nicely furnished and all have bathrooms, direct dial phones, mini-bars and television. The restaurant, overlooking the pool and garden, is most attractive. Local residents gather here for dinner to enjoy the excellent food and peaceful setting. The bar, in the old wine cellar, is cozy and inviting. The management provides personal touches and professional service. Enjoy the swimming pool, tennis courts and surrounding parklands. The hotel also provides conference facilities and sometimes caters to business groups either during the day or on an extended stay. Domaine d'Auriac's location affords a proximity to Carcassonne without being in the center of the bustling tourist attraction. Carcassonne is also a convenient stopover point when travelling between Provence and the Tarn, Basque or Perigord. *Directions: Located ninety-two kilometers southeast of Toulouse, four kilometers from Carcassonne, take the "Carcassonne Ouest" exit off the autoroute A61 and follow directions to "centre ville" and St Hilaire.*

DOMAINE D'AURIAC
Hôtelier: M & Mme B. Rigaudis
Route de St Hilaire, BP 554 Route de St Hilaire
11009 Carcassonne
Tel: 68.25.72.22 Telex: 500385 Fax: 68.47.35.54
23 Rooms - Dbl from 740F to 1340F
Closed: 14 January to 3 February
  Restaurant closed Sunday evenings low season
Credit cards: All major
Restaurant, pool, tennis
Region: Pyrénées Roussillon

Explore the medieval fortress of Carcassonne and then settle for an evening behind its massive walls in the intimate Hôtel de la Cité. Recessed into the walls near the Basilica St Nazaire, the hotel is on the site of the ancient episcopal palace and offers you the refined comfort of its rooms in a medieval atmosphere. The bar is a welcome spot to settle for a drink, its walls panelled in ornately carved wood and topped by beautiful and colorful murals that portray the life of days gone by. Breakfast is served in a room where tables are regally set on a carpet of Fleur de Lys under a beamed ceiling and surrounded by walls painted with shields and crests. The hotel's bedrooms, many of which open up onto the ramparts and a large enclosed garden, vary in price according to size, decor and view. Carcassonne is a magnificent fortress, completely restored to look as it did when first constructed centuries ago. It is impressive when viewed at a distance, rising above the vineyards at the foot of the Cevennes and Pyrénées, but even more spectacular when it can be explored on foot. Note: Although in principle the city is closed to all but pedestrian traffic, guests can enter the city by car (via Porte Narbonnaise), travel the Rue Mayrevieille, the rue Porte d'Aude and the rue St Louis and park at the hotel. *Directions: Carcassonne is located ninety-two kilometers southeast of Toulouse. The Hôtel de la Cité is found within the city ramparts.*

HÔTEL DE LA CITÉ
Hôtelier: Christophe Luraschi
Place de l'Église, 11000 Carcassonne
Tel: 68.25.03.34 Telex: 505296 Fax: 68.71.50.15
26 Rooms - Dbl from 960F to 1620F
Open: All year
Credit cards: AX, DC
Restaurant, parking
Hotel within city ramparts
Region: Pyrénées Roussillon

The village of Castillon du Gard sits on a knoll surrounded by grey-green olive trees and stretches of vineyards. Housed within medieval walls, the hotel, Le Vieux Castillon, runs the length of one small street in this village of sienna-tiled, sun-washed houses, so typical of Provence.   The first floor is a maze of tile floors, light sandstone archways, hallways and intimate sitting rooms. The renowned restaurant, Le Fumoir, overlooks the pool through arched windows. Lunch is sometimes served at tables set in a tiled courtyard. The staging of the pool is magnificent, set against a backdrop of the town ruins with vistas that sweep out over the countryside and neighboring villages. The bedrooms, found in the main building and in a neighboring annex, are furnished with floral wallpapers, complementing curtains and bedspreads and a tasteful mix of antiques and reproduction furniture. The style is one of Mediterranean elegance and leisure. Le Vieux Castillon is a remarkable accomplishment: eight years were spent to renovate a complex of village homes into this luxurious hotel. Care was taken to retain the character of the original buildings and, amazingly, stones were preserved, cleaned and reset within the walls. *Directions: From Avignon travel in the direction of Nîmes on the N86. At Remoulins take the D981 in the direction of Uzès and then travel two kilometers on D228.*

LE VIEUX CASTILLON
Hôtelier: Roger Traversac
Castillon du Gard, 30210 Remoulins
Tel: 66.37.00.77 Telex: 490946 Fax: 66.37.28.17
35 Rooms - Dbl from 740F to 1440F
Open: end of March to beginning of January
Credit cards: All major
Restaurant, tennis, pool
Region: Provence

Madame Gautier and her daughter, Delphine, were our gracious hosts at their restored château that dates from the twelfth and eighteenth centuries.   Set in a six-acre park, the main château houses the majority of guest bedrooms as well as a lovely restaurant with an abundance of fresh flowers, polished dark woods and antique furnishings.   The bedrooms are all furnished with refined taste: soft colors, antique or quality reproduction furniture sagely mixed with contemporary pieces and spotless, well-equipped bathrooms - all combining to provide a welcoming haven for the traveller.   Several bedrooms and beautiful apartments are located in a separate stone building that was commissioned to lodge the Knights of Malta, an elite corps of the French military in the twelfth century.   Their many different coats of arms are displayed on the shields in the small salon on the way to the luxurious rooms and suites which offer elegant and tranquil accommodations. These bedrooms are a bit more expensive than those in the château, but are larger, very quiet and have a view of the pool and/or garden.   Located just south of the picturesque wine capital of Beaune and just outside Chagny on N6, this twin towered château is atmospheric and peaceful, and displays an artistic woman's touch throughout.   *Directions: On the A6 from Paris, exit at Beaune and take the direction of Chalon sur Saône.   Coming from Lyon, exit at Chalon Nord and take the direction of Paris on the RN6.*

HÔSTELLERIE DU CHÂTEAU DE BELLECROIX
Hôtelier: Mme Evelyn Gautier
Route Nationale 6, 71150 Chagny
Tel: 85.87.13.86 Fax: 85.91.28.62
19 Rooms - Dbl from 590F to 990F
Open: February to 15 December
Credit cards: All major
Restaurant, park, swimming pool
Region: Burgundy

Chambord is the largest of the castles of the Loire Valley and very impressive in size and appearance. The castle stands dramatically on a large open expanse of lawn, bounded by forest. Although almost bare of furniture, it retains its grandeur and enchantment, especially at sunset or shrouded in the morning mist. Staying at the Hôtel du Grand Saint Michel provides an opportunity to explore the expanse of grounds surrounding Chambord either before you begin your day's adventures or at its end. It is one of the very few hotels in the Loire Valley that enjoys such a marvelous, close proximity to one of its castles. The Hôtel du Grand Saint Michel has an inviting terrace restaurant where many, hotel and château guests alike, enjoy a refreshing drink and snack. Indoors is an attractive restaurant and comfortable entry salon. Accommodation is surprisingly inexpensive. The rooms are simple in their country prints, basic in furnishings, but comfortable. Of the forty rooms a choice few look out through the surrounding lacy trees to the Château de Chambord. Of these, the corner rooms are the largest and should definitely be requested as they are no more expensive than the other rooms with a view. *Directions: Chambord is located twenty kilometers northeast of Blois by travelling the N956 south (four kilometers) and then the D33 east (sixteen kilometers).*

HÔTEL DU GRAND SAINT MICHEL
Hôtelier: Raymond Le Meur
Chambord, 41250 Bracieux
Tel: 54.20.31.31
40 Rooms - Dbl from 350F to 460F
Closed: 12 November to 28 December
Credit cards: VS, MC
Restaurant
Faces the Château de Chambord
Region: Loire Valley

Le Moulin du Roc is a small seventeenth- and eighteenth-century stone mill. With gardens sprawled along the river's edge, secluded even from the small village of Champagnac de Bélair, the setting of this small inn is picture-perfect. The fourteen rooms, although not large, are each stunning and the bathrooms all modern. One apartment is particularly enchanting: bridging the river below, it has a large room with a marvelous wood canopy double bed and an adjoining small room with a single bed. The bedroom windows overlook the lazy River Drome, the gardens and the beautiful birch-lined pastures. The small, captivating dining room utilizes the weathered old beams and wooden parts and mechanisms of the original mill in its decor. The atmosphere is intimate and the service is very attentive. Madame Gardillou is responsible for the kitchen and the exquisite cuisine. Preserving the traditions of fine gastronomy and employing established Périgord recipes and specialties, she has earned a coveted two-fork rating from Michelin. Menu prices are reasonable considering the excellence of the cuisine. Monsieur Gardillou is a most gracious and charming host. *Directions: Located thirty-three kilometers northwest of Périgueux, travel north on the D939 to Brantôme and from Brantôme six kilometers in the direction of Angoulème. Or from the village of Champagnac, travel northeast, six kilometers on D78 and D83.*

LE MOULIN DU ROC
Hôtelier: M & Mme Gardillou
24530 Champagnac de Bélair
Tel: 53.54.80.36 Telex: 571555 Fax: 53.54.21.31
14 Rooms - Dbl from 520F to 820F
Closed: mid-Nov to mid-Dec, mid-Jan to mid-Feb
  Restaurant closed: Tuesdays, & Wednesday lunch
Credit cards: All major
Restaurant, tennis court, pool, pedal boat
Region: Dordogne

François and Hedwige were on the front steps of their elegant château with their children as we drove up to Château des Briottières. The Valbrays are a charming, enthusiastic and artistic young couple who truly make their visitors feel like invited guests. Their grand home dates from 1773 and has been in François' family since 1820 when his great, great, great grandfather, the Comte de Valbray, resided here. Old family photos and portraits abound in the gracious salons and we were impressed by François' casual friendliness in spite of his noble heritage. It is hard to pick a favorite bedroom, as all are furnished in keeping with the style and mood of the château; however, a bedchamber, the Rose Room, is very special: feminine in decor, it was once inhabited by François' grandmother. Also, very special in their furnishings and outlook are the Lake Room and the Charles X Room. Downstairs the parquet floors, grand chandeliers, and marble fireplaces in the public rooms attest to a very rich and elegant heritage. The elegance of a bygone era continues as guests are privileged to dine at the one long candlelit table which is dressed with family silver and china. A stay of at least two days is recommended to fully appreciate the Valbrays' hospitality and the ambiance of this aristocratic setting. *Directions: From Angers (twenty-five kilometers) take the N162 north in the direction Laval. At Montreuil Juigné (seven and a half kilometers) take the D768 in the direction Feneu to Champigné. Château des Briottières is signposted from Champigné, located on the D290.*

CHÂTEAU DES BRIOTTIÈRES
Hôtelier: François & Hedwige de Valbray
Les Briottières, 49330 Champigné
Tel: 41.42.00.02 Telex: 720943 Fax: 41.42.01.55
8 Rooms - Dbl from 750F to 990F
Closed: 15 November to 15 January
Credit cards: All major
Restaurant - on a reservation only basis
Region: Loire Valley

The Champagne region of France produces a grape unique in the world. True champagne comes only from this beautiful region located just two hours east of Paris. In the heart of France's premier wine country, you may enjoy an excellent meal and taste some classic vintages at the Royal Champagne. Renowned for its cuisine, the restaurant of the Royal Champagne is very elegant, with tables set with white linen, crystal, silver and candlelight under a vaulted, beamed ceiling. A large fireplace warms the room and windows look out to spectacular views of the valley and surrounding vineyards. The bedrooms of the Royal Champagne are not traditional in decor, but modern and attractive. They are not exceptionally large and vary only in the color of the wallpaper, but they all have baths and small private terraces overlooking the vineyards. The village of Champillon Bellevue is set high on the hill amongst acres of terraced vineyards and located just a few kilometers north of Epernay, an important town in the Champagne region, making this a good base for champagne enthusiasts. *Directions: The Royal Champagne is a white stucco building, set just off the road that travels between Reims and Epernay. From Reims, take the direction Epernay south on the N51. Six kilometers before Epernay turn east towards Champillon ("Circuit Touristique - Route du Vignoble"). From Epernay take the direction Reims along the "Route Touristique".*

ROYAL CHAMPAGNE
Hôtelier: M Maral Dellinger
Champillon Bellevue, 51160 Ay
Tel: 26.52.87.11 Telex: 830111 Fax: 26.52.89.69
25 Rooms - Dbl from 800F to 1640F
Closed: 2 to 24 January
Credit cards: All major
Restaurant
Region: Champagne

In their family since 1742 the Marquis and Marquise de Longueil offer their château to overnight guests understandably with great pride and out of necessity to maintain this magnificent property. Built in 1650, the Château de Boussac is surrounded by a moat and pasture land. One gains access to the château by crossing a bridge and entering under the arched doorway into a central courtyard guarded by four regal turrets. Family treasures and photographs are very much in evidence and make you realize that the decor is not staged but real. If prior arrangements have been made, you can dine with the de Longueils in their family dining room, enjoying a delicious meal served on family china. Currently there are two suites and one single room for overnight guests and the family is in the process of renovating a fourth. The two suites are attractive and although not luxurious are commodious. Views from the rooms look out over the moat to surrounding gardens or pastures with grazing cattle. One cow actually peered in at us through the bathroom window as he munched on grass. *Directions: From Montluçon travel thirty-one kilometers east on N145 to Montmarault, continue northeast on the N145 a short distance in the direction of Moulins and then head east on the D46 for three and a half kilometers. Just past the town of St Marcel-en-Murat turn south on the D642. After the D642 crosses the A71, the Château de Boussac is sign posted and located just a short distance off the D642 to the southwest.*

CHÂTEAU DE BOUSSAC
Hôtelier: Marquis & Marquise de Longueil
à Target, 03140 Chantelle
Tel: 70.40.63.20 Fax: 70.40.60.03
5 Rooms - Dbl from 680F to 1050F
Open: 1 April to 15 November
Credit cards: VS
Table d'Hôte: 200F to 320F per person
Region: Auvergne

The Château de Prunoy enjoys a location relatively close to Paris and removed from the more touristy Loire area, thus is a favorite retreat for Parisian artists, writers and seekers of the good life in the country.　The elegant yet comfortable château is frequented by a fascinating and loyal clientele, no doubt drawn by the magnetic and charming presence of hostess Madame José Roumilhac.　Madame seems to weave a magic spell which slows the pace and imbues all with a sense of peace and tranquility, making sure that her guests feel "at home", free to wander the lovely, antique filled rooms and extensive grounds.　A tree-shaded walk down an overgrown lane leads to two enchanted ponds preserved in their natural state, appearing as they were in the sixteenth century when the original castle was built. Each bedroom is unique, and all are highly romantic, decorated and furnished with pleasing color schemes, lovely antiques and Madame's real flair for design, style and comfort. The Château de Prunoy's restaurant is light and airy with a floral motif, serving imaginative gourmet meals accompanied by attentive service.　Plan to stay more than one night here to truly unwind and experience the special ambiance that is the Château de Prunoy. *Directions: Travel north on the N6 from Auxerre, twenty-four kilometers to Joigny.　At Joigny, travel west on the D943 ten kilometers to Villefranche and then three kilometers south on the D18 to Prunoy.*

CHÂTEAU DE PRUNOY
Hôtelier: Mme José Roumilhac
Prunoy, 89120 Charny
Tel: 86.63.66.91 Fax: 86.63.77.79
14 Rooms - Dbl to 660F, Suites to 940F
Open: All year
Credit cards: All major
Restaurant, pool, grounds, ponds
Region: Western Loire Valley

Haute Provence is a region of France whose beauty is bounded by the snow-covered Alps, the fields of lavender and olive trees of Provence and the blue waters of the Riviera. Villages of soft stone and sienna tiled roofs cluster on hilltops and dot this picturesque landscape. Haute Provence is a beautiful region and serves as an ideal resting spot when travelling between the regions that bound it. La Bonne Étape is an old coaching inn, a grey-stone manor house with a tiled roof - blending beautifully and suited to the landscape. From its hilltop location, it enjoys panoramic views over the surrounding hills. Dating from the seventeenth century, the hotel has eleven bedrooms and seven apartments, all attractively decorated. The restaurant is recognized for the quality of its cuisine. Pierre Gleize and his son, Jany, employ local ingredients such as honey, lavender, herbs, lemon, pork, and rabbit to create masterpieces in the kitchen. Dine in front of a large stone fireplace and sample some of their specialties. But exceeding the praise for the cuisine are the superlatives guests use to describe the hospitality extended by your charming hosts, the Gleize family. *Directions: Château Arnoux is situated halfway between Digne and Sistern on the N85.*

LA BONNE ÉTAPE
Hôtelier: Pierre & Jany Gleize
Chemin du Lac
04160 Château Arnoux
Tel: 92.64.00.09 Telex: 430605
* Fax: 92.64.37.36*
18 Rooms - Dbl from 570F, Apt 1270F
Open: 15 February to 3 January
Credit cards: All major
Restaurant, bar, pool
Region: Haute Provence

Château de Chaumontel is an enchanting hotel that once belonged to the family of the Prince de Conde.   The castle gates and surrounding trees frame a breathtaking view of the castle.   Staged with a moat and a glorious expanse of green, lush grass and mounds of colorful flowers it is easy to understand why many French brides select the Château de Chaumontel as a setting for their wedding reception.   As a guest of the hotel one can also enjoy the romance of the castle's numerous bedchambers.   A labyrinth of narrow stairways winds up to rooms which are tucked under the beams or perhaps in one of the castle turrets.   All individual in their decor, the twenty rooms of the hotel are furnished with handsome antiques and pretty decorative prints.   A few of the bedrooms are a bit more private as they are located in a pavilion situated near the entrance.   The château has facilities to cater large parties and weddings but the guest dining room located in the castle proper is intimate and charming.   Tables are set before a large fireplace or on a warm day one can take advantage of the lovely white tables set in the garden. *Directions: Follow A1 from Le Bourget or Charles de Gaulle - Roissy airports to D9 then turn on N16 towards Luzarches and Chantilly.   Approximately eight kilometers before Chantilly a large sign indicates the Château - 200 meters further on.*

CHÂTEAU DE CHAUMONTEL
Hôtelier: M & Mme Patrick Rigard
21, rue André Vassord
Chaumontel, 95270 Luzarches
Tel: (1) 34.71.00.30 Telex: 609730
* Fax: (1) 34.71.26.97*
20 Rooms - Dbl from 540F to 900F
Open: All year
Credit cards: AX, VS
Restaurant, park
Region: Île de France

CHAUMONT SUR LOIRE   HÔSTELLERIE DU CHÂTEAU   Map: I

On the main road, opposite the gates that open to the road winding to the Château de Chaumont, you will discover the lovely Hôstellerie du Château.   An attractive, timbered building, the location of the hotel is its largest drawback, as it is hard to shut out the traffic noises from the rooms that overlook the road.   But for the Loire Valley the prices are moderate and from the moment you enter the hotel you will be charmed by the wood beamed interior, the glowing fire, the beautiful dining room, quaint salons and Gourdin's hospitality.   On a warm summer day tables are spread out under the trees in the front garden and provide an inviting spot to rest and enjoy a refreshing drink.   The hallways leading to the upstairs bedrooms are in need of some fresh paint, but the rooms are still quite attractive.   The least expensive rooms fall into the moderate price range and are smaller in size and overlook the road.   The more expensive rooms are worth a splurge as they are more commodious and overlook the hotel's back garden and pool and enjoy views of the passing Loire River.   All the rooms are decorated in warm and attractive colors and the bathrooms are modern.   The Hôstellerie du Château is a well-located hotel for exploring the castles of the Loire.   Accommodations are not luxurious, but comfortable and well priced.   *Directions: Chaumont sur Loire is located thirty-six kilometers northeast of Tours travelling the N751.*

HÔSTELLERIE DU CHÂTEAU
Hôtelier: M & Mme Gourdin
2, rue du Marechal de Lattre
Chaumont sur Loire, 41150 Onzain
Tel: 54.20.98.04 Fax: 54.20.97.98
15 Rooms - Dbl from 390F to 750F
Open: 1 March to end of November
Credit cards: VS
Restaurant, pool
Region: Loire Valley

Hôstellerie le Prieuré is a lovely château on the banks above the Loire. In season Le Prieuré caters to tours and buses do tend to invade the sense of days gone by. However, if you travel off season and can obtain a room in the castle proper you will be rewarded with a sense of regality. Stone steps wind up the castle turret to spacious rooms which are beautifully appointed with large windows set in thick stone walls opening up to fantastic vistas of the flowing Loire River. There are a few rooms built at the base of the château, called the terrace rooms, that open onto private patios. They are also handsome in their decor but not as luxurious in size. When heavily booked, Le Prieuré also offers more "motel-like" accommodations in bungalows found near the pool. The hotel claims that they advise guests when only bungalow rooms are available as they do not afford the castle experience that one would anticipate. The restaurant, an elegant room surrounded by windows, has earned a reputation for excellent cuisine. Situated in a large estate high above the Loire, this lovely hotel commands panoramic views of the river and makes a convenient base for exploring the enchanting Château de Saumur and western stretches of the Loire Valley. *Directions: From Saumur, travel northwest eight kilometers on D751 in the direction of Gennes.*

LE PRIEURÉ
Hôtelier: M P.H. Doumerc
Chênehutte les Tuffeaux, 49350 Gennes
Tel: 41.67.90.14 Telex: 720379
   Fax: 41.67.92.24
35 Rooms - Dbl from 790F to 1640F
Closed: 5 January to 1 March
Credit cards: VS, AX
Restaurant, pool, tennis, park
Region: Loire Valley

This hotel is in the town of Chenonceaux and within walking distance of its spectacular castle. The location of the Bon Laboureur et du Château affords one the opportunity to linger close to one of the most elegant of the Loire Valley's Renaissance châteaux. The hotel's accommodations are simple and moderately priced. Bedrooms are found in the building above the restaurant as well as in neighboring ivy-covered annexes. The bedrooms, all with either private bath or shower, vary in price depending on size and whether or not they overlook the road, garden or courtyard. Some of the rooms are decorated with traditional pieces while others are fresh with their brighter colors and modern furnishings. The hallways that lead to the bedrooms are attractively appointed with antiques and copper pieces. Behind a distracting glass partition, the hotel's restaurant is intimate and charming in its decor and offers an enticing menu. A second restaurant is planned for 1992. Managed for generations by the Jeudi family, the family is still very much behind the scenes, but chances are you will be received by an employee. The Bon Laboureur is more a town-hotel than country inn.
Directions: From Tours take N76 first following directions to Bléré and then on to Chenonceaux. Chenonceaux is located twenty-nine kilometers east of Tours.

BON LABOUREUR ET DU CHÂTEAU
Hôtelier: Jeudi Family
6, rue du Docteur Bretonneau
37150 Chenonceaux
Tel: 47.23.90.02 Fax: 47.23.82.01
29 Rooms - Dbl from 370F to 580F
Open: 15 March to 30 December
Credit cards: All major
Restaurant, pool
Region: Loire Valley

Chinon is a pretty riverside town with narrow cobblestoned streets which climb to the ruins of its crowning castle. This is where Jeanne d'Arc met Le Dauphin and is an interesting stop for any Loire Valley itinerary. The Hôtel Diderot is well located just off the Place Jeanne d'Arc in a residential district of town. The Hôtel Diderot is owned and managed by Theo Kazamias and his family who came to France from Cyprus ten years ago in search of a new life. He purchased and completely renovated the home. Off the entry way, a breakfast room set with country tables and chairs before a large fifteenth-century fireplace is where one enjoys breakfast complete with homemade jams and the chatter and good spirits of the many British travellers who frequent this hotel. An old wooden stairway and hallways with exposed walls and beams lead to eighteen of the bedrooms. Another room is found in the pavilion, and three additional rooms, converted from the stables, are located at street level and are equipped for handicap access. All of the bedrooms are furnished with a mixture of antique and contemporary pieces with bathrooms that are adequate and spotless. The Hôtel Diderot attracts bus groups and offers simple comforts and moderate prices. *Directions: Chinon is located forty-eight kilometers southwest of Tours. From Tours take the D751. In Chinon follow the road west along the River Vienne to Place Jeanne D'Arc. Circle round the Place and turn left on Rue Buffon.*

HÔTEL DIDEROT
Hôtelier: Theo Kazamias
4, rue Buffon, 37500 Chinon
Tel: 47.93.18.87 Fax: 47.93.37.10
25 Rooms - Dbl from 320F to 400F
Closed: 16 December to 14 January
Credit cards: All major
No restaurant
Region: Loire Valley

Travelling east from Tours on N76, look for signs before you reach Montrichard for the Château de Chissay in the small town of Chissay en Touraine.   At the top of a small hill, the arched stone entry way between twin towers is actually a side entrance to this "petite" château.   Walk through the vaulted stone walls over old cobblestones to reach the inner courtyard with its fountain and open cloister side which lets in cool breezes and looks out over a vista of the Loire Valley.   Tapestry covers the chairs in the intimate restaurant, and heavy antique furnishings dress the grand salons.   At the time of our visit the bedrooms were all occupied but a helpful management described them as all having private baths and beautifully traditional furnishings.   From the lovely decor and refined taste evident throughout the public areas of the château, we are sure the twenty bedrooms and seven apartments are very comfortable and pleasant.   Located in a twenty-acre estate, this romantic castle is a former royal residence containing a dungeon that dates from the eleventh century.   Despite its white stone walls and floors, and heavy, forbidding old wooden doors, the Château de Chissay provides a warm and luxurious ambiance from which to explore the many other châteaux of the Loire Valley. *Directions: From Tours travel forty-eight kilometers west of Tours in the direction of Chenonceaux and then Montrichard.   Chissay is located four kilometers before the town of Montrichard.*

CHÂTEAU DE CHISSAY
Hôtelier: M. Longet
Chissay en Touraine, 41400 Montrichard
Tel: 54.32.32.01 Telex: 750393 Fax: 54.32.43.80
27 rooms - Dbl from 700F, Apt to 1700F
Closed: January to March
Credit Cards: All major
Restaurant, pool, park
Region: Loire Valley

A converted mill, this ivy-covered complex of buildings is situated along the River Orne just downstream from the old stone bridge.   It is an idyllic setting ablaze with masses of flowers and the sound of the river tumbling past the former mill is quite soothing.   Le Moulin du Vey has a lovely terrace set with tables and shaded by a lacy willow tree.   If you choose to dine indoors, the restaurant is in an adjacent building.   Twelve bedrooms tucked away in the former mill could use a little sprucing up but they are comfortable and equipped with either private bath or shower.   Three kilometers from the mill is the Relais de Surone, an annex, where seven additional bedrooms are offered.   The Relais is an old home built in the style of a church or a priory.   Although away from the river and without a restaurant, the rooms of the Relais are more attractive and spacious than those of the Moulin.   Breakfast can be taken in the salon, in the bedroom, or, on a nice day, in the front garden.   Clécy le Vey is the capital of the beautiful district referred to as Swiss Normandy.   *Directions: Le Moulin du Vey is located two kilometers east of Clécy in the village of Le Vey.   The Relais is located on the other side of Clécy le Vey, just off the road that travels between Caen and Domfront (route D562).   Clécy is located thirty-seven kilometers south of Caen.*

LE MOULIN DU VEY
Hôtelier: Mme Denise Leduc
14570 Clécy le Vey
Tel: 31.69.71.08 Fax: 31.69.14.14
12 Rooms (Mill) - 7 Rooms (Relais)
*   Dbl from 420F to 640F*
Open: Moulin du Vey - 28 Dec to 30 Nov
*   Le Relais - Easter to October*
Credit cards: All major
Restaurant, park on river's edge
Region: Normandy

Colroy la Roche is a town typical of the Alsatian region.   The Hôstellerie la Cheneaudière, set on a hillside overlooking the town and surrounding valleys, was built to resemble a country tavern.   The bedrooms are very luxurious in their decor and appointments.   Beautiful wallpapers, handsome paintings, a tasteful blend of antique and contemporary furnishings and wall-to-wall carpets enhanced by Oriental rugs have all been selected and achieve an elegant environment in the bedrooms.   Each room is equipped with a telephone, television, mini-bar and remarkably spacious bathroom.   Many of the hotel's guest rooms also enjoy the privacy of a covered terrace.   Breakfast served on your own patio with views out over the village of Colroy is a treat.   The hotel has two dining rooms whose formal atmosphere is warmed by a large fire.   The cuisine is prepared under the supervision of Chef Jean Paul Bossee and includes specialties such as "millefeuille de foie gras & truffes" and "tartare de saumon sauvage".   The hotel has a large spacious lounge and a few elegant boutiques.   La Cheneaudière also organizes private hunting parties in the summer, autumn and winter months. *Directions: Colroy la Roche is located sixty-two kilometers southwest of Strasbourg.   Travel the D392 first in the direction of Molsheim, then Schirmeck.   Beyond Schirmeck at Saint Blaise la Roche take the D424 just a few kilometers to Colroy la Roche.*

HÔSTELLERIE LA CHENEAUDIÈRE
Hôtelier: M & Mme François
Colroy la Roche, 67420 Saales
Tel: 88.97.61.64 Telex: 870438 Fax: 88.47.21.73
32 Rooms - Dbl from 690F to 2100F
Open: March to December
Credit cards: All major
Restaurant, tennis, pool, sauna
Region: Alsace

Turn south off N89 (halfway between Périgueux and Brive) at Le Lardin and continue in the direction of Montignac for one kilometer to Conde where you turn east towards Coly on the D62. A sign before Coly directs down a private drive enclosed by cornfields to this old mill in its idyllic setting where tables are set in a garden bounded by stone walls, colorful flowers and a rushing stream. The flock of geese inhabiting a nearby lawn complete the postcard scene. The original core of this ivy-covered manor house was a forge and dates from the thirteenth century. Belonging to the Hamelin family for over three hundred years, the forge later became a mill and other sections were added with distinctive arched windows and doors. Family antiques decorate the salons, halls and bedrooms, including a magnificently tall grandfather clock on the stair landing. On the second floor the bedrooms are attractive in their simplicity and all have well appointed bathrooms. Since my first visit, the Hamelins have increased the number of rooms that they offer for overnight accommodation from six to ten and have built a lovely pool. Guests are expected to dine here and Madame will tailor her cuisine to the wishes of any on an extended stay. The Manoir d'Hautegente proves to be a picturesque, tranquil and convenient base from which to explore central Périgord. *Directions: (referenced above) Coly is located twenty-five kilometers southwest of Brive.*

MANOIR D'HAUTEGENTE
Hôtelier: Mme Edith Hamelin
Coly, 24120 Terrasson
Tel: 53.51.68.03 Telex: 550689 Fax: 53.50.38.52
10 Rooms - Dbl from 620F to 850F
Open: 15 November to 1 April
Credit cards: AX, VS, MC
Restaurant, riverside setting, pool
Region: Dordogne

The medieval village of Conques overlooks the Dourdou Gorge. Tucked off the beaten track, the village is glorious in the gentle light of evening or in the mist of early day. Conques' pride is an eleventh-century abbey, directly across from which is a simple hotel, the Ste Foy. The shuttered windows of our room opened up to the church steeples and we woke to the melodious sound of bells. The decor of the hotel is neat and attractive and one can't fault the location. For 1990 the Garcenot family has renovated a neighboring eighteenth-century building to increase their room offering from 20 to 34 rooms. The restaurant is no longer reserved exclusively for guests of the hotel and is open for breakfast, lunch and dinner. The interior restaurant is lovely and rustic in its decor, the walls hung with an exhibition of French, English and American paintings and on warm summer nights dinner is served family-style on a sheltered courtyard terrace. One can order à la carte or select from a well-chosen three- or four-course fixed menu at a very reasonable price. The restaurant offers a number of regional dishes. The Roquefort cheese produced in the area is exceptional and the house "salade verte aux noix et roquefort et huile de noix" is a perfect first course to any meal. A wide selection of fine French wines from the various provinces comprise the wine list. *Directions: Conques is located thirty-seven kilometers northwest of Rodez on the D901.*

HÔTEL STE FOY
Hôtelier: Marie France Garcenot
Conques
12320 St Cyprien
Tel: 65.69.84.03 Fax: 65.72.81.04
34 Rooms - Dbl from 414F to 684, Suite 1000F
Open: 10 April to 15 November
Credit cards: MC, VS
Restaurant, covered pool
Region: Lot & Aveyron

Vieux Cordes is an enchanting, medieval hilltop village.   It is a treasure and found at the center of this medieval city is the Hôtel du Grand Écuyer.   Once the home and hunting lodge of Raymond VII, Comte de Toulouse, this is a grand hotel that seems to improve with age.   Found along the upstairs hallway whose floors creak and slant, the fifteen bedrooms are very impressive in their decor.   Decorated with period furnishings, a few of the rooms boast magnificent four poster beds and some even enjoy large fireplaces.   The bedroom windows, set in thick stone walls, open on to glorious vistas of the surrounding countryside.   The reputation of the hotel's restaurant reflects the expertise of Monsieur Yves Thuriès, under whose direction and guidance selections from the menu are further enhanced by artful and creative presentation.   His specialty is desserts and they are divine in taste as well as presentation.   If you want to try your own talent in the kitchen, purchase a copy of his book, "La Nouvelle Patisserie".   Vieux Cordes is a gem.   It is a medieval village that proves to be a highlight of many a trip and the Hôtel du Grand Écuyer is the final polish that makes Cordes an ideal stopover for any itinerary.   The Thuriès family is responsible for the renovations of the Hôstellerie du Vieux Cordes located at the top of this charming village - much simpler in decor and very reasonably priced. *Directions: Cordes is a small medieval village located twenty-five kilometers northwest of Albi on the D600.*

HÔTEL DU GRAND ÉCUYER
Hôtelier: M Yves Thuriès
Rue Voltaire, 81170 Cordes
Tel: 63.56.01.03 Fax: 63.56.16.99
15 Rooms - Dbl from 710F to 1350F
Open: March to October
Credit cards: AX, DC, VS
Restaurant, Medieval city
Region: Tarn

An alternative for travellers who would like to avoid the crowds on the island of Le Mont Saint Michel, the ivy-clad, grey-stone Manoir de la Roche Torin is a lovely hotel.   This stately manor was a private residence for twenty-five years before it was converted to a hotel.   A short tree-lined drive past an ancient chapel on the front lawn leads to the front steps.   The highlights of this hotel are the mix of antique furnishings in the public rooms and the magnificent view from the dining room where one looks out over sheep grazing on the tidal grasslands to Le Mont Saint Michel.   The regional specialty known as "pre-salted lamb", sheep who have grazed on the salty grass, is roasted over a large open hearth in the restaurant. Two stately grandfather clocks watch over the dinner guests.   It is important to note that hotel guests are expected to dine in the Manoir's restaurant.   The twelve bedrooms of the Manoir de la Roche Torin are furnished with modern pieces and sometimes overly bright colors have been chosen for their decor.   The rooms, however, are clean, cheerful and reasonably priced.   All but one room is equipped with private bath.   Considering its location, priceless views and the warm welcome extended by the Barraux family, this hotel is a bargain and a tranquil haven near an otherwise congested tourist destination.   *Directions: Courtils is located nine kilometers east of Le Mont St Michel.   From Le Mont St Michel travel the "route de la baie" - the D43 and D275.*

MANOIR DE LA ROCHE TORIN
Hôtelier: M & Mme Barraux
Bas Courtils, 50220 Ducey "La Roche Torin"
Tel: 33.70.96.55 Fax: 33.48.35.20
12 Rooms - Dbl from 440F to 810F
Open: 15 March to 15 November
Credit cards: All major
Restaurant
Region: Normandy

Perched on a little hill in the middle of a lovely valley in Provence is the charming medieval village of Crillon le Brave comprised of only a cluster of weathered stone houses and a picturesque church. The town is completely non commercial except for one of Provence's jewels, the deluxe Hostellerie de Crillon le Brave which is terraced on the hillside just below the church. This small hotel of 20 rooms exudes an aura of elegance, yet there is nothing stuffy nor intimidating about staying here. The well-trained staff are all friendly and the ambiance is delightful. The restoration has been beautifully accomplished maintaining all the wonderful wood and stone textures which have been delightfully accented by the bold happy colors of provençal print materials. Fine country antiques are used throughout. The guest rooms too are prettily decorated in the same style and most have magnificent views of the countryside. The hillside location lends itself well to romance: the dining room is located in a medieval looking vaulted ceilinged room which opens out onto a splendid terrace where meals are usually served. Steps from the terrace a path leads down to a lower garden where a swimming pool invites one to linger on comfortable lounges and soak in the view. *Directions: In Carpentras follow signs toward Mount Ventoux and Bédoin on the D974. Travel 10 kilometers northeast and just before the village of Bédoin, take the left turn marked Crillon le Brave.*

HOSTELLERIE DE CRILLON LE BRAVE
Hotelier: Peter Chittick
Place de l'Eglise, 84410 Crillon le Brave
Tel: 90.65.61.61 Fax: 90.65.62.86
20 Rooms - Dbl 900F to 1300F
Open: from March to January
Credit cards: MC, VS, AX
Restaurant, swimming pool
Located: 40 km east of Avignon
Region: Provence

Hotel Descriptions

On an expanse of grounds, this lovely complex is a mix of stone and brick buildings, handsome with weathered timbers, lovely tile and slate roofs. Buildings stagger along a beautiful garden path and date from the fourteenth, fifteenth, and eighteenth centuries. Five rustically handsome double rooms and a suite with its own kitchen to house as many as four guests (private dinners can be arranged and served in the suite) open onto the expanse of grounds and overlook a small lake guarded by Balthazar the Swan. The Chahines have made their home in the larger, main house. For private functions a wonderful old room has been turned into a dining room whose tables are set round an ancient apple press. Madame Chahine personally coordinates art exhibitions in the summer months that are displayed in the marvelous old thirteenth-century barn and open to the public. Monsieur Chahine's strong and personal interest is understandable when you realize and recognize the paintings hung in his own home as those of his father, a famous painter, and he radiates a genuine pride as the only son and namesake. One month each year, concerts are also held in the thirteenth century timbered barn, acoustically excellent with its hard dirt floor. *Directions: Follow the D916 approximately twenty-eight kilometers northeast of Argentan and then travel two kilometers west on the C3 to the hillside village of Crouttes. Le Prieuré Saint Michel is located just beyond the village on the right hand side.*

LE PRIEURÉ SAINT MICHEL
Hôtelier: Monsieur & Madame Chahine
61120 Crouttes
Tel: 33.39.15.15 Fax: 33.36.15.16
5 Rooms - Dbl from 600F, Suite to 1200F
Open: All year
Credit cards: VS
Table d'Hôte: 250F per person including drinks
Region: Normandy

On the western outskirts of Paris, the Abbaye des Vaux de Cernay offers elegant accommodation and dining within the walls and ruins of a dramatic twelfth-century abbey. Sequestered at the end of a lovely forested drive that winds through the "Park Regionale de la Haute Vallée", surrounded by expanses of lawn and fronted by a serene lake, the setting is magnificent. Recently converted to a hotel, as an abbey, the Abbaye des Vaux de Cernay played an important role in French history. As a private residence, the Rothschild family took possession in the nineteenth century and was responsible for much of its restoration. Impressive ruins, vaulted ceilings, arched entries, massive wood doors, lovely antiques, grand wide hallways, a handsome mix of stone, tile and parquet floors and old stone walls are grand and imposing. The main dining room is very formal and intimate, set under the arches of the old abbey. Warmed by a large fireplace the restaurant walls are hung with beautiful paintings and the tables are set with red velvet chairs and only the best of linens, crystal and silver. The abbaye currently has sixty rooms to offer overnight guests. At the entrance gates, the stables were under renovation (Spring 1990) to accommodate by the end of the year an additional sixty guest rooms. *Directions: From Paris take the A6 then the A10 for approximately fourteen kilometers, direction of Chartres. Take the Les Ulis exit, direction of Gometz along the D35 and then the D40 through Les Molières and on to Cernay-la-Ville. The Abbaye is west of town.*

ABBAYE DES VAUX DE CERNAY
Hôtelier: Michel Lasserre
Cernay-la-Ville, 78720 Dampierre-en-Yvelines
Tel: (1) 34.85.23.00 Fax: (1) 34.85.20.95
60 Rooms - Dbl from 850F to 1750F, Suite to 3700F
Open: All year
Credit cards: AX, DC
Restaurant, park, lake, tennis, hunting, fishing
Region: Île de France

DOMME   HÔTEL DE L'ESPLANADE

The Dordogne River makes a panoramic journey through a r[...]
castles. The ancient village of Domme has for centurie[...]
hundred feet above the river and commands a magnificent[...]
itself is enchanting, with ramparts that date from the t[...]
narrow streets that wind through its old quarter and p[...]
century Hôtel de Ville. At the town center under the ol[...]
access to some interesting stalactite and stalagmite grottos. But [...]
come to Domme for its spectacular views and the best vantage point is from the
Terrasse de la Barre. Very near to la Barre, facing the church, is a hotel which
enables you to savor the village long after the tour buses have departed: the
Gillards extend a warm and friendly greeting at the Hôtel de l'Esplanade. René
Gillard is both your host and chef. In the dining room he'll propose some excellent
regional specialties that feature the delicious crepes, truffles, foie gras and local
fish. There are two restaurants to choose from, both attractive and very country in
decor. The hotel's twenty rooms, all with either bath or shower, are located in the
main building or in a neighboring annex that was once a building of the church and
dates from the seventeenth century. The bedrooms are simply decorated and
reasonably priced. *Directions: Domme is located seventy-five kilometers southeast of
Périgueux. From Sarlat-la-Canéda travel south to Cénac and across to Domme.*

HÔTEL DE L'ESPLANADE
Hôtelier: M René Gillard
24250 Domme
Tel: 53.28.31.41 Fax: 53.28.49.92
20 Rooms - Dbl from 440F to 890F
Closed: 13 November to 12 February
Credit cards: AX, VS, MC
Restaurant
Region: Dordogne

glance this hotel appears a typically French roadside restaurant, pretty with
al wood shutters and flower boxes overflowing with a profusion of red, pink
white geraniums at every window. The wonderful surprise one discovers is
at this restaurant also offers thirty-nine rooms in a quiet rear wing, all far
removed from any traffic noises. Beautifully appointed, all of the bedrooms have
private bath or shower and all rooms are equipped with direct-dial telephones and
mini-bars. The bedrooms are delightfully fresh in their decor, hung with pretty
flowered wallpapers and furnished in antique reproductions. With a good night's
rest in mind, the layout of the hotel was constructed so that all the bedrooms
overlook the garden. Fourteen of the accommodations are suites with private
patios in the very tranquil annex. The public areas, including the well known and
respected restaurant, are all very charming with many warm decorative touches and
tasteful antiques. Monsieur Patrick, the chef, is renowned in the region. The
Jean-Paul Perardel family manage the Aux Armes de Champagne with care and
taste. This is an ideal haven for overnight accommodations while touring the
Champagne district. *Directions: L'Épine is located forty kilometers southeast of Reims.
Take the N44 south from Reims to Châlons sur Marne and then the N3 east in the direction of
Metz. The hotel is situated eight kilometers from Châlons sur Marne on the N3.*

AUX ARMES DE CHAMPAGNE
Hôtelier: Denise & Jean-Paul Perardel
31, ave du Luxembourg, 51460 L'Épine
Tel: 26.66.96.79 Telex: 830998 Fax: 26.66.92.31
39 Rooms - Dbl from 485F to 895F
Closed: 5 January to 11 February
Credit cards: VS, MC
Restaurant, garden, mini-golf
Region: Champagne

Monsieur and Madame Treillou have opened up their home to guests. This ivy-covered former rectory is just across the cobblestone courtyard from the church. The reception area is a cozy sitting room with an oft used fireplace, warm tile floors and a gallery of treasured paintings. Madame Treillou was an antique dealer and had a shop housed in a wing of the building. The entire hotel is lovingly furnished with her selections of antiques which add a richness and warmth to the decor. Every bedroom is tasteful and unique and all have a lovely armoire. What were once the children's rooms have all been tastefully supplied with television, mini-bar, direct dial phones and all have a modern private bath or shower. Madame tends the lovely "English" garden, still in full bloom at the time of our fall visit. The tables in the garden courtyard invite a leisurely breakfast or an afternoon read. If the weather does not cooperate, a cozy fire is lit every morning in the open hearth fireplace of the breakfast room. Although Le Prieuré is near the main road that travels through Ermenonville, the mellow chimes of the adjacent church will temper any traffic noises. The Treillous are extremely gracious hosts and we are fortunate that they now offer their home to guests. *Directions: Located forty-seven kilometers northeast of Paris, take the A1 and exit at Survilliers. From Survilliers take the D922 north to Ermenonville. In town follow direction of Senlis on the N330 and you will come directly to Le Prieuré.*

HÔTEL LE PRIEURÉ
Hôtelier: Jean Pierre & Marie José Treillou
Chevet de l'Église, 60950 Ermenonville
Tel: 44.54.00.44 Telex: 145110 Fax: 44.54.02.21
11 Rooms - Dbl from 550F to 600F
Open: All year
Credit cards: Mc, VS, DC
No restaurant, garden
Region: Île de France

The vine-covered Hôtel Cro Magnon was built on the site where the skull of prehistoric Cro Magnon man was unearthed and a beautiful collection of prehistoric flints can be seen in the hotel.   Managed by the third generation of the Leyssales family, this is a tranquil country-style hotel with beautiful furnishings from the Perigord region.   The hotel has a large swimming pool, perfect for warm summer days, and a park of four acres.   There are twenty-three rooms, some of which are in the annex added in 1962.   Rooms are priced according to their location and size.   Back bedrooms in the annex look out through shuttered windows onto the expanse of colorful garden and pool.   The restaurant is truly delightful in its country French decor and the menu features Perigordian specialties that, alone, are a prime attraction of the region.   The hotel's front terrace is set under the shade of draping vines and is an ideal place to linger over lunch or enjoy an aperitif.   Les Eyzies is a popular tourist destination and the town is rich in accommodation.   The Cro Magnon hotel proves to be a choice and favorite of many which is a direct reflection on the standards of service and welcome set by the Leyssales family.   We continue to receive only words of praise from our readers who have experienced the hospitality of the Leyssales family for this lovely hotel.
Directions: Les Eyzies is located forty-five kilometers southeast of Périgueux. The Cro Magnon is located on the route from Périgueux at the entrance to the village.

HÔTEL CRO MAGNON
Hôtelier: M & Mme Jacques Leyssales
24620 Les Eyzies de Tayac
Tel: 53.06.97.06 Telex: 570637 Fax: 53.06.95.45
23 Rooms - Dbl from 460F to 900F
Open: end of April to mid-October
Credit cards: All major
Restaurant, pool, flower garden
Region: Dordogne

"The Annexe"

For more than a thousand years this majestic château has soaked up the sun and looked across the beautiful blue water of the Mediterranean. Rising thirteen hundred feet above sea level, the medieval village of Èze looks down upon Cap Ferrat and Nice. You can happily spend an entire afternoon on the secluded hotel terrace overlooking the pool and the stunning coastline vistas. In the sparkle of evening lights, the coastal cities seem to dance along the waterfront. The bedchambers open onto views of the Riviera or surrounding hillsides. Housed within the walls of this medieval village, the rooms are not grand or large, but tastefully appointed with modern conveniences. Enjoy a drink in the bar just off the pool while studying the day's menu selections. For lunch or dinner, a meal at the Château de la Chèvre d'Or is a wonderful experience because of the cuisine and the incredible views. The restaurant is popular with the local community and the many celebrities who have homes on the Riviera, so reservations are as difficult to get as room reservations. Attentive service, superb cuisine, beautiful views and a peaceful, serene medieval atmosphere make the Château de la Chèvre d'Or a hotel to which you will eagerly return. *Directions: Èze Village is located on the "Moyenne Corniche", the N7, between Nice and Monaco (thirteen kilometers east of Nice). Exit the Autoroute, A8, at La Turbie.*

CHÂTEAU DE LA CHÈVRE D'OR
Hôtelier: Pierre de Daeniken
Directeur: Randrianasolo Simon
Rue du Barri, 06360 Èze Village
Tel: 93.41.12.12 Telex: 970839 Fax: 93.41.06.72
11 Rooms - Dbl from 1600F to 2800F
Open: March to December
Credit cards: AX, VS, DC
Restaurant, lovely coastal views, pool
Region: Riviera

Monsieur Andre Rochat in the fabled tradition of Swiss excellence has renovated the former château of Prince William of Sweden and converted the magnificent residence into a hotel of superb luxury. The Château Eza is located in the medieval village of Èze, perched thirteen hundred feet above the coastline of the Riviera. The hotel's bedrooms are found in a cluster of buildings that front onto Èze's narrow, winding, cobble stoned streets. Most of the rooms have a private entry and blend beautifully as part of the village scene. Accommodation can only be described as extremely luxurious apartments or suites. The decor is stunning, with priceless antiques and Oriental rugs. Each room enjoys spectacular views and some have private terraces, extending out over the rooftops of the village, and wood-burning fireplaces. The Château Eza has a renowned restaurant with views and service to equal the excellent cuisine. A multi-level tea room with its hanging garden terraces is a delightful and informal spot for afternoon tea or a light meal. The Château Eza is a wonderful final splurge before departing France: the international airport at Nice is just fifteen minutes from Èze Village by the Autoroute. Note: As Èze is closed to all but pedestrian traffic look for the reception at the base of the village - it is easy to spot as two donkeys, "the bagagistes", are stabled out front. *Directions: Èze Village is located on the "Moyenne Corniche", the N7, between Nice and Monaco. Exit the Autoroute, A8, at La Turbie.*

CHÂTEAU EZA
Hôtelier: Andre Rochat
Rue de la Pise, 06360 Èze Village
Tel: 93.41.12.24 Telex: 470382 Fax: 93.41.16.64
11 Rooms - Dbl from 1360F, Suite to 3660F
Open: April to November
Credit cards: All major
Restaurant
Region: Riviera

The Hôstellerie du Château is a lovely and luxurious château hotel. Set in a magnificent park, fifty-five miles from the Charles de Gaulle - Roissy airport, the Hôstellerie du Château guarantees a peaceful night's rest whether it is your first or last night in France. The château has twenty-three individually decorated bedrooms to offer as accommodation. The decor is elegant. The walls are covered with beautiful materials that complement the bedspreads and drapes; the beds are large and comfortable; the bathrooms spacious; the location is peaceful and the views are splendid. Room twenty-nine, in the old tower, is decorated in feminine pinks and whites and offers views of the valley through its windows set deep in the old stone walls. Rooms twenty and twelve are both large, lovely apartments. Outdoor facilities include tennis courts and a new nine-hole golf course. Looking out onto the expanse of garden through lovely floor-to-ceiling windows, the restaurant is dressed in elegance with a display of beautiful linens, silver and crystal and offers a magnificent menu, with pastries too tempting to resist. The vaulted wine cellar maintains an excellent selection of fine French wines. *Directions: From Paris take the A4 and exit at Château Thierry following directions to Soissons. Then take the D967 north to Fère en Tardenois. The Hôstellerie du Château is located three kilometers outside Fère en Tardenois, ninety kilometers northeast of CDG Airport.*

HÔSTELLERIE DU CHÂTEAU
Hôtelier: Alain Fremiot
02130 Fère en Tardenois
Tel: 23.82.21.13 Telex: 145526 Fax: 23.82.37.81
23 Rooms - Dbl from 1000F, Suite to 1980F
Open: All year
Credit cards: AX, VS, DC
Restaurant, tennis, golf
Region: Champagne

At the heart of the Loire Valley, ideal for touring the châteaux, one could not choose a better spot than the Manoir du Grand Martigny. It offers location, comfort, charm and a warm welcome, all at a reasonable price.   Just west of Tours, the Grand Martigny is buffered from any noise by its own beautiful sixteen acre park.   The Desmarais purchased and renovated this sixteenth century home within the last decade and refurbished it with the intention of offering rooms to overnight guests.   The rooms are lovely, spacious, and very pretty in their decor and the bathrooms are luxurious.   Breakfast is served at a grand table in front of a large rustic fireplace in a room that adjoins a beautiful country kitchen.   When the house is full of guests, places are also set in the formal dining room.   A courtyard at the back, overlooked by its own turret, is a tranquil place for a morning croissant, and a games room is wonderful for children who aren't tired by "châteaux-hopping". Currently all the rooms are housed in the manor, but Henri has plans to eventually convert a free standing tower into a honeymoon retreat.   The Manoir du Grand Martigny makes for an ideal and charming base. *Directions: From Paris, leave the A10 at "Tours North" and drive to the Loire.   Do not cross the river but turn to the right on the north bank, N152 in the direction of Langeais.   The Manoir, signposted as "Chambre d'Hôte", is located on the north side directly off the N152 just five kilometers from Tours.*

MANOIR DU GRAND MARTIGNY
Hôtelier: Monsieur & Madame Henri Desmarais
Vallières, 37230 Fondettes
Tel: 47.42.29.87 Fax: 47.42.24.44
3 Rooms: Dbl from 400F to 650F*
  2 Suites: 900F* - * two night minimum
Open: 28 March to 12 November
Credit cards: None
No restaurant
Region: Loire Valley

La Régalido, converted from an ancient oil mill, is a lovely Provencal hotel, with its cream stone facade and sienna tile roof, whose shuttered windows peek out through an ivy-covered exterior. Running the length of this hotel is a beautiful garden bordered by a multitude of brilliantly colored roses. In the entry lovely paintings and copper pieces adorn the walls and plump sofas and chairs cluster before a large open fireplace. An arched doorway frames the dining room whose tapestry-covered chairs are placed round elegantly set tables and that now opens onto a veranda and the beauty of the rose garden. The inviting restaurant is renowned for the excellence of its regional cuisine and for its wine cellar. Monsieur Michel spends much of his day tending to the kitchen and is often seen bustling about the hotel, dressed in his chef's attire, but never too busy to pause for a greeting. His wife's domain is the garden - the French say that she has a "green hand" instead of just a "green thumb", and it shows. The bedrooms of La Régalido are very pretty in their decor and luxurious in size and comfort. Approximately half of the rooms enjoy the privacy of their own terrace and look out over the tile rooftops of Fontvieille. *Directions: From Avignon take the N570 south in the direction of Arles. Turn off the N570 ten kilometers before Arles on the D33 southeast to Fontvieille.*

LA RÉGALIDO
Hôtelier: Jean Pierre Michel Family
118, rue Frédéric Mistral
13990 Fontvieille en Provence
Tel: 90.54.60.22 Telex: 441150 Fax: 90.54.64.29
14 Rooms - Dbl from 570F to 1400F
Open: 1 February to 30 November
  Restaurant closed Mon & Tues lunch except in season
Credit cards: All major
Restaurant, converted oil mill
Region: Provence

The owner, Madame Hubert, describes Le Manoir du Stang as "not really a small hotel or inn, but a comfortable family home where we receive guests". Set behind its own moat and arched gateway and tower, it is, however, a dramatic home and affords some regal accommodation. A sixteenth-century manor house, Le Manoir du Stang is surrounded by well-tended flower gardens, a small lake, woods and acres of farmland. The interior furnishings manage to retain the original atmosphere of a private château. The hallway leading to the bedrooms is a bit motelish, but the rooms themselves are decorated in period pieces in keeping with the mood of the building. The hotel offers twenty-six rooms, all equipped with modern conveniences and comforts. The Louis XV dining room is handsomely appointed, with tables set before a large fireplace. Waitresses adorned in costumes of the southern coast of Brittany provide service and lend an air of festivity to the meal. Accommodation is offered on a demi-pension basis. *Directions: To locate take D783 between Concarneau and Bénodet, then follow D44 to the center of La Forêt Fouesnant and then V7 in the direction of Quimper. Less than a mile out of town watch for signs that will direct you down a long tree-lined drive to the manor.*

LE MANOIR DU STANG
Hôtelier: M & Mme Guy Hubert
29940 La Forêt Fouesnant (Finistère)
Tel: 98.56.97.37
26 Rooms - Dbl from 900F to 1100F
  Note: Price includes breakfast and dinner
Open: 2 May to 25 September
Credit cards: None
Restaurant, tennis, park
Region: Brittany

Located just around the corner from the Château de Gacé, a small château dating from the 1200s and 1400s on a green town square, Le Morphée is set behind tall iron gates and a driveway that circles a fountain from an ancient spring. This stately brick manor has two stories and our spacious room was tucked cozily under the eaves. It was a pretty room with exposed dark wooden beams and papered in a pink floral print with matching rose bedspreads and curtains. The bathroom was spotless and contained all the modern conveniences as well as thoughtful touches such as a small traveller's sewing kit. Downstairs we found an intimate dining room with a beautifully restored panelled ceiling. The sitting room across the main hall from the billiard room has another beautifully restored ceiling, a chandelier, decorative plaster relief work on the walls, a lovely parquet floor and a piano. The fortunate traveller will be treated to selections played by Madame Lecanu. Lavish praise for Le Morphée in the guest book attests to the main attraction of this hotel, the hospitality of its owner, Madame Lecanu. *Directions: From Argentan travel twenty-two kilometers east on N26 and then travel north twelve kilometers on the N138 in the direction of Rouen to Gacé.*

LE MORPHÉE
Hôtelier: Mme Lecanu
2, rue de Lisieux
61230 Gacé
Tel: 33.35.51.01 Fax: 33.35.20.62
10 Rooms - Dbl from 370F to 410F
Open: 1 March to 1 January
Credit cards: All major
No restaurant
Region: Normandy

Set across the street from a stretch of lawn that borders the meandering La Loire river, this is an attractive city hotel that is known for its restaurant. We chose to overnight in Gien in order to be first in line to visit the Gien Faience museum and factory which opens at 9:00 am. The hotel looked to be the best in town, and although we were just looking for a comfortable overnight, we were surprised and rewarded with exceptionally courteous service, and a clean and attractive room. All employees of the hotel seems to have taken a course in hospitality, from the girls cleaning the rooms who always wear a warm smile to the young man who appeared from the kitchen with a cold bottle of Evian, prompted only from the fact that he had seen us discard an empty bottle when straightening our car. Although not a country inn, but because Gien's faience might be an attraction for some, and because we were so impressed by the unsolicited warmth and service from the employees at the hotel, the Hôtel du Rivage deserves mention. All categories of rooms are reasonable in price, and the deluxe apartments afford a luxury of space. Our room overlooked the back parking area and was quiet. The rooms at the front enjoy river views but I would caution that they might be noisier with the passing traffic. *Directions: Gien is located on the Loire River sixty-four kilometers to the southeast of Orléans. Arriving from the northwest follow the D952 as it parallels the river through town. Just past the center of town, look for the Hôtel du Rivage, on the left hand side opposite the river.*

HÔTEL DU RIVAGE
Hôtelier: Monsieur & Madame Gaillard
1, quai de Nice, 45500 Gien
Tel: 38.67.20.53 Fax: 38.38.10.21
19 Rooms - Dbl from 410F to 730F
Open: All year (Restaurant closed 10 Feb to 15 Mar)
Credit cards: AX, DC
Restaurant
Region: Western Loire Valley

Just outside the medieval village of Gordes, in the direction of Sénanque, is a engaging complex of cream stone houses converted to an exclusive hotel. Set on the hillside the buildings sit amongst gardens and stretches of green lawn. The main building dates back to when it was a private home, regionally referred to as a "mas", and houses a beautiful restaurant and six bedrooms. The restaurant occupies most of the first floor. Tables are spaciously set before floor to ceiling windows that look out over the valley, in front of a magnificent stone fireplace or in a secluded corner. A quiet sitting room and bar are also available for guests' use. The Bergerie and Fermettes are neighboring, newly constructed buildings that offer luxurious suites and apartments as accommodation. With cream stone walls and tile roofs, the exteriors are attractively modeled after the original home and in keeping with the flavor of the region and all but two rooms in this section of the complex have a private terrace, patio or garden. The accommodations at the Domaine de l'Enclos are superlative, decorated with Provencal prints and treasured antiques. The bathrooms are spacious and equipped with every modern convenience. The Domaine's buildings are set to maximize views of the countryside and the setting is rural and tranquil. *Directions: Travelling the Autoroute, A7, take the Avignon Sud exit and then follow directions to Apt on the N573 and then D22 to Coustellet. From Coustellet travel north on D2 and D15 to Gordes.*

DOMAINE DE L'ENCLOS
Hôtelier: Patrick Sibourg
Route de Sénanque, 84220 Gordes
Tel: 90.72.08.22 Telex: 432119 Fax: 90.72.03.03
14 Rooms - Dbl from 520F, Apt to 2320F
Open: All year
Credit cards: All major
Restaurant, pool, tennis, park
Region: Provence

When the Konings family (whose home was Holland) asked a realtor to find a place for them to retire in Provence, they expected the search to take many years. Amazingly, the perfect property, a very old stone farmhouse with great potential charm, was found almost immediately. So, even though the timing was a bit sooner than anticipated, they bought the farmhouse and restored it into an absolute dream. The six guest rooms are in a cluster of weathered stone buildings which form a small courtyard. The name of each room gives a clue as to its original use such as "The Old Kitchen", The Hayloft", "The Wine Press", etc. Arja Konings has exquisite taste and each room is decorated using country antiques and Provençal fabrics. Most conveniently, the Konings' son, Gerald, (who was born in the United States, is a talented chef. He oversees the small restaurant which is delightfully appealing with massive beamed ceiling, tiled floor, exposed stone walls and country-style antique furnishings. The dining room opens onto a terrace which overlooks the swimming pool. *Directions: Gordes is located about 38 kilometers northeast of Avignon. From Gordes, head east the D2 for about 2 kilometers. Turn right (south) on D156. In just a few minutes you will see La Ferme de la Huppe on your right.*

LA FERME DE LA HUPPE
Hôtelier: Family Konings
Route 156
84220 Gordes
Tel: 90.72.12.25 Fax: 90.72.01.83
6 Rooms - Dbl from 500F
Closed: January to 15 March
Credit cards: MC, VS
Gourmet restaurant
Region: Provence

Gordes is a very picturesque village whose terraced buildings cling to a rocky hillside that is dominated by its church and château. Located less than twenty miles east of Avignon and in the heart of Provence, this medieval village is worth a detour for a visit regardless of one's base of exploration. Since 1970 the Vasarely Museum (closed Tuesdays), which focuses on the evolution of painting and cinema art, has been installed inside the walls of the old château. The narrow streets stumble through town and shelter a number of interesting art and craft shops. Should you decide to stay in Gordes, La Mayanelle is a moderately priced hotel and enjoys a central location at the heart of this medieval village. Monsieur Mayard extends a warm welcome: he is your host as well as chef for the hotel's lovely restaurant. La Mayanelle's ten bedrooms are small (room number four being the largest), but comfortable and pleasing in their decor. Since the hotel is perched on the side of the village, the bedrooms whose windows open out to the Luberon Valley enjoy some magnificent views. I was here at the time of a festive wedding reception and had the only room not occupied by a wedding guest. *Directions: Gordes is located thirty-eight kilometers east of Avignon. Travelling the Autoroute, A7, take the Avignon Sud exit and then follow directions to Apt on the N573 and then D22 to Coustellet. From Coustellet travel north on D2 and D15 to Gordes:*

LA MAYANELLE
Hôtelier: M Mayard
84220 Gordes
Tel: 90.72.00.28
10 Rooms - Dbl from 340F to 480F
Closed: 3 January to 3 March
* Restaurant closed Tuesdays*
Credit cards: All major
Restaurant
Region: Provence

A small sign directed me along a dirt road and through a small town as I searched for the Château de Roumégouse. I was not certain I had followed the sign correctly. Suddenly, a large majestic tower, peering above the treetops, revealed the location of the château. A very cordial Monsieur Lauwaert, who speaks perfect English, was the only person at the château when I arrived. I wrongly assumed that due to the isolated location of the hotel, no one knew about it: as it turned out, the reason for the lack of guests was that Monsieur Lauwaert had closed for the season a week earlier. When open, the hotel and restaurant are very popular - even Pompidou and de Gaulle have dined here. Monsieur and Madame Lauwaert retired five years ago and the management of the château is now in the capable hands of their daughter and her husband, Monsieur and Madame Laine. Elegant furnishings are found throughout. In keeping with the mood of the castle, the bedroom suites are extremely handsome while the dining rooms are in Louis XV decor. In summer dinner is served on the terrace overlooking the Lot Valley. The Laines request that overnight guests lunch or dine at the hotel. *Directions: Gramat is located fifty-three kilometers southeast of Brive. To locate the château, travel southeast from Brive on the N20 and N140. The château is located four and a half kilometers before Gramat.*

CHÂTEAU DE ROUMÉGOUSE
Hôtelier: M & Mme Laine
Rignac, 46500 Gramat
Tel: 65.33.63.81 Telex: 532592 Fax: 65.33.71.18
16 Rooms - Dbl from 520F to 1050F
Open: April to beginning of November
* Restaurant closed Tuesdays*
Credit cards: All major
Restaurant, pool
Region: Dordogne

The Château de Locguénolé, surrounded by acres of woodland, is dramatic and isolated. Standing proud, the property of this stately manor extends down to the edge of the Blavet. This château has been the family home of the de la Sablière family since 1600 and today Madame de la Sablière runs it as an exclusive hotel. The hotel glories in the tradition and heritage of the family's pride and possessions. Antiques abound. Many of the bedrooms have majestic fireplaces and all have lovely views. The service and attention to detail is very professional and refined, befitting the high standards outlined by the prestigious Relais et Châteaux chain of hotels. The restaurant of the hotel is set in the formal dining room. Denis Le Cadre presents a wonderful menu complemented by an excellent wine list (both expensive). Two minutes by car from the Château, isolated on the silent moors of Brittany, the Residence Kerniaven, a genuine Morbihan cottage, shelters twelve additional luxurious rooms. Set on the southern coast of Brittany, Hennebont is a convenient base from which to explore the region and the Château de Locguénolé makes your base a luxurious and extremely comfortable one as well. *Directions: Hennebont is located ten kilometers east of Lorient. To locate the château, travel east from Lorient on the N165 and then south from Hennebont, four kilometers on D781.*

CHÂTEAU DE LOCGUÉNOLÉ
Hôtelier: M. Bruno de la Sablière
Route de Port-Louis
56700 Hennebont
Tel: 97.76.29.04 Telex: 950636 Fax: 97.76.39.47
36 Rooms - Dbl from 740F to 2080F
Open: 2 February to 2 January
Credit cards: All major
Restaurant, pool, tennis, saunas, bikes
Region: Brittany

Honfleur is one of the world's most picturesque port towns and I am certain that you will want to spend time here. On the outskirts of town, in a residential district, I have recommended the moderately priced Hôtel l'Écrin and just outside of town, the very expensive and excellent La Ferme St Siméon. Should these hotels be full, or if your budget needs some monitoring, there is an alternate, budget selection, the Hôtel du Dauphin. Off St Catherine's Square just near the port, the hotel has a central location, but the port is teeming with activity so a quiet night's sleep is not guaranteed. The rooms of the hotel are very simple and spartan in their decor, but clean and inexpensive. A maze of stairways and confusing double doors ramble through the building and lead to the various rooms. Flower boxes adorn the timbered facade. The Hôtel du Dauphin has an informal bar and cafe, but no restaurant: however, there are numerous cafe-restaurants that specialize in fish bordering the scenic harbor. The Hôtel du Dauphin offers basic, clean and inexpensive accommodation at the heart of picturesque Honfleur. *Directions: Arriving from Paris (one hundred eighty kilometers) take the Autoroute, A13, direction Caen via Rouen. Exit the Autoroute at Beuzeville and travel north on the D22 and then west on the D180 to Honfleur.*

HÔTEL DU DAUPHIN
Hôtelier: Michel François
10, Place Pierre Berthelot
14600 Honfleur
Tel: 31.89.15.53 Fax: 31.92.48.57
30 Rooms - Dbl from 320F to 400F
Closed: January
Credit cards: AX, VS
Budget hotel, no restaurant
Region: Normandy

An alternative to the very expensive Relais et Châteaux Hôtel, La Ferme St Siméon, located outside the town of Honfleur, is the moderately priced Hôtel l'Écrin. This hotel is conveniently located within walking distance of the picturesque harbor, yet benefits from the quiet of a residential district. We've chosen this hotel, converted from a private home, because of its location and price. However, the decor would be considered by many to be overly ornate. We felt it would be difficult to improve upon the following description provided by one of our readers, Bill Simpson:

"Our room was very large, convenient, with all the amenities. The bathroom was completely modern and well-equipped. The staff was friendly and helpful. The decor, to say the least, was flamboyant. Red velvet and gilt, lavishly applied, the fanciest French furniture, a multitude of paintings of all descriptions and a wide-ranging assortment of decorations including stuffed birds, a larger-than-life size painted statue of a Nubian slave and a smiling portrait of Maurice Chevalier."

Honfleur is truly one of France's most picturesque port towns and the Hôtel l'Écrin offers a quiet, convenient, moderately priced, if colorful, base. *Directions: Arriving from Paris (one hundred eighty kilometers) take the Autoroute, A13, direction Caen via Rouen. Exit the A13 at Beuzeville, travel north on the D22, then west on the D180 to Honfleur.*

HÔTEL L'ÉCRIN
Hôtelier: M & Mme Jean-Louc Blais
19, rue Eugène Boudin, 14600 Honfleur
Tel: 31.89.32.39 Fax: 31.89.24.41
20 Rooms - Dbl from 350F to 870F
Open: All year
Credit cards: AX, VS, DC
No restaurant
Region: Normandy

Set on the coastal hills just outside the picturesque port town of Honfleur, La Ferme St Siméon is a lovely seventeenth-century Normandy home with flower boxes adorning every window. Recently seventeen new rooms have been added, set in the same gardens where painters such as Monet, Boudin and Jongkind set up their easels and were lodged by the famous Mrs. Toutain. Of these new rooms, three are suites and, like the other rooms, all are individually styled and handsomely decorated with fine antiques. The intimate decor of the restaurant is beautifully accented by a beamed ceiling and colorful flower arrangements decorate each table. The chef, Jean Pierre de Boissière, has earned recognition in some of France's most prestigious restaurants and utilizes the high quality fresh produce for which the region is famous to make the most of his talents in creating exquisite dishes. Offered on an à la carte basis, the cuisine is delicious and expensive. Reservations for the hotel as well as for the restaurant are a must and should be made well in advance. On the outskirts of Honfleur, it is a convenient base from which to explore enchanting Honfleur, and the D-Day beaches and Monet's home at Giverny are both just an hour's drive away by car. *Directions: From Paris (one hundred eighty kilometers) take the Autoroute, A13, direction Caen via Rouen. Exit the A13 at Beuzeville, travel north on the D22, then west on the D180 to Honfleur. La Ferme is located just outside Honfleur on the coastal road (D513) in the direction of Deauville.*

LA FERME ST SIMÉON
Hôtelier: M & Mme Roland Boelen
Rue Adolphe-Marais, 14600 Honfleur
Tel: 31.89.23.61 Telex: 171031 Fax: 31.89.48.48
39 Rooms - Dbl from 1160F, Suite to 4080F
Open: All year
Credit cards: VS
Tennis, countryside estate, new pool, sauna
Region: Normandy

Winding through the foothills of the Vosges Mountains, the wine route of Alsace is extremely picturesque. It meanders through delightful towns and is exposed to enchanting vistas of a countryside carpeted with vineyards and dotted by neighboring towns clustered around their church spires. The village of Itterswiller, nestled on the hillside amongst the vineyards, is a wonderful base from which to explore the region and the Hôtel Arnold is a charming country hotel. The accommodation and restaurant are in three separate buildings. Although the color wash of the individual buildings varies from white to soft yellow to burnt red, each is handsomely timbered and the window boxes hang heavy with a profusion of red geraniums. Most of the twenty-eight bedrooms are located in the main building of the Hôtel Arnold set just off the road on the edge of the village. The bedrooms are at the back of the hotel and look out over the surrounding vineyards. On the town's principal street, standing next to the hotel's restaurant, the Winestub Arnold, is a selection of lovely rooms in La Réserve. Set under lovely old beams with provincial cloths and decorative flower arrangements adorning the tables, the Winestub Arnold is an appealing place to dine on regional specialties and the estate's wines. *Directions: From Strasbourg, take the N392 and continue on the N425 thirty-nine kilometers south to Epfig and then travel a few kilometers west to Itterswiller on the D335.*

HÔTEL ARNOLD
Hôtelier: Mme Marlene Arnold
Route du Vin, 67140 Itterswiller
Tel: 88.85.50.58 Telex: 870550 Fax: 88.85.55.54
28 Rooms - Dbl from 380F to 695F
Open: All year
  Restaurant closed Sundays & Mondays
Credit cards: VS, MC
Region: Alsace

The Château du Plessis is a lovely, aristocratic country home, truly one of France's most exceptional private châteaux-hôtels and a personal favorite. Madame Benoist's family have lived here since well before the revolution, but the antiques throughout the home are later acquisitions of her great, great, great grandfather, as the furnishings original to the house were burned on the front lawn by the revolutionaries in 1793. Furnishings throughout the home are elegant, yet the Benoists also establish an atmosphere of homey comfort. Artistic fresh flower arrangements abound and one can see Madame's cutting garden from the French doors in the salon that open onto the lush grounds. The well-worn turret steps lead to the beautifully furnished accommodations. In the evening the large oval table in the dining room provides an opportunity to enjoy the company of other guests and the country-fresh cuisine of Madame Benoist. She prepares a four course meal and Monsieur Benoist selects a different regional wine to complement each course. The Benoists are a handsome couple who take great pride in their home and the welcome they extend to their guests. *Directions: To reach La Jaille-Yvon travel north of Angers on N162 and at the town of Le Lion d'Angers clock the odometer eleven kilometers further north to an intersection, Carrefour Fleur de Lys. Turn east and travel two and a half kilometers to La Jaille-Yvon and the Château du Plessis on its southern edge.*

CHÂTEAU DU PLESSIS
Hôtelier: M & Mme Paul Benoist
49990 La Jaille-Yvon
Tel: 41.95.12.75 Fax: 41.95.14.41
8 Rooms - Dbl from 580F to 730F
Open: 1 March to 1 November
Credit cards: All major
Restaurant by reservation only
Region: Loire Valley

Nestled in the countryside just a few kilometers outside Tours, the Hôtel du Château de Beaulieu is well located for visiting the castles of the Loire Valley. The formal garden setting is highlighted by vividly colored flowers and nearby, public swimming pool and tennis courts. A somewhat Oriental theme pervades in the grand entry hall and on the staircase where collections of Oriental war spears, tapestries and carpets are displayed. The nine bedrooms in the château and ten in a nearby pavilion annex are attractively appointed and are priced according to size, view and whether they have a bath or a shower (less expensive). The management requests guests stay here on a demi-pension basis. There are two menus offered daily priced at 185F and 215F as well as a "Menu Gastronomique" at 280F and a "Menu Degustation" at 380F. Dinners are enjoyed in the gracious dining room surrounded by fresh flowers and attentive waiters. Reduced rates are offered for guests who stay three or more days. Comfortable and atmospheric, this hotel offers a château ambiance without the higher prices of its more luxurious neighbors. *Directions: Located just five kilometers to the southwest of Tours, take the D86 and then D207 from Tours following signs to Villandry.*

HÔTEL DU CHÂTEAU DE BEAULIEU
Hôtelier: Jean-Pierre Lozay
Route de l'Epend
37300 Joué lès Tours
Tel: 47.53.20.26 Fax: 47.53.84.20
19 Rooms - Dbl from 456F to 746F
Open: All year
Credit cards: All major
Restaurant
Public pool and tennis courts adjacent
Region: Loire Valley

Kaysersberg is one of Alsace's greatest splendors. The village sprawls up the hillside and the Hôtel l'Arbre Vert is tucked away along a street in Haut Kaysersberg. This delightful country inn whose facade is colored by boxes of overflowing geraniums has been a family business for three generations. The Hôtel l'Arbre Vert is a simple, comfortable inn, rustic in its decor and reasonably priced. The atmosphere is friendly and the Kieny and Wittmer families extend a personal welcome. Monsieur Kieny who supervises the kitchen offers a number of interesting Alsatian specialties that are complemented by the regional wines. Even if the cuisine weren't such a gastronomic delight it would be a memorable treat to dine in the charming, country restaurant. The hotel also has a cozy wine cellar where one can sample some of the famous as well as local Alsatian wines. Should the Hôtel l'Arbre Vert be full, the Hôtel la Belle Promenade (tel: 89.47.11.51), directly across the square, is also attractive, a bit more modern in decor, but benefiting from the same gracious and hospitable management.

Directions: Kaysersberg is located eleven kilometers northwest of Colmar by travelling the N83 and N415. L'Arbre Vert is located in Haute Kaysersberg.

HÔTEL L'ARBRE VERT
Hôteliers: Kieny & Wittmer Families
1, Rue Haute du Rempart
68240 Kaysersberg
Tel: 89.47.11.51
23 Rooms - Dbl from 332F to 414F
14 Rooms (Annex - Belle Promenade)
Closed: January
Credit cards: MC, VS
Restaurant
Region: Alsace

Just inside the walls of the charming village of Kaysersberg is a wonderful, recently opened hotel, the Résidence Chambard. Each of the rooms is decorated differently, the majority with an emphasis on regal luxury. (A few annex rooms are a bit modern but comfortable, and one should specify a preference when making reservations.) Of the twenty bedrooms, two (rooms 206 and 207) are lovely apartments, well worth the additional nominal surcharge. Room 206 is particularly enchanting with a turret sitting area. Just off the entrance hall is a lovely lounge, and downstairs in the basement is a charming bar. The Restaurant Chambard is in a separate building, just in front of the hotel. This is Pierre Irrmann's pride and joy. The decor is handsome: high-back, tapestry-covered chairs set round intimate tables before a large, open stone fireplace. It has earned three forks and one toque from Michelin. Specialties of the house include "foie gras frais en boudin", "turbot au gingembre frit" and "mousse chambard" and the wine list highlights some delicious Rieslings and Pinot gris. *Directions: Kaysersberg is located eleven kilometers northwest of Colmar by travelling the N83 and N415.*

HÔTEL RÉSIDENCE CHAMBARD
Hôtelier: Pierre Irrmann
13, rue du Général de Gaulle
68240 Kaysersberg
Tel: 89.47.10.17 Telex: 880272
*   Fax: 89.47.35.03*
20 Rooms - Dbl from 650F to 850F
Closed: 1-21 Mar and 22 Dec to 4 Jan
*   Restaurant closed Mondays, Tuesday lunch*
Credit cards: All major
Restaurant
Region: Alsace

Perched regally above the flowing River Dordogne, the Château de la Treyne has been renovated and returned to its earlier state of grandeur. A fairy-tale fortress, the château will enchant you with its presence, its grace, its regal accommodation and excellent restaurant. Michèle Gombert-Devals has opened her home to a privileged few, not as a hotel, but, more intimately, as a "château-prive". Set on three hundred acres of parkland formal French gardens stage the entry of the Château de la Treyne. Inside, heavy wood doors, wood panelling and beams contrast handsomely with white stone walls and the rich, muted colors of age-worn tapestries. Public rooms are furnished dramatically with antiques and warmed by log burning fires. In summer, tables are set on a terrace with magnificent views that plunge down to the Dordogne. On brisk nights, the dining room is romantically lit with candlesticks and tables are elegantly set with silver, china and flowers. Guests are to make reservations on a demi-pension basis. The château's bedrooms are all luxuriously appointed and furnished. Individual in their decor, size and location, the windows of the rooms open either onto dramatic river views or onto the lovely grounds. *Directions: From Souillac on the N20 take D43 three kilometers west towards Lacave - Rocamadour: just over the bridge are the gates to the château.*

CHÂTEAU DE LA TREYNE
Hôtelier: Mme Michèle Gombert-Devals
Lacave, 46200 Souillac
Tel: 65.32.66.66 Telex: 531427 Fax: 65.37.06.57
12 Rooms - Dbl from 1020F to 1720F
Closed: January to Easter
Credit cards: All major
Restaurant, pool, tennis
Region: Dordogne

Château de Brindos is a superb Spanish-style castle in the Basque region. It is an attractive white building with an orange tile roof that sits sheltered in its own expanse of green park. The medieval hall, grand salon and dining rooms are impressive. Of the fifteen luxurious bedrooms it is hard to choose a favorite but rooms seventeen (a corner room facing the lake with an antique four-poster canopy) and eleven (a large room, with twin beds, decorated in gold, with a round salon) are exceptional. The facilities (pool, tennis courts, practice golf course) and refined service make the Château de Brindos more of a resort than hotel. An afternoon can easily be spent lounging poolside and ordering exotic drinks. The Château de Brindos is situated on the Lac de Brindos with its own dock at the lake where ducks and swans set a graceful scene. The Château de Brindos stages a very romantic setting. *Directions to the hotel are from Biarritz, located just five kilometers away. From the city, follow the N10 in the direction of the airport, and turn off to Lac de Brindos just after the airport or "aérogare".*

CHÂTEAU DE BRINDOS
Hôtelier: M & Mme Vivensang
Lac de Brindos
64600 Anglet
Tel: 59.23.17.68 Telex: 541428 Fax: 59.23.48.47
15 Rooms - Dbl from 1000F to 1350F
Open: All year
Credit cards: All major
Restaurant
Pool, tennis, practice golf
Region: Basque

In the heart of a picturesque hill town at the foot of a castle once home to the infamous Marquis de Sade, Monsieur Court de Gebelin offers exquisite accommodation in his atmospheric seventeenth century home. Monsieur has spent several years lovingly restoring and improving his house to achieve a harmonious mix of historic surroundings with the latest in modern conveniences. Bedrooms are furnished in understated good taste, and feature subdued lighting and luxurious private baths. Each room is unique in its design and decor, with the high level of comfort and attention to detail remaining uniform throughout. As an added luxury for guests, Monsieur has installed a small, jewel-like swimming pool beside the upstairs terrace where guests are invited to relax after a day of sightseeing, or simply to escape summer's midday heat. This is not a hotel, but a luxurious bed and breakfast type accommodation. The sincere, warm welcome offered by Monsieur Court de Gebelin and his mother complete the perfection of the unforgettable "Relais du Procureur". *Directions: From Avignon or Cavaillon take N100 towards Apt, turning right at the village of Lumières following signs for Lacoste. Once in the village, the route to the "Relais du Procureur" is well-marked, although the narrow old streets can be difficult to navigate in a large car.*

"RELAIS DU PROCUREUR"
Hôtelier: Monsieur Court de Gebelin
Rue Basse
84710 Lacoste
Tel: 90.75.82.28 Fax: 90.75.86.94
  * Reservations by phone or fax only
7 Rooms - Dbl from 460F to 630F
Open: All year
Credit cards: All major
No restaurant, pool, tennis (5km away)
Region: Provence

The lovely Château d'Urbilhac, set high above the town, is a beautiful château with extensive grounds and a stunning swimming pool surrounded by statues. Very reasonable in price, the château attracts European families on holiday who appear very "at home" here and comfortable in their regal surroundings. Madame Xompero, the owner, extends a gracious welcome and genuinely cares that her guests enjoy their holiday. There is no lift and the bedrooms are scattered on three floors. We stayed in a small room on the third floor which was once the servants' quarters. There are a number of more spacious, grand rooms: fourteen and fifteen both have beautiful antique double beds, twelve, a corner room, has antique twin beds and twenty-four has twin brass beds. The dining room is small and friendly and the menu boasts a number of regional specialties - beautifully prepared and thoughtfully served. Removed from any tourist destination, the Château d'Urbilhac offers calm and quiet, a perfect hideaway for those who want to relax. *Directions: Lamastre is located forty kilometers northwest of Valence travelling the D533. The château is tucked in the wooded hills above Lamastre: travel the D2, Route de Vernoux, for two kilometers.*

CHÂTEAU D'URBILHAC
Hôtelier: Mme Xompero
Route de Vernoux, 07270 Lamastre
Tel: 75.06.42.11 Fax: 75.06.52.75
13 Rooms - Dbl from 1000F to 1100F*
  *includes dinner
Open: 1 May to 8 October
Credit cards: All major
Restaurant, gorgeous pool, tennis
Region: Rhône Valley

We were greeted with a smile by the chef himself, ready to welcome guests eager to sample his cuisine.   Monsieur Crotet who had a successful restaurant in Nuits St Georges was not looking to move, but happened on what is now the Hôstellerie du Levernois and decided a change was meant to be.   He has done a fabulous job bringing back to glory a lovely property that was abandoned for three years.   The restaurant features in the original house.   A green and blue pattern, designed specifically for the restaurant, splashes a wash of color in the drapes, table cloths and china.   Crystal, linen and silver add elegance.   Outside, bountiful yellow pansies color the garden yellow and are a perfect complement to the yellow and white striped cushions.   The twelve bedrooms are all found in a modern addition, a garden path's distance from the restaurant.   Expecting a modern hotel wing, I was pleased to find the bedrooms exceptional in their decor and comfort.   Lovely floral prints have been selected and set off the beams and stucco walls.   All on one level, the rooms either look out over an expanse of lawn, or for a little less money, onto a small band of garden that buffers the parking area.   Each room is spacious and has its own patio.   Breakfast is served in the rooms or on the patio. *Directions: Levernois is a small town located just a few kilometers to the southeast of Beaune on the D970 in the direction of Verdun-sur-le-Doubs and Levernois.   Turn left after the autoroute overpass.*

HÔSTELLERIE DE LEVERNOIS
Hôtelier: Monsieur & Madame Jean Crotet
Route de Verdun-sur-le-Doubs
Levernois, 21200 Beaune
Tel: 80.24.73.58 Telex: 351468 Fax: 80.22.78.00
12 Rooms - Dbl from 940F to 1140F
Closed: Christmas, New Years & 15 days in Aug
Credit cards: All major
Restaurant, tennis, garden
Region: Burgundy

Levernois is a country village located a five-minute drive on D970 from Beaune. Here the ivy-clad Hôtel le Parc offers a countryside alternative for those travellers seeking to guard their pocketbook as well as avoid city noises. Madame Christine Oudot owns and manages the hotel with pride and care. The flower garden and small park are scrupulously tended as are all facets of the hotel. The twenty rooms are almost always full with returning clients, who also enjoy congregating before dinner in the convivial bar near the cheerful entry salon. Prettily papered hallways lead to the simple, but charming bedrooms, all but one of which have their own spotlessly clean bath or shower. Antique pieces are strategically placed throughout the hotel, especially in the breakfast room which boasts an old country hutch filled with colorful plates, a large antique mirror and matching wooden tables and chairs which look out through French doors onto the flower-filled courtyard. Reserve early in order to be able to enjoy the warm hospitality of the Moreau-Tanrons in this tranquil setting. *Directions: Travel five kilometers southeast of Beaune on Route de Verdun-sur-le-Doubs D970 and D111.*

HÔTEL LE PARC
Hôtelier: Mme Christine Oudot
Levernois
21200 Beaune
Tel: 80.24.63.00
20 Rooms - Dbl from 200F to 435F
Open: All year
Credit cards: None
No restaurant
Region: Burgundy

Domaine de Beauvois is a fifteenth- and seventeenth-century château surrounded by a lovely wooded estate of three hundred and fifty acres. Its forty rooms are furnished with antiques and offer you a holiday equal to that enjoyed by the many lords and ladies who came to the Loire Valley for relaxation long ago. It was once a residence for the knights of the fifteenth century and there are some very historical rooms with exposed old stone walls in the original tower. The ceiling of one bedroom looks up dramatically to the original old oak beams that form a stunning pattern and a chamber once occupied by Louis XIII has its own fireplace and a vaulted ceiling. From the bedrooms one looks down over a pool surrounded by grass, over a courtyard, its reflecting pool and fountain or up to the dense forest. On most nights one large, beautiful room whose floor to ceiling windows overlook the courtyard terrace is elegantly set for dinner. There is also, however, a smaller, more intimate dining room. The service is professional and it is worth asking the "sommelier" for a tour of the remarkable wine cellar. For sports enthusiasts there are also tennis courts, lovely marked trails in the surrounding forest and fishing nearby. *Directions: Take the N152 north out of Tours (right bank of the River Loire) in the direction of Saumur. Twelve kilometers after leaving Tours turn right at the Port de Luynes on the D49. Traverse Luynes and then continue on the D49 in the direction of Clere les Pins for two kilometers to the Domaine.*

DOMAINE DE BEAUVOIS
Hôtelier: Jean Claude Taupin
Route 49 Cléré les Pins, 37230 Luynes
Tel: 47.55.50.11 Telex: 750204 Fax: 47.55.59.62
40 Rooms - Dbl from 980F to 1450F
Open: 15 March to 15 January
Credit cards: All major
Restaurant, pool, tennis, park
Region: Loire Valley

Within a renaissance setting, encased in the walls of Old Lyon, this hotel is unique in Europe and has been described as a masterpiece. Housed in four buildings, that once belonged to the Duc de Bourgogne, the decor of the Cour des Loges is a stunning contrast of modern and old. Old stone walls and massive beams stage a backdrop for bright fabrics, chrome, glass and dried flowers. Tapas is the hotel's one informal restaurant that offers light fare. Money was not spared in outfitting the accommodations. Double windows buffer city noises, automatic shutters block out the light, televisions offer CNN, mini bars are stocked with complimentary beverages and snacks, and bathrooms are ultra modern. Accommodations are expensive and surprisingly small and in some cases where bathrooms are located on a terraced level, within the room, should be reserved for intimate travel companions. Popular with businessmen, this hotel is also perfect for the traveller. Located at the heart of Vieux Lyon, from the Cours des Loges one can easily explore a city rich in history and art. *Directions: Travel south on A6 through Lyon, take the Vieux Lyon exit immediately after the Tunnel Fourvière. Follow the Quai Fulchiron to where it becomes the Quai Romain Rolland. At the Pont de la Feuillée (bridge), turn left on Rue Octavio-Mey and then make a hard left in front of the Gare Saint-Paul on the Rue F.-Vernay. The hotel's welcome office is located on the left. As the hotel is located in a pedestrian zone, park here and arrangements will be made for your car and luggage.*

COUR DES LOGES
Directeur: Jean-François Piques
2,4,6,8 rue du Boeuf, 69005 Vieux Lyon
Tel: 72.42.75.75 Telex: 330831 Fax: 72.40.93.61
63 Rooms and Suites - 1250F to 3100F
Open: All year
Credit cards: All major
Restaurant, sauna, pool, garden, parking
Region: Rhône Valley

Château de la Caze is a fairytale fifteenth-century castle, majestically situated above the Tarn.   With its heavy doors, turrets and stone facade, it is a dramatic castle and yet intimate in size.   It was not built as a fortress, but rather as a honeymoon home for Sonbeyrane Alamand, a niece of the Prior François Alamand. She chose the idyllic and romantic location and commissioned the château in 1489. Today this spectacular château offers accommodation and now one will be royally attended to by Madame and Mademoiselle Roux.   Inside the château vaulted ceilings, rough stone walls, tile and wood-planked floors are warmed by tapestries, Oriental rugs, dramatic antiques, paintings, copper, soft lighting and log-burning fires.   Each bedroom in the castle is like a king's bedchamber.   Just opposite the château "la Ferme" offers six additional, attractive apartments.   Room six, the honeymoon apartment of Sonbeyrane, is the most spectacular room: it has a large canopied bed and an entire wall of windows overlooking the Tarn and its canyon. On the ceiling there are paintings of the eight sisters who later inherited the château, and according to legend, were very beautiful, having secret rendezvous each night in the garden of the castle with their lovers.   The restaurant enjoys spectacular views of the canyon.   *Directions: La Malène is located forty-two kilometers northeast of Millau by travelling the N9 and D907.   From La Malène travel northeast five and a half kilometers on D907.*

CHÂTEAU DE LA CAZE
Hôtelier: Mme & Mlle Roux
La Malène, 48210 Ste Enimie
Tel: 66.48.51.01 Fax: 66.48.55.75
19 Rooms - Dbl from 750F, Suite to 1050F
Open: May to November, Restaurant closed Tuesdays
Credit cards: AX, VS, DC
Restaurant
Region: Tarn

For fifteen hundred years the Manoir de Montesquiou was the residence of the Barons de Montesquiou. With the canyon walls at its back the Manoir de Montesquiou faces onto the street in the small town of La Malène at the center of the Tarn Canyon. This is a moderately priced château hotel, not luxurious but very traditional in furnishings. The welcome and service is warm and friendly. The Manoir de Montesquiou serves as a delightful and comfortable base from which to explore the spectacular beauty of the Tarn Canyon, "Gorges du Tarn". Here you can enjoy a wonderful meal and then climb the tower to your room. All the bedrooms are with private bath and those that overlook the garden at back are assured a quiet night's rest. Each bedroom is unique in its decor, some with dramatic four-poster beds, and the carvings on the headboard in room six are magnificent. Although the setting and accommodation of the Manoir de Montesquiou are not as spectacular as the Château de la Caze, it is a less expensive alternative and well located at the heart of the Tarn Canyon. With the Manoir de Montesquiou as a base, you can venture out by day to boat, fish, hunt, explore and walk. *Directions: La Malène is located forty-two kilometers northeast of Millau by travelling the N9 and then the D907. The Manoir is located five and a half kilometers northeast of La Malène by continuing on the N907.*

MANOIR DE MONTESQUIOU
Hôtelier: M Bernard Guillenet
La Malène
48210 Ste Énimie
Tel: 66.48.51.12
12 Rooms - Dbl from 390F to 680F
Open: April to October
Credit cards: DC, VS
Restaurant
Region: Tarn

Château de Marçay is a fifteenth-century fortress that was transformed into a luxurious hotel in 1970.   It is a dramatic castle, built of stone, with twin end turrets, situated six kilometers south from Chinon following the D116 and surrounded by its own vineyards, enjoying the quiet and calm of the lovely Vienne Valley which creates a restful and welcoming environment.   There are twenty-seven bedrooms in the château and eleven in a modern "motel" annex.   In the château the rooms are unique and lovely.   Room eleven is spacious with twin beds and a dark red color scheme that blends with the richly dark wooden beams.   Room twenty-five is a plain double room, but the bathroom is magnificent, larger than the room itself, located in one of the end turrets with blue and white tiles, beamed walls and ceiling. In the public areas the Château de Marçay has a lovely salon with comfortable chairs set before the warmth of a large fireplace, high stools gathered around an inviting bar and a very elegantly staged restaurant.   Plan on spending the quiet hours of early evening on the terrace that overlooks the serene Vienne Valley.   On the expanse of grounds that surrounds the château, guests will find a large swimming pool, tennis courts and a pretty garden.   The Château de Marçay is a very luxurious, reasonably expensive château-hôtel. *Directions: Leaving Tours take the D751 to Chinon.   Traverse Chinon and then take the D116 six kilometers south to Marçay.*

CHÂTEAU DE MARÇAY
Hôtelier: Patrick Ponsard
Marçay, 37500 Chinon
Tel: 47.93.03.47 Telex: 751475 Fax: 47.93.45.33
35 Rooms - Dbl from 1050F to 1730F
Closed: mid-January to mid-March
Credit cards: All major
Restaurant
Pool, tennis, park, vineyard & wine cellar
Region: Loire Valley

The Château de la Fredière, on the hillside overlooking the surrounding farmland and village of Ceron, is a pretty cream stone château with delicate end turrets and a silvery grey slate roof. Very reasonable in price, there are six guest rooms located in the nineteenth-century château and four in a modern building located at the end of the driveway overlooking the nine hole golf course. The rooms in the château are attractive and comfortable in their furnishings. Their size and whether or not they have a full bath are reflected in their price. The four rooms in the annex are found above the clubhouse and restaurant. Very inexpensive, the rooms in the annex can be noisy and are very basic with only a sink and shower and a shared toilet down the hall. Madame Charlier is a charming and attentive hostess. Her son maintains the golf course and her daughter-in-law oversees the restaurant. (Dinners are on a reservation-only basis.) A bountiful continental breakfast is served in the dining room before the fireplace or at an intimate table set in the turret round, or on pretty days, in the morning sun on the terrace. Not luxurious, the Château de la Fredière, instead, offers comfortable, reasonably priced accommodation and a friendly welcome. *Directions: Travel north on the D482 seventy-one kilometers from Roanne. At Marcigny travel west on the D990 to Urbisse, then north to Ceron.*

CHÂTEAU DE LA FREDIÈRE
Hôtelier: Mme Edith Charlier
Céron, 71110 Marcigny
Tel: 85.25.19.67 Fax: 85.25.35.01
6 Rooms in the Château - Dbl from 310F to 630F
4 Rooms in the Clubhouse - Dbl from 200F
Closed: 20 to 28 December
Credit cards: None
Restaurant, golf
Region: Rhône Valley

Timbered houses, window boxes colored with geraniums, and sloping vineyards are typical of the Alsace region of France.   Marlenheim is praised as a typical Alsatian village and the Hôstellerie du Cerf represents the typical Alsatian inn.   It is in fact an old coaching inn at the start of the Route du Vin d'Alsace.   Settle in one of its nineteen pleasantly furnished bedrooms or in one of the three more spacious apartments.   Dine indoors in the cozy elegance of the restaurant or in the sheltered courtyard, bordered by a multitude of flowers, under the skies that bless the region's grapes.   This reasonably priced hostelry highlights local specialties. Both father and son, Robert and Michel, supervise the kitchen and their recommended "carte de marche", a menu that changes daily based on the freshest produce, meats and fish available, is always enticing.   Both the hotel and restaurant are closed on Tuesdays and Wednesdays, but breakfast, lunch and dinner are served the rest of the week.   Family pride and the desire to maintain a tradition of fine Alsatian cuisine inspire Robert and Michel Husser to keep an excellent kitchen.   The Hôstellerie du Cerf is a charming roadside inn and a perfect base from which to explore the vineyards of Alsace. *Directions: Marlenheim is located twenty kilometers west of Strasbourg travelling the N4.*

HÔSTELLERIE DU CERF
Hôtelier: Robert Husser
30, Route du Général de Gaulle
67520 Marlenheim
Tel: 88.87.73.73 Fax: 88.87.68.08
22 Rooms - Dbl from 410F to 700F
Open: All year except one week in Feb
  Closed weekly: Tuesday & Wednesday
Credit cards: AX, VS
Restaurant
Region: Alsace

There is an enchantment about this beautiful castle high above Mercuès and the Lot Valley. Once you have seen it you will not be able to take your eyes away or to drive through the valley without stopping. It appears to beckon you. Here you can live like a king with all the modern conveniences. The château has been restored and decorated in keeping with formal tradition. The thirty-two guest rooms in the château are magnificent - the furnishings are handsome and the windows open to some splendid valley views. Unique and priced accordingly, room 419 (in a turret) has windows on all sides and a glassed-in ceiling that opens up to the beams. In recent years an additional twenty-two rooms have been added in the newly constructed annex, the Hôtel des Cèdres. Here bedrooms are modern in decor and less expensive. Enjoy a memorable dinner in the elegantly beautiful restaurant. The Vigouroux family own vineyards which produce sumptuous wines bottled under the Château de Haut Serre label. They have just built some large cellars under the gardens connecting the château to store their produced and acquired wines. *Directions: Located eight kilometers from Cahors take the D911 from Cahors to Mercuès and then turn right at the second light.*

CHÂTEAU DE MERCUÈS
Hôtelier: M Georges Vigouroux
Directeurs: Yves & Brigitte Buchin
Mercuès, 46090 Cahors
Tel: 65.20.00.01 Telex: 521307 Fax: 65.20.05.72
32 Rooms (castle) - Dbl from 714F to 1914F
22 Rooms (Cèdres) - Dbl from 550F to 900F
Open: 1 April to 15 November
Credit cards: All major
Restaurant, pool, tennis, park
Region: Lot

The Château de Meyrargues was once the stronghold of the mightiest lords in Provence.   Built in the shape of a horseshoe, this large, imposing stone fortress is reached by taking a small winding road from the center of Meyrargues.   Large heavy doors open on the outside to the central courtyard and inside to the lofty entry halls and sparsely decorated hallways that lead to various wings of the château and its eight bedrooms and three apartments.   It is impressive in a château of its size and age that thirteen of the fourteen rooms are handsomely decorated with period furnishings.   The pride and effort of new ownership are wonderfully apparent in the fresh decor, the newly refurbished bathrooms and the standard of service and comfort.   The entire hotel is fit for nobility and the cuisine that originates in the château's charming kitchen hung with heavy copper pans is delicious.   One can savor traditional French cuisine in one of the two restaurants or on the wonderful terrace that enjoys spectacular valley views.   A swimming pool and outdoor grill have just been added and tennis courts are available nearby.
Directions: The Château de Meyrargues is a dramatic castle-hotel located just fifteen kilometers north of the city of Aix en Provence.   Take the A51 to the Sisterton exit, N96, and follow signs the short distance farther to Meyrargues.   The château is easy to spot, crowning the village.

CHÂTEAU DE MEYRARGUES
Hôtelier: M. Bernard Sobelman
Directeur: M. Eric Roubi
13650 Meyrargues
Tel: 42.57.50.32 Fax: 42.63.43.99
11 Rooms - Dbl from 900F to 1400F, Apt to 2500F
Closed for renovation until May 1, 1992
Closed annually: January
Credit cards: AX, VS, MC
Restaurant
Region: Provence

Overpowered by the walls of the towering Jonte Canyon, the picturesque houses of Meyrueis huddle along the banks of the River Jonte.   From this quaint village you take a farm road to the enchanting Château d'Ayres.   Hidden behind a high stone wall, the château has managed to preserve and protect its special beauty and peace.   Built in the twelfth century as a Benedictine monastery, it has been burned and ravaged over the years and at one time was owned by an ancestor of the Rockefellers.   It was purchased by recent owners when Monsieur Teyssier du Cros came to the castle to ask for the hand of his wife and recognized the grounds where he had played as a child.   The Teyssier du Cros family operated the Château d'Ayres for a number of years until they sold it in the late 1970s to a young and enthusiastic couple, Jean-François and Chantal de Montjou, under whose care and devotion the hotel is managed today.   Now there are twenty-four beautiful bedchambers instead of the original two.   Works of art are created in the kitchen daily.   The Château d'Ayres, its character formed by so many events and personalities, is a lovely and attractive hotel.   *Directions: Meyrueis is located forty-two kilometers east of Millau by travelling the N9 to the D907 to the D996. Travel east from Meyrueis for one and a half kilometers on D57.*

CHÂTEAU D'AYRES
Hôtelier: Comte & Comtesse de Montjou
48150 Meyrueis
Tel: 66.45.60.10 Fax: 66.45.62.26
24 Rooms - Dbl from 500F to 800F
Open: 1 April to 4 November
Credit cards: DC, VS, AX
Restaurant, tennis, pool (1991)
Region: Tarn

Relais la Métairie is a charming country hotel nestled into one of the most irresistible regions of France, the Dordogne. La Métairie is an attractive soft yellow stone manor set on a grassy plateau. Views from its tranquil hillside location views are of the surrounding farmland and down over "le cingle de Trémolat", a scenic loop of the River Dordogne. The nine bedrooms and one apartment are tastefully appointed and profit from the serenity of the rural setting. Rooms open onto a private patio or balcony terrace. The bar is airy with a decor of white wicker furniture. The restaurant is intimate and very attractive with tapestry-covered chairs and a handsome fireplace awaits you in the lounge. In summer grills and light meals are served on the terrace by the swimming pool. Relais la Métairie is found on a country road that winds along the hillside up from and between Mauzac and Trémolat, and, without a very detailed map, a bit of a struggle to find. We found the reception to be somewhat cool, but will hope for a warmer welcome on our next visit as this is a lovely country inn with an idyllic, peaceful setting. *Directions: From Trémolat travel west on the C303 and then the C301 to La Métairie. Both Trémolat and Millac are approximately fifty kilometers south of Périgueux.*

RELAIS LA MÉTAIRIE
Hôteliers: Mme Françoise-Vigneron
Directeur: M Gerard Culis
Millac, 24150 Mauzac
Tel: 53.22.50.47 Telex: 572717 Fax: 53.22.52.93
10 Rooms - Dbl from 650F to 1080F
Open: 1 April to 15 November
  Closed: Tuesdays October to 15 November
  Restaurant closed Tuesdays at lunch
Credit cards: MC, VS
Restaurant, pool, park
Region: Dordogne

Alongside a small lake with lily pads, ducks and a few colorful rowing boats is the quaint Les Moulins du Duc, dating from the sixteenth century. This charming mill once belonged to the Dukes of Brittany. Under beamed ceilings, looking out to the garden and small stream, the dining is enchanting: both the atmosphere and specialties provide the ingredients for a perfect evening. The owner, Monsieur Quistrebert, is ever present. He bustles about ensuring that the service is professional and attentive. Guest rooms are found in stone cottages that are spaced along a pathway following the course of the babbling stream. On a recent visit we found the grounds and the gardens absolutely beautiful in a multitude of color but were disappointed to find the original bedrooms a bit musty in smell and in need of refurbishing. Additional cottages have been built and house some lovely apartments, attractive and equipped with modern bathrooms, lofts, sitting areas and often a fireplace. The apartments, however, are not spacious and seem a bit overpriced. Les Moulins du Duc for the most part is extremely charming, does enjoy an idyllic setting and boasts an excellent restaurant. I will hope that reviews from readers contradict my findings and that fresh paint and carpets will precede my next visit. *Directions: Moëlan sur Mer is located ten kilometers south of Quimperlé by travelling the D16 south and the D24 west. To find the mill, travel two kilometers northwest from the village of Moëlan sur Mer. Signs for the mill are well posted.*

LES MOULINS DU DUC
Hôtelier: Quistrebert Family
29350 Moëlan sur Mer
Tel: 98.39.60.73 Telex: 940080 Fax: 98.39.75.56
27 Rooms - Dbl from 650F to 1315F
Closed: mid-January to end of February
Credit cards: All major
Excellent restaurant, indoor pool
Region: Brittany

Haute Provence is a beautiful region of rugged terrain and villages of warm sandstone buildings and tiled roofs, nestled between the Riviera, the Alps and Provence. Monsieur and Madame Vernet built Le Calalou in the shadow of Moissac to match the village architecturally and blend beautifully into the landscape. Madame Vernet is a perfectionist and the guests benefit as she demands that rooms be spotlessly clean, the public areas fresh, the garden immaculately groomed and the terrace swept. Monsieur Vernet is very approachable and the staff nice and accommodating. The bedrooms are simple and basic in their decor, but have very comfortable beds, a modern bathroom and look out over the swimming pool to spectacular valley views or open on to a private terrace. One can dine either in the glass-enclosed restaurant, a smaller more intimate dining room or on the garden terrace. During season, May through mid-September, the Vernets request that guests stay at Le Calalou on a demi-pension basis. Off season, take advantage of the hotel's proximity to the village of Tourtour, "village dans le ciel", and discover its many charming restaurants tucked along medieval streets. *Directions: From Aix en Provence take the St Maximin exit off the Autoroute A8 and follow the D560 northeast to Barjols and then on to Salernes. At Salernes take D31 north to Aups and from Aups it is just five kilometers on D9 to Moissac-Bellevue. Moissac-Bellevue is located approximately eighty-six kilometers from Aix.*

HÔTEL LE CALALOU
Hôtelier: M & Mme Armande Vernet
83630 Moissac-Bellevue
Tel: 94.70.17.91 Telex: 461885 Fax: 94.70.50.11
40 Rooms - Dbl from 554F to 914F
Open: 1 March to 1 November
Credit cards: All major
Restaurant, pool, tennis
Region: Haute Provence

Château d'Artigny is world-famous for its cuisine and accommodation. This is a grand and luxurious château hotel whose stature rivals its regal neighbors - Azay le Rideau, Chambord, Amboise. The public rooms are elegant and spacious with their high ceilings, ornate furnishings, crystal chandeliers, gilded fixtures and Oriental carpets. The restaurant is formal in atmosphere, decor and service. There are thirty-eight rooms and seven apartments in the château and eight bedrooms in an annex on the river's edge. The Château d'Artigny hosts a number of enchanting musical "soirees" from November to March. The evenings have become very popular, beginning with a cocktail at 7:30 pm and featuring the concert a half an hour later. One can also enjoy the concert followed by a romantic candlelit dinner. Contact the château for their season schedule of events and for reservation information. The Château d'Artigny will please those who seek luxury: for those in search of a country inn the Château d'Artigny might prove a bit too formal. *Directions: Located twelve kilometers south of Tours, take the Autoroute A10 and exit at Montbazon - Chambray les Tours. Continue south on the N10 to Montbazon. The hotel is located just outside Montbazon, to the southwest on D17.*

CHÂTEAU D'ARTIGNY
Owner: René Traversac
Hôtelier: Alain Rabier
37250 Montbazon
Tel: 47.26.24.24 Telex: 750900 Fax: 47.65.92.79
53 Rooms - Dbl from 940F, Apt to 3160F
Open: 9 January to 30 November
Credit cards: VS only
Restaurant, pool, tennis
Region: Loire Valley

Domaine de la Tortinière has a relaxed and inviting atmosphere and provides everything needed to make wonderful lasting memories. The château, built in 1861, has an intricate exterior, a lovely swimming pool and grounds that invite exploration and contain a path which was once a Roman road. The bedrooms combine the height of elegance with comfort. You might choose one of the castle's dramatic turret rooms or perhaps settle under beams in a cozy apartment in the neighboring pavilion. Located at the entrance to the property is an annex with a few ultra-modern rooms which are not as convenient nor as charming as those in the main castle. The dining room is small and attractive and the cuisine is excellent. Madame Olivereau-Capron, your charming hostess, runs the hotel with the help of her three children: Sophie, Xavier and Gregoire. In recent years the château has sponsored five-day cooking classes that serve as an introduction to fine regional cuisine. Recipes are selected from those served at the finest tables among the privately owned châteaux and manors of the Touraine. Instruction includes preparation of complete menus and one has the opportunity to dine with the owners in their châteaux. For reservations and information, please contact the hotel direct. *Directions: The château is located just off the N10, two kilometers north of Montbazon and ten kilometers south of Tours.*

DOMAINE DE LA TORTINIÈRE
Hôtelier: Mme Olivereau-Capron
Les Gués de Veigné, 37250 Montbazon
Tel: 47.26.00.19 Telex: 752186 Fax: 47.65.95.70
21 Rooms - Dbl from 470F to 1250F
Open: 1 March to 20 December
Credit cards: MC, VS
Restaurant, swimming pool, garden paths, tennis
Region: Loire Valley

Overlooking the scenic river Loir and the pastoral valley beyond, on the site where Richard the Lion Heart installed his troops at the end of the twelfth century, stands the stately Château de la Voûte. Termed a bed and breakfast by the owners, the quality of its comfort and the elegance of its furnishings rival some of France's loveliest château-hôtels. It was a treat to explore each of the five bedrooms, all with private bath, as they are individual and outstanding in their decor, having received the artful attention of Claude and Jacques. Gorgeous antiques, handsome fabrics, lovely carpets and original art are coordinated beautifully. Although there are no public rooms available to guests, with good beds, welcome seating areas and excellent lighting the spacious rooms are as comfortable as they are attractive and an inviting retreat. A breakfast feast is served on the garden terrace or in the bedrooms before the large windows whose shutters open up to the freshness of the morning. In the evening it is an enjoyable walk down the garden path and a short stroll along the village street to an outstanding country restaurant, Le Cheval Blanc. Charming, convenient and reasonably priced, Le Cheval Blanc is a welcome bonus as the Château de la Voûte does not serve meals other than breakfast. (Chef: Michel Coyault, tel: 54.72.58.22, closed: Monday night and Tuesdays) *Directions: From Tours take the N10 north to Vendôme and then travel west on the D917 to the village of Troo.*

CHÂTEAU DE LA VOÛTE
Hôteliers: Claude Venon & Jacques Clays
à Troo, 41800 Montoire
Tel: 54.72.52.52
5 Rooms - Dbl from 400F to 500F
Open: All year
Credit cards: VS
No restaurant
Region: Loire Valley

The Château de la Salle is tucked romantically away in the scenic countryside of Cotentin, Normandy.   Once part of a private estate, this thirteenth-century stone mansion has only ten bedchambers all of which are spacious, with either a bath or a shower, and are handsomely decorated with period pieces.   There are two rooms furnished with dramatic four-poster beds: one (reserved for honeymoon couples) remains in its authentic condition, historically romantic but a bit small, and the second has been enlarged to fit a double mattress.   The small restaurant has a few heavy wooden tables and tapestry-covered chairs positioned before a large open fireplace.   The dining room occupies what was once the kitchen, actually very modern for its time.   Take notice of the well.   If you are lucky perhaps you will secure the table next to the hearth where a small wooden door at table height opens to expose a small round oven where pastries were once baked.   Views look out through windows set deep in the thick stone walls.   This is a jewel of a château tucked away in the quiet of the rural Normandy landscape.   Our arrival coincided with a wet, grey day but we were greeted by Madame Lemesle with a warm welcome and found an inviting fire blazing in the grate. *Directions: Located thirteen kilometers southeast of Coutances.   From Coutances, take D7 towards Villedieu and then head for Cerisy la Salle on D27.   A small road, D73, will turn off before Cerisy and continues on to the château just outside Montpinchon.*

CHÂTEAU DE LA SALLE
Hôtelier: Mme Cecile Lemesle
50210 Montpinchon
Tel: 33.46.95.19 Fax: 33.46.44.25
10 Rooms - Dbl from 680F to 1280F
Open: 20 March to 15 November
Credit cards: AX, VS
Restaurant
Region: Normandy

If you want to stay on the island of Mont St Michel, I recommend the Hôtel Mère Poulard. The hotel is found immediately on the left as you enter the town gates. You will be tempted inside by the aroma and cooking display of the famous Mère Poulard omelet. The cheery bright restaurant is famous for this omelet, created here almost a century ago by Mère Poulard. The preparation of the omelet can be seen from the street and is an attraction in its own right. The eggs are whisked at a tempo and beat set by the chef and then cooked in brightly polished copper pans over a large open fire. The restaurant is open for both lunch and dinner and reservations are strongly recommended. Although the restaurant is found inside the walls of the fortress of Mont St Michel and does not enjoy a view of the encircling landscape, its menu far surpasses any other on the island both in quality and price. Dramatic in its presence and setting, Mont St Michel is understandably a popular tourist destination and in the tourist season is mobbed with people, particularly at midday. You can stay overnight at the Hôtel Mère Poulard and experience the town in the quiet of the early morning and late evening hours. The small bedrooms are comfortable and simply furnished. The hotel remains one of the nicest on the island. Management requests that reservations are made on a demi-pension basis. *Directions: Le Mont St Michel is located sixty-six kilometers north of Rennes travelling the N175.*

HÔTEL MÈRE POULARD
Hôtelier: M Vannier
BP 18 Grand Rue, 50116 Mont St Michel
Tel: 33.60.14.01 Telex: 170197 Fax: 33.48.52.31
27 Rooms - Dbl from 400F to 1600F
  Demi-pension only
Open: All year
Credit Cards: All major
Region: Normandy

Whenever I hear the name Le Moulin de Mougins, I recall the charm and splendor of this small inn. The hotel, a sixteenth-century oil mill, is located in a quiet setting just off the main road from Cannes - only a few miles from the bustling Côte d'Azur. The accommodation is described by the owner himself as providing "comfort and quiet as in a friend's house". With the focus on the restaurant, the inn has only five apartments for overnight guests. The accommodation is extremely pleasant, with a cozy country ambiance. The cuisine is prepared by the owner, Roger Vergé. Blessed by the sun of the French Riviera, produce is bountiful and meats, fish, herbs, vegetables and fruits are picked up fresh every morning and dictate the selections on the menu. Here one can experience truly fine French dining, and service is very attentive. If you would like to return home with souvenirs of your holiday visit the boutique which Denise Vergé has opened offering delicacies created by her husband, antiques and gift items. For those who want to learn how to cook some of the entrees they have sampled, Monsieur Vergé has a cooking school above his other restaurant, L'Amandier. Five- and ten-day courses are offered. *Directions: Mougins is located just seven kilometers to the north of Cannes off the N85.*

LE MOULIN DE MOUGINS
Hôtelier: M Roger Vergé
Notre Dame de Vie
06250 Mougins
Tel: 93.75.78.24 Telex: 970732 Fax: 93.90.18.55
5 Rooms - Dbl from 950F to 1450F
Open: 20 March to 20 November
  Restaurant closed Mondays
Credit cards: AX, DC, VS
Gourmet restaurant, cooking school
Region: Riviera

This is a lovely, intimate château that still vibrates the warmth of a family home. The Mascureau family grew up here and their photos tell a story of the laughter that must have echoed up the circular stone stairway.   Off the entry is a handsome dining room where guest meals are served by prior arrangement.   One enters into the salon on the other side where large oil paintings of previous generations look down on the sitting area.   Upstairs off the first landing are two handsome armoirs and an impressive collection of pistols.   The bedrooms are spacious, look out over the grounds, enjoy nooks and crannies tucked under the eaves and bathrooms nestled in the turrets.   Of the four bedrooms, two have adjoining rooms without bath for an accompanying child.   One is a child's fantasy - tucked in the turret round.   On the grounds is a lovely family chapel.   The first of many daughters was married last summer, not in the chapel but in the town church, and when I asked if rooms would return to the family with the promise of grandchildren, I was informed that there were many rooms to be occupied in this stately château that I did not see. Madame de Mascureau is a beautiful hostess, very gracious, very warm and currently taking classes to learn English and better welcome her guests.   *Directions: Located twenty kilometers to the northwest of Le Mans.   Travelling the motor way, at Le Mans exit the A81 at "Le Mans-Ouest".   At Coulans-sur-Gée, follow direction of Conlie for six kilometers.   After the village of Saint-Julien, you will see a sign on the right for the château.*

CHÂTEAU DE LA RENAUDIÈRE
Hôtelier: Monsieur & Madame de Mascureau
72480 Neuvy en Champagne
Tel: 43.20.71.09
4 Rooms - Dbl from 580F to 780F
Open: May to October
Credit cards: None
Table d'Hôte: 100F to 150F per person
Region: Northern Loire Valley

I visited the Château de Noizay the week it was being readied to open.   Noizay is a quiet town on the north side of the Loire River to the west of Amboise and this is a lovely, intimate château tucked on the hillside.   In fact incredibly this now intimate château played a role in a turbulent period of French history.   It was here in 1560 at the Château de Noizay that Castelnau was held prisoner by the Duc de Nemours after a bloody assault in town.   Castelnau was then taken to Amboise where heads were guillotined and then speared and displayed on the balcony of the château, a day referred to as the massacre that marks the defeat of the calvinists.   The Château de Noizay now enters a new era as a hôstellerie.   Fourteen rooms, found up a grand central stairway, have been decorated with attractive fabrics and period furnishings and coupled with modern bathrooms.   From the smallest third floor rooms tucked under the eaves looking out through small circular windows, to the more dramatic and spacious second floor bedchambers, accommodations are commodious and quiet.   Off the entry, an elegant dining room decorated in a warm yellow and soft blue promises gastronomic cuisine and an impressive wine cellar.   The grounds of the château include a lovely forested park, formal garden, pool and tennis courts.   *Directions: Cross the Loire River to the north from Amboise, then travel west on the N152 approximately ten kilometers and then turn north on D78 to Noizay.*

CHÂTEAU DE NOIZAY
Directeur: François Mollard
37210 Noizay
Tel: 47.52.11.01 Telex: 752715 Fax: 47.52.04.64
14 Rooms - Dbl from 760F to 1140F
Open: 15 March to 18 November
Credit cards: All major
Restaurant, pool, tennis, park
Region: Loire Valley

If not for our determination we would never have found this lovely château.   Set in a meadow, tucked off the closest public road by a long gravel and dirt path, miles from any city and a good distance from the neighboring hamlet that shares its address, this is a place to escape to.   It has everything a castle should have: a moat, a bridge, turrets and hallways filled with items that promise stories of five generations of the du Peyroux family.   This is their family home and they offer to guests three rooms which are located down one long hallway, cluttered with paintings, old books, chairs, and tables.   Each room has been decorated with family furnishings and enjoys the quiet of the rural setting.   From the windows of a lovely room with a double bed decked with a blue spread one can overlook the moat; this room has a small alcove furnished with a child's bed.   A grand twin-bedded room overlooks the gardens and a first floor apartment is spacious with the convenience of an adjoining children's room, decorated in a charming blue and white motif.   Breakfast is served in a formal sitting room on the first floor.
Directions: Travelling the D309 from Le Mans, at Parcé-s-Sarthe turn north on the D57.   In Avoise cross the bridge to the south of town, travel up a small road and turn right at the first street at the top of the hill.   Château de Dobert can be seen down on the left of this small country road and its entrance should be signposted. Note: Accommodation by reservation only.

CHÂTEAU DE DOBERT
Hôtelier: Monsieur & Madame du Peyroux
Avoise, 72430 Noyen sur Sarthe
Tel: 43.92.01.52
3 Rooms - Dbl from 400F to 550F
2 Children's Rooms - 175F
Open: May to July, August to November
Credit cards: None
Table d'Hôte: 170F to 250F
Region: Northern Loire Valley

Ideally situated on the tourist route that winds through the chalky plains of the "Haute de Côte de Nuits", just northwest of the center of Nuits St Georges as you travel the Route de Meuilley for one and a half kilometers, La Gentilhommière is a charming and very reasonably priced hotel. The hotel can be seen set just a short distance off the road, but as it is built in the pale grey stone so typical of the region it blends beautifully with the landscape. The reception, restaurant and bar are found in the former sixteenth-century hunting lodge. Staged handsomely, the upstairs restaurant is lovely. Tapestries cover the dramatic stone walls and high-back tapestry chairs set round heavy wood tables add character to the decor. The bedrooms are in a newly constructed wing that stretches along a trout stream, behind the former lodge. All the rooms are identical in style and size and vary only as to whether they have a double bed or twin beds. The furnishings are simple, functional, but pleasant. The rooms, although not spacious, are comfortable and all are equipped with private bath. La Gentilhommière is a pleasant inn set on the wine route of Burgundy, offering travellers an excellent location, a scenic setting and attractive rates. *Directions: Nuits St Georges is located seventeen kilometers north of Beaune. Take the N74 to Nuits St Georges. Once in town follow direction of Meuilley on the D25. La Gentilhommière is signposted.*

LA GENTILHOMMIÈRE
Directeur: Jack Vanroelen
Route de Meuilley Ouest
21700 Nuits St Georges
Tel: 80.61.12.06 Telex: 350401 Fax: 80.61.30.33
20 Rooms - Dbl from 450F to 480F
Open: All year, Restaurant closed Mondays
Credit cards: All major
Restaurant, pool, tennis
Region: Burgundy

Once a hunting pavilion of the Count de Rostaing, the Domaine des Hauts de Loire is a beautiful château opened this past decade as a hotel.   It is managed and owned by Madame Bonnigal.   The Domaine des Hauts de Loire is a few miles away from the Loire River, bounded by six acres of park and forest.   A private, wooded drive leads up to this elegant hotel.   With its grey slate roof and ivy-covered facade the regal home is framed by trees and reflected in a small lake that fronts it.   The château has twenty-two large, elegantly decorated rooms and four exceptionally lovely apartments - all with spacious modern bathrooms - and a lovely dining room. Accommodations are located in the château as well as in a lovely, timbered annex. The public salons are quiet, and elegantly furnished with antiques.   The restaurant is gorgeous, with soft pastel linens, silver candlesticks, silver and china dressing every table.   Everything about this château says "luxury".   *Directions: Onzain is located to the northeast of Tours by travelling forty-four kilometers on the N152.   From the town of Onzain take the D152 then turn north on D1 and travel three kilometers in the direction of Herbault.*

DOMAINE DES HAUTS DE LOIRE
Hôtelier: Pierre Alain Bonnigal
41150 Onzain
Tel: 54.20.72.57 Telex: 751547
*   Fax: 54.20.77.32*
26 Rooms - Dbl from 800F to 1500F,
*   7 Apts from 1750F to 1950F*
Open: 1 March to 1 December
Credit cards: AX, VS
Restaurant, pool, tennis
Region: Loire Valley

Vieux Pérouges is a charming, medieval village with the atmosphere of a time long gone by.   In one of the quaint old timbered buildings that lean out over the narrow, cobblestoned streets, you will find a captivating restaurant, the Ostellerie du Vieux Pérouges.   Traditional and regional cuisine of the Bressane and Lyonnaise districts which are the pride of the chef are served in the thirteenth-century dining room of this charming hotel.   Enhancing the atmosphere are waiters dressed in regional costumes.   Open for breakfast, lunch and dinner, the restaurant also profits from a wine cellar with a wonderful selection of fine Burgundies.   The bedrooms are located in two separate buildings.   The fifteen rooms in the manor, "Au St Georges et Manoir", are fabulously decorated with antiques and a few even have their own garden.   The annex, "a l'Annexe", houses more simply decorated rooms - not as attractive as those in the main building, but quite pleasant and perhaps more appealing since they are less expensive.   *Directions: Pérouges is located thirty-nine kilometers northeast of Lyon.   Take the Autoroute A42 from Lyon and exit at Pérouges.   Pérouges is located six and a half kilometers to the northeast by taking the D65 to the D4.*

OSTELLERIE DU VIEUX PÉROUGES
Hôtelier: M Georges Thibaut
Place du Tilleul, Vieux Pérouges
01800 Pérouges
Tel: 74.61.00.88 Telex: 306898 Fax: 74.34.77.90
28 Rooms - Dbl from 600F to 1100F
Open: All year, Restaurant closed Wednesdays
Credit cards: VS
Restaurant, lovely old timbered building
Region: Rhône Valley

A wonderful feeling of contentment and continuity with days gone pervades the senses as one approaches via the long, tree shaded drive leading to the gates of the du Fayet de la Tour's family home. The imposing grey stone castle is a former fortress dating from medieval times, and thus sits on a hillside affording an incomparable vista over the misty hills of the Auvergne countryside. Since their home is classified as an historical monument, some of the rooms have been kept in their original state and are open to the public for viewing. Authentic furniture, wallpapers and upholstery transport guests back in time. Guest rooms are accessed via the old tower's large, winding stone staircase and are comfortably furnished, all with private baths. A tennis court and lovely gardens overlooking the panoramic view offer restful diversion. For all its history and grandeur, the Château de la Vigne is still very much a family home, presided over by the energetic, unpretentious Madame du Fayet de la Tour. A modern-day madonna incarnate, Madame and her talented husband have six adorable children who are all delightfully personable and attractive. A stay here is a peaceful experience, "away from it all", surrounded by the warm and friendly du Fayet de la Tour family.

Directions: Located one hundred twenty kilometers southwest of Clermont Ferrand. From the town of Mauriac, take D681 to the small hamlet of Ally, direction Pléaux. Just before reaching Ally, look for a sign and driveway on the left to the Château de la Vigne.

CHÂTEAU DE LA VIGNE
Hôteliers: M and Mme du Fayet de la Tour
Ally, 15700 Pléaux
Tel: 71.69.00.20
2 Rooms, 1 Suite - Dbl from 500F to 800F
Open: June through September
Credit cards: None
No restaurant, tennis, views
Region: Auvergne

This handsome stone manor is the result of one man's lifelong dream and years of hard work.   Monsieur Bernard had a vision of what a château should be and has created it here in Pleugueneuc.   Château de la Motte Beaumanoir is an oasis in the heart of Brittany's farmland, set in sixty acres of forest and pasture, facing its own private lake and moat. Éric Bernard, the son, manages the château and welcomes and escorts guests to one of the château's eight bedchambers.   Each room is different in its decor, but all reflect the artistry of Monsieur Bernard and offer luxury, spaciousness and modernly appointed bathrooms.   The large bedroom windows frame enchanting scenes of either the lake or forest.   In the evening, the Bernards often host a convivial aperitif for all guests in their living room.   If dining, guests are then escorted to a light and airy salon where tables are set before French doors opening on to the lake. Le Château de la Motte Beaumanoir is a private home offering rooms to paying guests and does not provide the formality and variety of service associated with a hotel.   But to wake in the morning to the sound of swans taking flight and to have received the gracious hospitality of the Bernard family is truly a unique and memorable experience.
Directions: Leave Rennes on the RN137 - direction of St Malo.   It is thirty-five kilometers to Pleugueneuc.   Traverse the village and continue for two kilometers to the first stoplight.   Turn left on D78 towards Plesder.   Located forty kilometers from Rennes.

CHÂTEAU DE LA MOTTE BEAUMANOIR
Hôtelier: Bernard Family
35720 Pleugueneuc
Tel: 99.69.46.01 Fax: 99.69.42.49
8 Rooms - Dbl from 450F to 990F
Open: All year
Credit cards: VS, MC, AX
Restaurant - requested to dine at least one night
Region: Brittany

The Auberge du Vieux Puits, although set on a main road in the town of Pont Audemer, is an endearing, timbered inn that shelters a melange of charming rooms in which to dine and a back wing of rooms that overlook an oasis of "Shakespearean" garden.   L'Auberge du Vieux Puits translates to mean the inn of the old well and is a typical Normandy home dating from the seventeenth century. It was used as a tannery in the nineteenth century, was converted to an inn in 1921 and has been in the Foltz family for two generations. Madame Foltz is an attractive and gracious hostess and Monsieur Foltz has established himself as a highly acclaimed chef who oversees the kitchen.   The restaurant is divided into a multitude of alcoves where tables are set under low, heavy beams, before a large open fireplace and surrounded by copper, paintings and antiques.   Of the original twenty bedrooms, all but eight were destroyed in World War II.   These eight rooms are small, modest, yet extremely charming.   Five of the bedrooms have showers.   In 1985 another timbered wing was renovated to accommodate six bedrooms, slightly more contemporary in decor, all with private bath.   This is a "restaurant with rooms" and guests are asked to dine at the restaurant.   *Directions: Arriving from Paris-Rouen on the A13 take Pont-Audemer-Nord.   At the light follow direction of Caen.   At the bridge, continue straight on.   The Auberge is located 300 meters on the left.*

L'AUBERGE DU VIEUX PUITS
Hôtelier: M & Mme Foltz
6, rue Notre-Dame du Pré, 27500 Pont Audemer
Tel: 32.41.01.48
14 Rooms - Dbl from 282F to 500F
Open: 19 Jan to 1 Jul & 11 Jul to 15 Dec
  Restaurant closed Mondays and Tuesdays
Credit cards: VS, MC
Excellent restaurant, lovely garden
Region: Normandy

Tucked away in the beauty and quiet of the Black Mountains is a fantastic hotel - the Château de Montlédier.   Once you've arrived at the Château de Montlédier and developed a taste for the splendor and elegance it offers, you will not want to leave and when you do, you will resolve to return.   With just nine guest rooms the Château de Montlédier is intimate in size and atmosphere.   The accommodations are magnificent in their furnishings, luxuriously appointed, with commodious, modern bathrooms.   "Raymond", with its two stunning canopied beds, is one of the loveliest bedrooms.   The restaurant of the hotel is staged in the cellar: cozy and intimate, it is a romantic setting in which to sample the excellent cuisine.   The château also has a lovely swimming pool with views of the surrounding woodlands. The Château de Montlédier is a superb hotel, where everything - service, decor, cuisine - is done to perfection and with superb taste. *Directions: Mazamet is located forty-seven kilometers north of Carcassonne.   The Château de Montlédier is five kilometers from Mazamet.   From Mazamet take the D88 in the direction of Béziers, exit at Mazamet in the direction of Angles.*

CHÂTEAU DE MONTLÉDIER
Hôtelier: Chantal Thiercelin
Route d'Anglès, Mazamet
81660 Pont de Larn
Tel: 63.61.20.54 Telex: 531833
9 Rooms - Dbl from 500F to 650F
Closed: January
* Restaurant closed Sunday night & Mondays*
Credit cards: AX, DC
Restaurant, pool, park
Region: Tarn

The Moulin de la Gorce is set amongst rolling farmland. This sixteenth-century mill has been converted to a lovely countryside hotel and a superb restaurant. In the various buildings clustered along the edge of a quiet pond and brook are luxurious, antique-furnished bedrooms whose walls are hung with tapestries. (The tapestries are hand-painted replicas from a factory in Rambouillet, and are for sale.) The wallpapers and materials chosen for the decor are sometimes overbearing, but the rooms are all with private bath or shower and very comfortable. A few open onto a grassy terrace. The restaurant, intimate in size, is romantically furnished in soft pastel tones: tables are set before a lovely fireplace and the restaurant's atmosphere is surpassed only by the unusually beautiful presentation of each course. The care and attention to detail that the Bertranet family strive for is evident throughout. There are currently only six rooms in the mill but the Bertranets have built an additional three in an adjacent building. A lovely retreat, and, as a result, a bit difficult to find. Please note that the Bertranet Family does ask that overnight guests dine at the restaurant of the inn. *Directions: From St Yrieix La Perche travel on the D704 northeast out of town in the direction of Limoges ten kilometers, and then turn right and travel two kilometers to La Roche l'Abeille. La Roche l'Abeille is located thirty-nine kilometers to the south of Limoges.*

MOULIN DE LA GORCE
Hôtelier: M & Mme Bertranet
87800 La Roche l'Abeille
Tel: 55.00.70.66 Fax: 55.00.76.57
9 Rooms - Dbl from 550F to 780F
Closed: January
Credit cards: AX, DC, VS
Restaurant (from 200F to 450F)
Region: Sud-Limousin, near Dordogne

Hotel Descriptions

During the Middle Ages the Château d'Isenbourg was the cherished home of the prince bishops of Strasbourg and more recently it was owned by wealthy wine growers. On the hillside above the town of Rouffach, the château is still surrounded by its own vineyards. There are forty bedrooms, nine of which are modern additions that overlook either the vineyards, the wide plain of Alsace or the castle park. A number of rooms are exceptionally elegant with massive, hand-painted ceilings: room two is an especially beautiful apartment. Room fourteen is as expensive but is also impressive in furnishings. The grounds feature a large swimming pool and tennis courts. The kitchen is the domain of the château's young and remarkable chef. You can appropriately savor a delicious meal and fine Alsatian wines (select from the château's own reserve) in the vaulted fifteenth-century wine cellar or on the panoramic terrace. An open-air luncheon is offered in summertime. Between October and January you might want to plan your stay around one of the musical evenings that the hotel sponsors. The soirees begin at 7:30 pm over a cocktail and the concerts begin punctually at 8:00 pm, followed by a candlelit dinner. An indoor swimming pool was a welcome addition in 1990.
Directions: Travel south from Colmar ten kilometers on the N83 in the direction of Cernay. Exit at "Rouffach Est". The Château d'Isenbourg is located just to the north of town.

CHÂTEAU D'ISENBOURG
Hôtelier: M Daniel Dalibert
68250 Rouffach
Tel: 89.49.63.53 Telex: 880819
  Fax: 89.78.53.70
40 Rooms - Dbl from 800F to 1850F
Open: 9 March to 15 January
Credit cards: VS
Restaurant, pool, tennis
Region: Alsace

Deep in the heart of France is the elegant Château de la Commanderie, one of the finest French châteaux open to guests, its comforts challenging those of the finest hotels. Count and Countess de Jouffroy-Gonsans are gracious and hospitable hosts who obviously take great pride and pleasure in welcoming guests to their historic château, in the Count's family since 1630. The Countess has artfully redecorated the entire castle with imaginative style, utilizing beautifully complementing color schemes in upholstery fabrics and wallpapers. Each room is unique, but all are decorated with impeccable taste and flair. Lovely collectibles, antiques and objets d'art grace the bedrooms and public areas. Warm, personal touches such as bowls of potpourri, cologne, bath gels and soaps add comfort and convenience to the modern bathrooms. In the evening, the Count and Countess serve an aperitif in the salon before the fire, and then escort guests into an elegant dining room and host a delightful dinner party. A stay with the de Jouffroy-Gonsans is truly a chance to experience a taste of aristocratic country life. The Count and Countess even offer hunting and riding parties, season permitting. *Directions: Farges-Allichamps is located approximately thirty-five kilometers south of Bourges. From Bourges, travel in the direction of Montluçon on N144, turning off before the town of St Amand-Montrond at Bruère-Allichamps and following signs to the small village of Farges-Allichamps. Look for signs to the Château de la Commanderie.*

CHÂTEAU DE LA COMMANDERIE
Hôtelier: Cte and Ctesse B. de Jouffroy-Gonsans
à Farges-Allichamps, 18200 St Amand-Montrond
Tel: 48.61.04.19 Fax: 48.61.01.84
9 Rooms and Suites - 850F to 1200F
Open: All year, reservations important in off-season
Credit cards: AX, VS
Table d'Hôte: 300F per person including drinks
Region: Berry, Center of France

Monsieur Kubens-Millet has recently retired from Paris and restyled his country home in a tiny half-timbered hamlet into a charming country inn. Across the country lane from the old cemetery and church, the Auberge du Prieuré is a former rectory. Its thatched roof, half-timbers, windows hung heavy with geraniums, odd angles and interesting sections dating from the thirteenth century lend much character to this peaceful inn. The low-ceilinged dining hall offers a wide variety of Madame Kubens-Millet's gourmet specialties. The centuries-old aroma of a log-burning fire mingles with the mouth-watering scents from the kitchen. One sits in the restaurant, which is very rustic in decor, on pew benches and tapestry chairs at long trestle tables placed in the firelight. In the morning, one is tempted to join the flock of ducks and geese in the lush back garden that faces the rose-covered stone wall of the auberge. Monsieur Kubens-Millet proudly showed us all of his seven bedrooms including one commodious duplex. The accommodations all have spotless and modern bathroom facilities (no easy task in a building of its age), large comfortable beds and dark beamed ceilings and are accented by handsome antique furnishings. Colors are muted earth tones and there is a very masculine touch to the decor. *Directions: Located eleven kilometers southeast of Deauville. From Deauville take the D513 east across the bridge to Trouville and then head south on the D74 and then the D17 to the village of St André d'Hébertot.*

AUBERGE DU PRIEURÉ
Hôtelier: M & Mme Kubens-Millet
St André d'Hébertot, 14130 Pont l'Evêque
Tel: 31.64.03.03
7 Rooms - Dbl from 400F to 620F
Open: All year
Credit cards: VS, MC
Restaurant, pool
Region: Normandy

Beyond the ruins of a medieval arched gateway, the Hôte
at the foot of St Cirq Lapopie, is an engaging inn whose cha
artistic owners, the Matuchets. Fresh and simple ii
whitewashed walls contrast handsomely with dark wooden be
floors - strikingly reminiscent of the Mediterranean. Thick sto..
shuttered windows frame the idyllic scene of St Cirq Lapopie perched high a.
wide band of the meandering Lot River. The restaurant is limited in seating, so n
is wise to make reservations well in advance in order to savor Marie-Françoise's
delicious and fresh regional cuisine - one can select from an à la carte menu. It is
incredible how efficient and creative Marie-Françoise can be in the confines of her
small kitchen. François's talents are in the field of music. A piano and string
instruments decorate the intimate, candlelit restaurant, and his own recordings
stage a romantic mood. St Cirq Lapopie is truly one of France's most picturesque
villages. With only forty-four year-round residents, this hamlet of steep, narrow,
winding cobbled streets, sun-warmed tile roofs, mixture of timber and stone
facades, and garden niches is a postcard-perfect scene. It is wonderful to find an
inn which so perfectly complements the beauty of this village. *Directions: St Cirq
Lapopie is located thirty-three kilometers east of Cahors by travelling the D653 and then the
D662.*

HÔTEL DE LA PÉLISSARIA
Hôtelier: François & Marie-Françoise Matuchet
St Cirq Lapopie, 46330 Cabrerets
Tel: 65.31.25.14
8 Rooms - Dbl from 440F to 690F
Open: 1 Apr to 15 Nov, Restaurant closed Thursdays
Credit cards: VS, MC - closed Thursday
Gourmet restaurant
Region: Lot

...rge du Sombral is a small country inn facing onto the main square of the ...sque village of St Cirq Lapopie. In such a small, remote village it was ...zing to learn that editors of *Gourmet* and *Le Figaro* had already discovered the ...uberge and praised it for its restaurant. It is owned by the Hardevelds, with Monique a charming hostess and Gilles the acclaimed chef. Café tables are set on the front porch and provide an inviting spot to linger and enjoy a cool drink after an afternoon of exploring the narrow and steep cobbled streets of the village. Inside, the restaurant is furnished with a melange of country tables and chairs set on a warm tile floor, watercolors that paint country scenes and a glorious, enormous, central arrangement of flowers. Offered are a number of well priced menus or a tempting à la carte selection. The wine list highlights excellent regional wines. The inn's bedrooms are found at the top of a wooden stairway. All are with bath or shower and they are clean, basic and many look out over the rooftops of St Cirq Lapopie. During high season (May through September) the Hardevelds offer rooms on a demi-pension basis only. The Auberge du Sombral is a little inn with a stone facade and simple accommodations offering both moderately priced rooms and superb country French cuisine. *Directions: St Cirq Lapopie is located thirty-three kilometers east of Cahors by travelling the D653 and then the D662.*

AUBERGE DU SOMBRAL
Hôtelier: M & Mme Gilles Hardeveld
St Cirq Lapopie, 46330 Cabrerets
Tel: 65.31.26.08
8 Rooms - Dbl from 370F to 570F
Open: 1 April to 15 November
Credit cards: VS, MC
Restaurant
Region: Lot

The wine town of St Émilion was introduced to us in all its splendor.   It was a day that the town was dressed with banners, filled with music and laughter and visited by all the dignitaries of the region.   It was a warm day in late September, a day to commence the "vendage" - the beginning of the wine harvest.   The day was captivating and we fell in love with the town.   Crowning a hillside with vistas that stretch out to the surrounding vineyards, St Émilion is a medieval village of tradition, long considered the capital of the Bordeaux wine region.   The Hôtel Plaisance opens on to the square, in the shade of the church, and its walls have echoed over the centuries the first church bells commemorating the start of the wine harvest.   To stay here one could not be more central to the activity and the town's events.   The hotel has only twelve rooms, most of which were understandably occupied at the time of our visit.   All are individual in decor and from their windows views extend out over vineyards and the maze of tile rooftops. The dining room is lovely and extremely popular, with tables set against windows whose views appear to plunge over the valley. Service is gracious and accommodating.   La Plaisance is the place to stay in town and St Émilion is the most charming town of the Bordeaux wine region.   *Directions: St Émilion is located thirty-nine kilometers east of Bordeaux. Take the N89 east to Libourne and then travel the D936 in the direction of Bergerac. St Émilion is signposted to the north off the D936.*

HÔSTELLERIE PLAISANCE
Hôtelier: Louis & Samira Quilain
Place du Clocher, 33330 St Émilion
Tel: 57.24.72.32 Telex: 573032 Fax: 57.74.41.11
12 Rooms - Dbl from 660F to 1299F
Closed: January
Credit cards: AX, VS
Restaurant
Region: Dordogne

Hôtel de Chantaco is a lovely Spanish villa in an isolated quiet position on the outskirts of St Jean de Luz, a picturesque port town, on the road that winds up into the Basque hills and some truly charming villages.   Facing a challenging eighteen-hole golf course, the hotel serves as an ideal retreat for golfers.   For those who want to settle in Basque, the Hôtel de Chantaco offers a comfortable and well-located retreat.   Architecturally, the hotel blends beautifully with the region.   Just off the road, but against a backdrop of greenery, this cream-stone, tile-roofed villa has shuttered windows and arched entryways draped with vines.   The decor is austere but well suited to this weathered villa.   The grand entry and salons are airy, spacious and classically furnished.   The hotel was full when we visited and so we were able to view only a few additional rooms but found them individual and comfortable in decor.   The restaurant, El Patio, is inviting and the service is friendly.   For its accommodation, restaurant and service, the Hôtel de Chantaco adds to the enchantment of the Basque province. *Directions: Leave the Autoroute A63 at St Jean de Luz Nord, then travel east on Avenue de Chantaco on the D918. Continue half a kilometer to the small lake and the golf course.*

HÔTEL DE CHANTACO
Hôtelier: Claude Libouban
Golf de Chantaco
64500 St Jean de Luz
Tel: 59.26.14.76 Telex: 540016 Fax: 59.26.35.97
24 Rooms - Dbl from 950F to 1750F
Open: April to November
Credit cards: AX, DC, VS
Restaurant, faces golf course
Region: Basque

La Chapelle St Martin is a small grey-wash manor that rests on a velvet green lawn. Although there is very little exterior ornamentation (even the shutters are painted to blend with the facade) the interior decor is very ornate and detailed. Colorful patterned wallpapers, complementing carpets, paintings hung in heavy gilt frames, lavish chandeliers, tapestries and miniature statues decorate the rooms of the hotel. Known for its restaurant, La Chapelle St Martin serves meals in three elegant, small dining rooms. The setting and service is formal, with lovely porcelain, crystal, china and silver used to enhance the presentation of Chef Yves Leonard's masterful creations. La Chapelle St Martin is only a few minutes from Limoges, a city famous for its porcelain. Although many guests venture from Limoges for dinner, the manor does have eleven rooms to accommodate overnight guests. The bedrooms are decorated with the same flavor as the restaurant and public rooms. Very commodious, the rooms are all with private bath and look out onto the hotel gardens and greenery. The surrounding farmland and two ponds complete the storybook atmosphere of La Chapelle St Martin. *Directions: La Chapelle St Martin is located twelve kilometers northwest of Limoges by travelling the N147 and D35.*

LA CHAPELLE ST MARTIN
Hôtelier: M Jacques Dudognon
St Martin du Fault, 87510 Nieul
Tel: 55.75.80.17 Fax: 55.75.89.50
11 Rooms - Dbl from 750F to 1500F
Open: March to January
  Restaurant closed Mondays
Credit cards: VS
Outstanding restaurant, tennis
Region: Dordogne

La Colombe d'Or is located opposite the main square at the gates to the fortified town of St Paul de Vence. The hotel is attractive and elegant in its rustic ambiance, the theme of its decor focusing around the colors of the home and region. Antiques worn over the years to a warm patina are placed on terra cotta floors, set under rough wooden beams before open fireplaces. Walls are washed white, heavy wooden doors contrast handsomely and throw pillows, wall hangings, and flower arrangements add colors of rusts, oranges, browns and beiges. The hotel also boasts a fantastic collection of art. In the past a number of now famous painters paid for their meals with their talents - and now the walls are hung like a gallery and the reputation of the inn dictates that the value of the art complements the cuisine. The restaurant of La Colombe d'Or is both excellent and attractive. Dine either in the intimacy of a room warmed by a cozy fire or on the patio whose walls are draped with ivy at tables set under the shade of cream umbrellas. In the evening, stars and candles illuminate the very romantic setting. The entrance to the fortified town of St Paul de Vence is just up the street from La Colombe d'Or. After a day of sightseeing, return to La Colombe d'Or and enjoy its refreshing pool set against a backdrop of aging stone wall and greenery. *Directions: St Paul de Vence is located twenty kilometers northwest of Nice. From the Autoroute A8 either from Cannes or Nice, exit at Cagnes Sur Mer and then travel north on the D6 and D2.*

HÔTEL LA COLOMBE D'OR
Hôtelier: M & Mme Roux
Place de Gaulle, 06570 St Paul de Vence
Tel: 93.32.80.02 Telex: 970607 Fax: 93.32.77.78
25 Rooms - Dbl from 1070F to 1360F
Closed: 5 November to 20 December
Credit cards: All major
Restaurant, pool, art collection
Region: Riviera

Le Hameau is an old farm complex set on the hillside just outside the walled city of St Paul de Vence. The whitewashed buildings, tiled roofs aged by years of sun, shuttered windows, arched entryways, heavy doors and exposed beams all create a rustic and attractive setting. The bedrooms of this inn are found in four buildings clustered together amidst fruit trees and flower gardens. Each building has its own character and name: L'Oranger, L'Olivier, Le Pigeonnier and La Treille. Three of the largest bedrooms have a small room for an infant and the attraction of their own balcony (rooms one and three with twin beds and two with a double bed). Of the rooms, eleven, with antique twin beds and a lovely view onto the garden, was my favorite. I was very impressed with the quality of this provincial inn. Monsieur Xavier Huvelin is a charming host and is graciously attentive to the needs of his guests. Le Hameau does not have a restaurant but a delicious country breakfast can be enjoyed in the garden or in the privacy of your room. I highly recommend Le Hameau as a wonderful inn and a great value. *Directions: St Paul de Vence is located twenty kilometers northwest of Nice. From the Autoroute A8 either from Cannes or Nice, exit at Cagnes Sur Mer and then travel north on the D6 and D2.*

HOTEL LE HAMEAU
Hôtelier: M & Mme X. Huvelin
528, Route de la Colle
06570 St Paul de Vence
Tel: 93.32.80.24 Telex: 970846
16 Rooms - Dbl from 440F to 760F
Credit cards: All major
Open: February to 15 November
No restaurant, terraces, gardens
Lovely new pool overlooking the coastal hills
Region: Riviera

Les Orangers welcomes you to St Paul de Vence. Nestled amongst olive and orange trees, the hotel has a view looking back to the village of St Paul de Vence and down towards the French Riviera. The hotel is not located within the walls of St Paul de Vence, but just on its outskirts, on the Route de la Colle. A lovely large living room serves as a welcoming place to settle: a handsome antique hutch, comfortable sofa and chairs and a cozy fireplace tempt one to linger while mapping out the day's itinerary. Monsieur T. Franklin's loving touch is especially apparent in the nine charming bedrooms which are in a building off the reception area. Pretty provincial prints have been chosen to adorn the beds and frame the windows while lovely antiques and Oriental rugs warm the rustic tile floors. Bathrooms are all spotlessly clean and supplied with fresh country soaps and fresh, soft towels. Although the hotel is no longer associated with the restaurant, Les Oliviers, located just below it on the hillside, there are numerous eating places to choose from in the medieval walled village of St Paul. Since each of the bedrooms at Les Orangers has its own terrace, with grape vines entwined in the corner and the fragrance of orange blossoms wafting from below, there is no place more romantic to enjoy a country breakfast. *Directions: St Paul de Vence is located twenty kilometers northwest of Nice. From the Autoroute A8 either from Cannes or Nice, exit at Cagnes Sur Mer and then travel north on the D6 and D2.*

LES ORANGERS
Hôtelier: M T. Franklin
Chemin des Fumerates, 06570 St Paul de Vence
Tel: 93.32.80.95
9 Rooms - Dbl from 550F to 750F
Open: All year
Credit cards: None
No restaurant
Region: Riviera

For many years one of our favorite places to stay has been Le Moulin de l'Abbaye in the located in the Dordogne region of France. The exceptionally talented owners, Cathy and Regis Bulot, have now opened a second hotel in the near the French riviera in the heart of the medieval village of St Paul de Vence. The charming mood is set as soon as you enter the hotel and see the cozy lounge - appealingly decorated in a French country provençal theme. The bedrooms are located on the upper three floors. Because the hotel is built within the shell of one of the very old houses, the rooms are not large, yet each is tastefully decorated and offer every amenity such as beautiful linens, fluffy towels, terry cloth robes, refrigerator, televisions, fine soaps, etc. This is not your standard unimaginative hotel where every room is the same. Instead each has its own personality. Two of our special favorites are a corner room, decorated in pretty provençal, Pierre Deux-style print fabrics and an especially romantic room, tucked under the eaves on the top floor with views out over the quaint jumble of tiled roof tops. One of the guest rooms has a small terrace. Another bonus, La Baronnie restaurant serves gourmet meals either inside, or during the summer on an enchanting terrace. *Directions: St Paul de Vence is located twenty kilometers northwest of Nice. From the Autoroute A8 either from Cannes or Nice, exit at Cagnes Sur Mer and then travel north on the D6 and D2.*

HOTEL LE SAINT-PAUL
Hôtelier: Cathy & Regis Bulot
86, rue Grande, 06570 Saint Paul de Vence
Tel: 93.32.65.25 Telex: 461683 Fax: 93.32.52.94
15 Rooms & 3 suites from 750F to 1700F
Open: All year
Credit cards: AX, DC, VS
Restaurant, La Baronnie
Located 20 km NW of Nice
Region: Riviera

Dining in the care of Marc Meneau is truly an enchanting and memorable experience. Relax and study the daily offerings in the salon, subtle in its soft beiges, greys, well-placed mirrors and abundance of green plants. Casual yet quietly elegant, the restaurant looks out onto outdoor greenery through floor-to-ceiling windows. Tables are set with soft pastel linen, stunning flower arrangements, elegant crystal and silver. Marc Meneau is a tall, handsome man, who sports a tie under his chef's white and is ever-present to welcome guests before attending to his culinary creations. His lovely wife, Françoise, graciously supervises the attentive, professional staff of waiters. She bustles about to extend greetings, pour wine, assist with the service and offer a welcoming smile. Shadowed by his devoted Doberman, Volt, Marc Meneau reappears in the lounge after dinner to relax with guests over coffee. For those fortunate enough also to secure a room reservation, there are thirteen beautifully appointed bedrooms upstairs, traditional in furnishings. There are an additional three suites and five bedrooms, lovely and more rustic in decor, situated in a renovated mill just three hundred meters from the reception. *Directions: L'Espérance is located three kilometers southeast of Vézelay on D957.*

L'ESPÉRANCE
Hôtelier: Marc & Françoise Meneau
St Père sous Vézelay, 89450 Vézelay
Tel: 86.33.20.45 Telex: 800005
* Fax: 86.33.26.15*
21 Rooms - Dbl from 650F to 1200, Suite to 2800F
Closed: January to mid-February
* Restaurant closed Tuesdays & Wednesday lunch*
Credit cards: All major
Restaurant
Region: Burgundy

The Château des Alpilles was purchased a few years ago by the Bons and they have renovated this magnificent manor to its former state of grandeur. The Château des Alpilles is grand, with high ornate ceilings, decorative wallpapers and tall windows draped with heavy fabrics. The public rooms are attractively decorated with period pieces. The breakfast room has been beautifully renovated and blends beautifully with the rest of the home. Upstairs tiled hallways hung with tapestries lead to the fourteen lovely bedrooms. Soft, subdued colors such as rose and Dutch blue have been selected for fabrics and papers. Large armoirs, beds, desks and chairs arrange easily in the spacious rooms, each with private bath, and make for a very comfortable stay. The corner rooms are especially nice with four large shuttered windows overlooking the shaded gardens that are planted with a multitude of exotic species of trees. On the top floor, the Bons suggest three smaller rooms that share a bath and toilet as ideal accommodation for children. The Bons have also renovated a small chapel and an adjacent farmhouse into a beautiful apartment. In summer for a midday meal a barbecue of lamb, beef or pork and large salads are offered poolside. The rest of the year, although the Château des Alpilles does not have a restaurant, meat and cheese platters, omelets, foie gras and wines are available. *Directions: From Avignon travel south on N570 and N571 to St Rémy. Leave town to the west on the D31.*

CHÂTEAU DES ALPILLES
Hôtelier: Mme & Mlle Bon
Route D31, 13210 St Rémy
Tel: 90.92.03.33 Telex: 431487 Fax: 90.92.45.17
19 Rooms - Dbl from 710F to 1350F
Open: Easter to 10 November & Christmas week
Credit cards: All major
No restaurant, pool, tennis, sauna
Region: Provence

Fairytale in its setting and the luxury of its decor the Château d'Esclimont is a memorable and convenient choice (only sixty-five kilometers from Paris) for either beginning or end to your countryside travels.   Not inexpensive, but well priced for what it offers, the Château d'Esclimont is spectacular.   Hidden off a small country road, a private drive winds through handsome gates and then round to expose a stunning château framed by trees and reflected in a beautiful lake graced with swans.   Turrets, moats, stone bridges, towers and sculptured facades create a fanciful world of its regal past.   Thirty-two rooms are located in the main château, all decorated regally with beautifully coordinating fabrics and handsome furnishings.   Whether tucked into turret rounds or under the eaves of the third floor rooms looking out through dormer windows, the accommodations are spacious and equipped with private baths.   Also very attractive in their decor and setting, another twenty-four rooms are found in the "Dungeon", the "Pavilion de Chasse" and the "Grande Ecuries" - all stately buildings separated from the château by the moat.   The Château d'Esclimont has a number of elegant rooms for dining and meetings.   Although often hosting small tours and conferences, guests receive individual attention and excellent service. *Directions: From Paris take the A10 direction Chartres.   Exit the A10 at Ablis, take the N10 to Essars.   At Essars turn on the D101 in the direction of Prunay six kilometers to St Symphorien.*

CHÂTEAU D'ESCLIMONT
Hôtelier: Nicole and Raymond Spitz
28700 St Symphorien-le-Château
Tel: 37.31.15.15 Telex: 780560 Fax: 37.31.57.91
56 Rooms - Dbl from 755F to 2660F
Open: All year
Credit cards: VS
Restaurant, pool, tennis, park, gardens
Region: Île de France

The true French meaning behind their saying "chez soi" can be defined and experienced at the Hôstellerie du Levézou. This is a simple hotel housed within the walls of a fourteenth-century château and lovingly run and managed by the entire Bouviala family: parents, sons, daughters and the dog. The Bouvialas do not boast a hotel of luxurious comfort, but rather a place where one can enjoy good food and comfortable accommodations at a reasonable price. Monsieur Bouviala's pride is his restaurant. Inviting in its decor the dining room is lovely and, when the weather permits, outdoor seating is set on a terrace that extends out in front of it. The focal point of the restaurant is a large fireplace where Monsieur Bouviala grills his delicious specialties. The thirty bedrooms of the Hôstellerie du Levézou are basic, cheerful in their decor, a few with private bath or shower and all extremely reasonable in price. At the heart of the ancient fortified village of Salles Curan, with a beautiful view over Pareloup Lake and the countryside, the Hôstellerie du Levézou, once the medieval summer residence of the Bishops of Rodez, offers a friendly welcome and good-value lodging. *Directions: Located thirty-seven kilometers northwest of Millau, travel north from Millau on the D911 turning off in the direction of Salles Curan and Lac de Pareloup.*

HÔSTELLERIE DU LEVÉZOU
Hôtelier: M David Bouviala
12410 Salles Curan
Tel: 65.46.34.16 Fax: 65.46.01.19
20 Rooms - Dbl from 250F to 350F
Open: 1 April to 15 October
* Restaurant closed Sunday evenings & Mondays*
Credit cards: All major
Restaurant, fourteenth-century château
Region: Tarn

Captivating L'Abbaye de Ste Croix was built in the ninth and twelfth centuries. For seven hundred years it was a residence of Cistercian monks but abandoned and left to ruin in the nineteenth century.   In 1969 it was purchased and converted into a hotel by the Bossard family.   Sprawling along the contours of the hillsides of Provence, the abbey commands a peaceful and idyllic location and enjoys a splendid panorama over the surrounding countryside.   Vaulted ceilings, antiques, tiled floors and open fires warm the atmosphere of the abbey.   A labyrinth of narrow stairways, low, small arched doorways and stone passageways lead to the rooms that are named for saints.   Since the bedrooms' history dates back to when they accommodated Cistercian monks who came to savor the peaceful setting and facilities, they tend to be a bit small and dark, with deep-set windows that peek out through thick stone walls.   A few enjoy the extension of a private terrace.   The restaurant opens up to spectacular vistas out over the Salon Valley and highlights Provencal cuisine.   *Directions: L'Abbaye is located five kilometers to the northeast of Salon de Provence following D16 and a private drive.*

L'ABBAYE DE STE CROIX
Hôtelier: Bossard Family
Route du Val de Cuech
13300 Salon de Provence
Tel: 90.56.24.55 Telex: 401247
   Fax: 90.56.31.12
19 Rooms - Dbl from 970F to 1140F
   5 Apts to 1910F
Open: March to November
Credit cards: All major
Restaurant, large pool
Region: Provence

Nestled in the area bordering Spain, the Hôtel Arraya has captured the tradition and rustic flavor of this Basque region. Long ago the hotel was founded to provide lodgings for pilgrims on the road to Santiago de Compostela. Today it accommodates guests who have fallen in love with this dear inn and return time and again. The Hôtel Arraya is decorated with an abundance of seventeenth-century Basque antiques and is a comfortable and hospitable country manor. The entry, lobby and breakfast nook are charming. Cozy blue and white gingham cushions pad the wooden chairs that are set round a lovely collection of antique tables. The restaurant offers regional Basque specialties to tempt you: "ravioles de xangurro", "piquillos emplis d'une farce de champignons des bois, servis avec un fin ragoût aux palourdes", "petites truites au jambon, nappées d'une courte sauce au vinaigre et à l'ail", "Agneau aux pochas", "foie de canard frais poêlé aux cèpes", "fromages des Montagnes" and "pastiza", a delicious Basque almond cake filled with cream or black cherry preserve. The bedrooms are all individual in decor and size but are attractive with their white-washed walls, exposed beams and pretty fabrics. The hotel is managed by Paul Fagoaga who welcomes his guests as friends in the traditional way, round the "zizailua", or bench near the fire. *Directions: Exit the Autoroute A6 at St Jean de Luz. Follow directions to St Pée sur Nivelle on RN10. After five kilometers turn right to the village of Ascain and then take the Col de St Ignace to Sare.*

HÔTEL ARRAYA
Hôtelier: M Paul Fagoaga
Sare, 64310 Ascain
Tel: 59.54.20.46 Fax: 59.54.27.04
21 Rooms - Dbl from 510F to 590F
Open: 1 May to 5 November
Credit cards: AX, VS, MC
Restaurant
Region: Basque

The Domaine de Bassibé is a hotel you have to stay at to realize its charms. Set in a region popular for its health spas and resorts, the hotel is a beautiful vine covered homestead. The setting, atop a gently rolling hill overlooking the countryside of Geroise, is extremely restful and serene. The use of large floral prints dominates the bedroom decor, quite modern in contrast to the character of the building. After a morning by the pool and an exquisite lunch served at the poolside with luxurious linens, crystal and china I felt quite ready to recommend the hotel to you. The staff are extremely hospitable, making the Bassibé a romantic hideaway as well as an ideal holiday spot for families. The restaurant in the converted stables proves popular with guests and locals alike. The rough wooden beams have been painted in fresh white and contrast attractively with the warm orange color of the walls. Tables are spaciously set on a tile floor around a warming log fire: on warm afternoons they are placed in the courtyard under the shade of low hanging trees. On a Sunday, locals will linger here an entire afternoon over a delicious meal.

Directions: To reach the hotel, travel nine kilometers south from Aire sur l'Adour on N134 in the direction of Pau and then continue on D260. Or from Pau travel north on the N134 approximately thirty-five kilometers to the D260.

DOMAINE DE BASSIBÉ
Hôtelier: Olivier & Sylvie Lacroix
32400 Segos
Tel: 62.09.46.71 Telex: 531918
  Fax: 62.08.40.15
9 Rooms - Dbl from 660F to 1300F
Open: All year
Credit cards: AX, VS, DC
Restaurant, pool
Region: Basque

If business or pleasure brings you to Nantes, stay in this converted thirteenth-century abbey on the town's outskirts.   L'Abbaye de Villeneuve might also serve as a good point to bridge the distance between a tour of Brittany and the Loire Valley. A tree-lined drive leads up to L'Abbaye de Villeneuve, a grand, two-story dwelling set a good distance from the main road.   High ceilings and handsome furnishings impose a formal air and fit the mood of this stately home.   Two intimate dining rooms offer guests a lovely atmosphere in which to dine. Service is very professional, befitting the elegant table settings and grand cuisine. A massive stone stairway winds up to the abbey's eighteen bedrooms: these accommodations are luxuriously furnished, with vast windows offering views of the grounds.   Each room is equipped with direct dial phone, television and lovely, modern bathrooms. Although the grounds are lacking in color, there is a small circular wading pool on the back lawn.   *Directions: Travel southeast out of Nantes, following the direction of La Rochelle-Bordeaux and then La Roche Sur Yon.   At the second stoplight, follow direction Viais.*

L'ABBAYE DE VILLENEUVE
Hôtelier: Philippe Savry
Directeur: M. Lesmarie
Route de Sables d'Olonne
44840 Les Sorinières
Tel: 40.04.40.25 Telex: 710451
  Fax: 40.31.28.45
18 Rooms - Dbl from 720F to 1300F
Open: All year
Credit cards: VS, AX, DC
Restaurant, wading pool
Region: Loire Valley

On a recent trip to France I discovered the Hôtel des Rohan just around the corner from Strasbourg's stunning cathedral. On a pedestrian street, this charming hotel has a lovely foyer and a salon where breakfast is served. The thirty-six beautiful rooms have either private bath or shower, direct-dial phone, radio, television and mini-bar. The hotel is decorated in seventeenth- and eighteenth-century style. Tapestries adorn the walls, and in the bedrooms the style is either Louis XV or rustic. The location is quiet, ideal for exploring Strasbourg on foot. The narrow streets are a maze that winds in the shadow of leaning, timbered buildings and in the shade of the lacy trees that grow beside the river. The shops are delightful with their beautiful displays of Alsatian specialties such as wines, foie-gras, sausages and costumes. The Hôtel des Rohan is without a restaurant and so one is free to investigate the numerous sidewalk cafes and cozy restaurants that Strasbourg is famous for. Being at the heart of the city's old quarter is also the hotel's one drawback - one must park elsewhere. Nearby parking areas convenient to the hotel are at the Place du Château, the Place Gutenberg (underground) and the Rue du Viel Hôpital (except on Wednesdays and Saturdays when there is a flea market). *Directions: Located at the center of town.*

HÔTEL DES ROHAN
Hôtelier: Rolf & Nicole Van Maenen
17-19, rue du Moroquin
67000 Strasbourg
Tel: 88.32.85.11 Telex: 870047 Fax: 88.75.65.37
36 Rooms - Dbl 410F to 700F
Open: All year
Credit cards: VS
No restaurant
Region: Alsace

L'Auberge du Père Bise combines a traditional welcome, exquisite cuisine (some of the best in the region) and a beautiful location to ensure an enjoyable holiday. This shingled, three-story, ivy-covered inn is charming through and through and has offered first class accommodation and service since 1901. At L'Auberge du Père Bise, angled on a small peninsula with terraces and gardens that extend to the water's edge, one can enjoy an idyllic setting of lake, mountains and a large, wooded park. Most of the rooms overlook the lake and many enjoy a private balcony. Accommodations are charming and at the same time luxurious in their comfort. This lovely auberge is not a discovery but rather long praised and recognized by many to be one of the finest inns in France. Sadly, François Bise passed away in 1984, but his widow and daughter carry on the tradition of excellence that he established and has long been associated with this lakeside inn. Even if the setting didn't warrant a visit, Michelin's three toque rating for the restaurant indicates that it alone is worth a dining detour. *Directions: Located fifty-six kilometers south of Geneva. Travelling the N201 south from Geneva follow the eastern shore of Lac d'Annecy at Annecy on the D909 to Talloires.*

L'AUBERGE DU PÈRE BISE
Hôtelier: Charlyne & Sophie Bise
Route de Port a Gauche, Talloires
74290 Veyrier du Lac
Tel: 50.60.72.01 Telex: 385812 Fax: 50.60.73.05
34 Rooms - Dbl from 1300F, Apt to 3800F
Closed: 15 February to 15 November
* Feb to May: Restaurant closed Tue, & Wed lunch*
Credit cards: AX, VS, DC
Restaurant, faces lake, park
Region: Alps (listed on map under Rhône Valley)

La Tonnellerie, renovated from a wine-merchant's house, is situated on a small road near the church in the country village of Tavers.   Just three kilometers away from the medieval city of Beaugency and only an hour and a half's drive from Paris by the autoroute, the Hôstellerie de la Tonnellerie proves to be an ideal starting point for visiting the châteaux of the Loire Valley.   Although the inn is located on a village street, there is very little traffic through Tavers and most of the bedrooms overlook an oasis of garden.   Two wings of the building extend back and border a central courtyard ablaze with flowers and a lovely, refreshing pool.   On the first floor of one wing is La Tonnellerie's restaurant which features regional specialties as well as "nouvelle cuisine" and this is where, a century ago, coopers made barrels for the wine merchants.   The atmosphere of this lovely restored home is enhanced by antiques, arrangements of flowers, lovely watercolors and decorative wallpapers. The decor is warm and inviting and the welcome extended by the Aulagnon family is very gracious. *Directions: Beaugency is located twenty-eight kilometers southwest of Orléans.   The hotel is situated three kilometers to the southwest of Beaugency on N152.*

HÔSTELLERIE DE LA TONNELLERIE
Hôtelier: M & Mme Aulagnon
12, rue des Eaux-Bleues
Tavers, 45190 Beaugency
Tel: 38.44.68.15 Telex: 782479
*   Fax: 38.44.10.01*
26 Rooms - Dbl from 700F to 1100F
Open: April to mid-October
Credit cards: VS, MC
Restaurant, pool, garden
Region: Loire Valley

La Bastide de Tourtour is situated on the outskirts of Tourtour, "le village dans le ciel", and actually guards a position even higher than the "village in the heavens". From its vantage point one can enjoy unobstructed vistas of the surrounding countryside of Haute Provence. The region is lovely and the village with its cobbled streets, galleries, tempting shops, cozy restaurants and inviting cafes a delight to explore. The location of La Bastide de Tourtour is ideal, and so I was therefore extremely disappointed to find it in need of refurbishing and the welcome somewhat stiff on a recent visit. However, I was unable to find a better substitute, and so continue to include it in the book with the hopes that conditions will improve in the near future. A grand circular staircase, with old implements for weaving, spinning, etc. - "brocante", adorning each floor's landing, winds up to the hotel's accommodations. All of the Bastide's bedrooms have private terraces and profit from the hotel's greatest offering - its panoramic views: the scope and direction of the view is a direct factor in determining rates. The decor as well as the view varies from room to room. The restaurant is attractive, with tables set under arches and beamed ceilings and, when weather permits, tables are set on its terrace.

Directions: Located twenty kilometers northwest of Draguignan. Leaving Draguignan follow directions of Flayosc/Salernes, cross Flayosc and continue towards Salernes. After seven kilometers take the road to the right in the direction of Tourtour.

LA BASTIDE DE TOURTOUR
Hôtelier: Etienne & Francine Laurent
Route Draguignan, 83690 Tourtour
Tel: 94.70.57.30 Telex: 970827 Fax: 94.70.54.90
25 Rooms - Dbl from 640F to 1400F
Open: March to November
Credit cards: AX, VS, DC
Restaurant, pool, tennis, jacuzzi, weight room
Region: Haute Provence

On a hilltop overlooking neighboring islands is a charming hotel managed and run by a delightful couple.   In 1977 Gerard and Danielle Jouanny purchased a home, then put their energy and creative effort into renovating and opening it as a hotel in 1978.   The Ti Al-Lannec still feels like a home away from home, from the smell of croissants baking to the personal touches in the decor.   The restaurant is lovely and opens onto glorious views of the coast.   The public rooms have been thoughtfully equipped to accommodate the hobbies of the guests and the unpredictable moods of the weather.   There are jigsaw puzzles, books and games, in addition to a swing on the lawn and a large outdoor chess set.   From the back lawn there is a path that descends to the beach.   Children are obviously welcome.   The hotel was full when I visited, but as I viewed a number of occupied rooms, there were few that did not have a cherished stuffed animal warming the pillow.   Most of the rooms look out to the sea and the Jouannys have recently completed the addition of balconies and terraces to almost all of them.   I saw an especially lovely corner room, eleven, with spacious twin beds and fantastic views.   I was very impressed by the Ti Al-Lannec but I am not at all certain the Jouannys' warm welcome didn't touch me even more.   *Directions: Trébeurden is located nine kilometers northwest from Lannion on the D21 and D65, and Lannion is located eighteen kilometers to the northwest from Guingamp on the N167.*

TI AL-LANNEC
Hôtelier: Gerard & Danielle Jouanny
Allée Mezo Guen, 22560 Trébeurden
Tel: 96.23.57.26 Telex: 740656 Fax: 96.23.62.14
29 Rooms - Dbl from 710F to 990F
Open: 15 March to 15 November
Credit cards: AX, VS, DC
Restaurant, lovely sea views
Region: Brittany

A picturesque farm converted to hotel and restaurant, La Verte Campagne can offer you a delicious meal in a room with a cozy fireplace and comfortable accommodation. The dining room is intimate and charming. Under heavy beams, worn copper and decorative plates adorn the exposed stone walls of this eighteenth-century Normandy farmhouse. Tables huddle around the warmth of the room's large open fire. In centuries past the fireplace served as the stove and it was here that large kettles of food were cooked. La Verte Campagne has only eight bedrooms, most of them quite small, but then so is the price. Room seven with twin beds and bath, and six with a double bed and bath, are the largest bedrooms. Room one, on the other end of the scale, is the smallest; tiny in fact. It has a delicate pink print wallpaper and just enough room to sleep. Room three, one of the medium-sized rooms, is the one I liked most. It has one bed and is decorated with bright red and white checks. *Directions: La Verte Campagne is a bit difficult to find, which also contributes to its charm: Trelly is located twelve kilometers south of Coutances. From Trelly, travel southeast one and a half kilometers on D539.*

LA VERTE CAMPAGNE
Hôtelier: Mme Meredith
Hameau Chevallier
Trelly, 50660 Quettreville
Tel: 33.47.65.33
8 Rooms - Dbl from 250F to 400F
Closed: 15 November to 10 December
*   and 15 February to 1 March*
Credit cards: VS
Charming restaurant, small farmhouse
Region: Normandy

Nestled on a picturesque bend of the Dordogne, referred to as the "Cingle de Trémolat", is the sleepy, tobacco-growing village of Trémolat.   Tucked off a quiet street that leads into the center is Le Vieux Logis et Ses Logis des Champs. Opening up on one side to farmland, this charming hotel has a pretty back garden with a small stream.   The Giraudel-Destord family has lived in this ancient, ivy-covered farm complex for four hundred years.   The current Mme Giraudel-Destord opened the family home to guests thirty-five years ago; her charm dominates the atmosphere and she still arranges flower bouquets for the breakfast trays each morning.   Her son Bernard continues her fine traditions.   The bedrooms have recently been redecorated and are located in various buildings about the property.   Each room has an individual theme for its decor and everything matches, down to the smallest detail.   A favorite is decorated in large red and white checks: the duvets, the pillows, the curtains, and the canopy on the four-poster bed.   The restaurant is in the barn and the tables are cleverly positioned within each of the stalls.   *Directions: Trémolat is located fifty-four kilometers south of Périgueux.   From Périgueux travel south on the N139 and at Le Bugue travel southwest on D31 to Trémolat.*

LE VIEUX LOGIS ET SES LOGIS DES CHAMPS
Hôtelier: Bernard Giraudel-Destord
24510 Trémolat
Tel: 53.22.80.06 Telex: 541025
  Fax: 53.22.84.89
23 Rooms - Dbl from 780F to 1230F
Open: 15 December to 14 January
  and 15 February to 14 November
Credit cards: All major
Restaurant, conference room
Region: Dordogne

Manoir de l'Hormette is a beautiful farmhouse in Aignerville. The garden setting is very restful, protected and enclosed by the stone walls. The grounds are meticulous, beautifully groomed and planted. Inside, the warmth of the family and their welcome is evident in the decor and their thoughtful touches. A loft bedroom with sitting room below is found on the first floor. The second floor of the main house offers a double room, a twin room, and a small single room with sleigh bed. An apartment in the separate cottage has its own living room, darling wood table, tv, single day bed in living room, twin bedded room, double room and one bath. The kitchen is a masterpiece and Monsieur's collection of homemade vinegars sit above the window ledge. The dining room is very handsome, and outside tables await a sunny morning for a wonderful breakfast repast. *Directions: Located fifteen kilometers northwest of Bayeux off the N13. Travelling the N13 from Bayeux to Isigny, take the "Aignerville" exit to the left. Six hundred meters from the highway, at the first cross-road, turn left. The Manoir is 150 meters on the right at the second white fence.* Note: As this book goes to press, the Corpets have informed me that they have a new apartment that accommodates four to five persons and a studio for two to offer overnight guests.

MANOIR DE L'HORMETTE
Hôtelier: Monsieur & Madame Yves Corpet
Aignerville, 14710 Trévières
Tel: 31.22.51.79 Fax: 31.22.75.99
3 Rooms, 2 Cottages with kitchen, 1 Studio
  Dbl from 550F to 1100F
Open: End of March to end of December
Credit cards: VS, MC
Table d'Hôte: 220F per person
Region: Normandy

In the middle of a beautiful valley, with mountains towering as much as five thousand feet on either side, the medieval town of Trigance clings to a rocky spur. The Château de Trigance is found within the walls and ruins of the ancient castle that crowns the village. The restorations and extent of the work involved to prepare this eleventh-century fortress as a hotel are fully appreciated after seeing the before and after photographs. At present there are ten rooms which are tucked behind thick stone walls of the ancient fortress. The accommodation is definitely not luxurious, often a bit dark and austere with beds tucked right up against the ancient stone walls, but the setting and atmosphere is unique with an authentic medieval flavor. One can now even reserve a large room in the round tower that overlooks the village. The restaurant is renowned for its fine cuisine. Monsieur and Madame Thomas are in charge of the hotel in its magnificent setting under the warm blue skies of Haute Provence. The location is convenient for touring the spectacular Gorges du Verdon: pack a picnic and spend a day driving the canyon at leisure. Roads travel either side of the Gorges du Verdon. Views plunge down to narrow stretches where the river forges a path and to calmer, wider sections where the Verdon pauses to create glistening, dark, blue-green pools. A spectacular journey. *Directions: Trigance is located forty-one kilometers north of Draguignan. Leave Draguignan in the direction of Castellane on the D955.*

CHÂTEAU DE TRIGANCE
Hôtelier: M & Mme Jean Claude Thomas
83840 Trigance
Tel: 94.76.91.18 Fax: 94.47.58.99
10 Rooms - Dbl from 570F to 920F
Open: 16 March to 11 November
Credit cards: All major
Restaurant, enclosed in medieval walls
Region: Haute Provence

On the northeastern boundaries of the Loire Valley and its numerous, more famous castles, the Château de Valençay is an impressive and less frequented château. Built on the vast terraces that dominate the Nahon Valley, this majestic Renaissance château is impressive, with a large central pavilion flanked by four imposing round dome towers.   The expanse of grounds hosts a zoological garden. The Hôtel d'Espagne is located adjacent to the gates that open up to the Château de Valençay.   In Napoleon's time this marvelous villa was once the hideaway of the exiled Spanish princes. Isolated and enchanting with its vine-covered walls, cobbled courtyard, covered terrace bordered by beautiful flowers, gardens and elegant rooms, it is still possible to make it your own secret hideaway.   Since 1875, the gracious Fourre family have been welcoming guests into their home and serving them royally.   The bedrooms are attractive and comfortable, decorated with lovely prints and matching fabrics. Although individual in size and decor, the rooms are all equipped with private bathrooms and located in wings of the hotel that border a peaceful inner courtyard.   The Hôtel d'Espagne is highly regarded and praised for its cuisine and the dining room is romantic in its decor and atmosphere. *Directions: Travel south from Blois, fifty-five kilometers, on the D956 to Valençay.*

HÔTEL D'ESPAGNE
Hôtelier: Fourre Family
9, rue Château, 36600 Valençay
Tel: 54.00.00.02 Telex: 751675 Fax: 50.00.12.63
17 Rooms - Dbl from 510F to 1060F
Open: mid-March to mid-November
Credit cards: AX, MC, DC
Restaurant, inner courtyard
Region: Loire Valley

In a region famous for its food, Restaurant Pic stands out for its excellent cuisine. This is in the true sense a "restaurant with rooms" as the hotel portion consists of two bedrooms and two apartments - all provided simply for the convenience and comfort of those fortunate guests who reserved early and who have come to sample the culinary delights of the restaurant. Father and son, Jacques and Alain, are masters in the kitchen, a reputation that is acclaimed the world over. Madame Pic is ever present to offer a welcoming smile and ensure that guests are content while her husband and son are busy creating in the kitchen. For such a renowned restaurant, the ambiance is surprisingly not stuffy or overly formal, but congenial - a direct reflection of and compliment to the Pic family. The Hôtel-Restaurant Pic does not offer accommodation on a demi-pension basis, but does have three good value menus or one can always order a la carte. In summer, meals are served in the shady garden. *Directions: Valence is located ninety-nine kilometers south of Lyon. To reach the hotel take the Valence-Sud exit off the autoroute in the direction of "Centre Ville" and continue on to the Avenue Victor Hugo where the Hôtel-Restaurant Pic is located.*

HÔTEL-RESTAURANT PIC
Hôtelier: M Jacques Pic
285, Avenue Victor Hugo
26000 Valence
Tel: 75.44.15.32 Fax: 75.40.96.03
4 Rooms - Dbl from 900F to 1300F
Open: All year
  Restaurant closed Wednesdays and Sunday nights
Credit cards: AX, DC, VS
Restaurant with rooms
Region: Rhône Valley

Hotel Descriptions

A beautiful drive winds up to this magnificent, grey-turreted château - the first impression is captivating. The Château de Castel Novel offers superlative service and accommodation and, to top it off, the cuisine is superb. This is the country of such delicacies as "foie gras", truffles, veal and a delightful variety of mushrooms. Jean Pierre Faucher, who served his chef's apprenticeship in the region and at some of France's finest restaurants, offers you a wonderful menu. The bedrooms are cozy and beautifully maintained. They are few in number, and I found as they were shown to me that each one became my "favorite" in the order visited. They are all marvelous, but different. One is impressive if you like to sleep in a turret; another has a pair of magnificent, spiraling wooden four-poster beds; and yet another has twin beds, two balconies and a lovely view. The Parveaux family have added ten garret rooms in an annex called La Metarie du Château. These rooms are less luxurious in furnishings but are offered at a reduced rate. Built in the fourteenth and fifteenth centuries, the Château de Castel Novel is set in a garden of fifteen acres with a swimming pool, tennis courts and a practice area of three holes for golfers. The hotel is professionally and graciously managed by Albert Parveaux and his charming wife, Christine. *Directions: Travel ten kilometers to the northwest from Brive la Gaillarde on D901 in the direction of Objat.*

CHÂTEAU DE CASTEL NOVEL
Hôtelier: M Albert Parveaux
Varetz, 19240 Allassac
Tel: 55.85.00.01 Telex: 590065 Fax: 55.85.09.03
37 Rooms - Dbl from 900F, Apt to 1640F
Open: 27 April to 14 October
Credit cards: AX, VS, DC
Restaurant, pool, tennis, bikes
   Jogging trails, 3-hole practice green
Region: Dordogne

Vence is a quaint little town of narrow streets, intriguing passageways and tempting craft and specialty shops. Located in the hills above the resort towns of the Riviera, Vence enjoys a quieter setting and medieval ambiance. It is a perfect base from which to explore neighboring hilltop villages such as the fortified St Paul de Vence and its Maeght Foundation, the perfume center of Grasse, and the charming Biot which has recently earned a reputation for fine glassware. Look for the largest tree in Vence and there you will find L'Auberge des Seigneurs. This is a delightful inn, located on a quiet side street at the center of Vence. The inn is charming in its decor and country ambiance: heavy old beams are exposed in the ceilings and walls are whitewashed. Copper plates, pans and bed warmers adorn the walls, while provincial prints cover the tables and lovely antique pieces are used handsomely. Wooden doors, rich in their patina, a large stone fireplace and striking flower arrangements complete a scene in the restaurant and salon that is intimate and cozy. Up a creaking stairway are ten delightful, small rooms. Inexpensive in price, the bedrooms are a true bargain - comfortable and simply decorated with pretty country prints. *Directions: From Nice travel southwest on the N98 to Cros de Cagnes and then travel north on the D36 to Vence. Vence is located twenty-two kilometers to the northwest of Nice.*

L'AUBERGE DES SEIGNEURS ET DU LION D'OR
Hôtelier: M Pierre Rodi
Place du Frêne, 06140 Vence
Tel: 93.58.04.24
10 Rooms - Dbl from 350F to 400F
Open: 2 December to 15 October
  Restaurant closed Sunday evenings, Mondays
Credit cards: All major
Restaurant
Region: Riviera

Looking up from the town of Vence you can see the Château St Martin sitting on the hillside a few kilometers away. The Château St Martin stands behind the historical ruins of an old drawbridge, tower and wall, giving the hotel a feeling of the past, while a beautifully located swimming pool and tennis courts provide the pleasures of the present. The castle ruins hint at a past which stretches back to Roman times. The present castle was built in 1936 to combine the maximum in comfort with the refinement and beauty of residences of old. The accommodation is so luxurious and spacious the rooms are appropriately referred to as suites. If you prefer solitude, there are also small Provencal country houses on the estate. A well-known cook is in charge of this most famous kitchen. All products from the estate are at his disposal: fresh eggs, fruit and vegetables picked daily and oil from one thousand-year-old olive trees. Sample his splendors at tables set on a wide, outdoor terrace and enjoy a one hundred-kilometers vista down to the Côte d'Azur. Although indoors, an elegant restaurant looks out through floor to ceiling windows and enjoys the same breathtaking panorama. The Château St Martin is for those seeking sheer luxury and the finest of service. *Directions: From Nice travel southwest on the N98 to Cros de Cagnes and then travel north on the D36 to Vence. From Vence, travel to the north, two and a half kilometers on D2, the Route de Coursegoules. Vence is located twenty-two kilometers to the northwest of Nice.*

CHÂTEAU ST MARTIN
Directeur: Mlle Brunet
Avemie des Templiers, 06140 Vence
Tel: 93.58.02.02 Telex: 470282 Fax: 93.24.08.91
25 Rooms - Dbl from 1160F to 3200F
Open: mid-March to mid-November
Credit cards: All major
Restaurant, pool, tennis, park
Region: Riviera

The Dordogne, a favorite region of France, has an abundance of small country inns. It is difficult to isolate a favorite hotel as each has an individual style, charm and appeal.   Since each deserves special attention, the only "sensible" solution is to make repeated visits to the Dordogne in the hopes of savoring them all.   As a result I have one more "gem" - the Manoir de Rochecourbe.   It is with special pleasure that I include and recommend it, as the wife of the owner, Madame Roger, is also the sister of Madame Bonnet of the delightful Hôtel Bonnet in Beynac.   The Manoir de Rochecourbe, a dainty château with its one single turret, belonged to Madame Roger's grandmother and most of the furnishings are original or from Monsieur Roger's family. Surrounded by its own lacy garden, it seems appropriate that each of the seven rooms is named after a flower.   Climb the turret to your chamber.   Only the smallest room does not have an en-suite bathroom. Although the hotel does not have a restaurant, simple meals are sometimes prepared by request and served in the small, intimate dining room.   This is indeed a lovely hotel and the welcome is delightfully consistent and characteristic of this gracious family.   *Directions: Vezac is located sixty-four kilometers southeast of Périgueux. Vezac is a small town located on the road between Sarlat-la-Canéda and Beynac.*

MANOIR DE ROCHECOURBE
Hôtelier: M & Mme Roger
Vezac, 24220 St Cyprien
Tel: 53.29.50.79
5 Rooms - Dbl from 360F to 460F
Open: 15 June to 15 September
Credit cards: VS
No restaurant
Region: Dordogne

Considered to be one of France's most picturesque villages, Vézelay is a "must" today just as it was in the Middle Ages when it was considered an important pilgrimage stop. Perched on the hillside overlooking the romantic valley of the Cousin, Vézelay is a wonderful place to spend the afternoon, enjoy a countryside picnic, or, if afforded the luxury of time, to linger and spend the evening. A popular choice for a hotel is the Poste et Lion d'Or, a hillside inn that sits just outside the village gates and walls. Poste et Lion d'Or is believed to have existed as a post house in the Middle Ages, accommodating those who awaited the opening of the village drawbridge. Throughout the hotel there are remembrances from times more recent than the days of knights in armor. The bedrooms in the main building are lovely and decorated with handsome antiques. An ivy-clad annex is surrounded by a sprawling English garden. Here the rooms are quiet but the decor is modern. Like the hotel, the restaurant has an intriguing blend of old and modern decor. The Remillet family purchased the hotel in 1988 and succeed to welcome you and expertly manage this comfortable hillside inn. *Directions: Vézelay is located fifteen kilometers from Avallon. From Avallon take the D957 west in the direction of Vézelay.*

HÔTEL POSTE ET LION D'OR
Hôtelier: Remillet Family
Place du Champ de Foire
89450 Vézelay
Tel: 86.33.21.23 Telex: 800949 Fax: 86.32.30.92
45 Rooms - Dbl from 320F to 760F
Open: 10 April to 8 November
Credit cards: All major
Restaurant
Region: Burgundy

It is fitting that the engaging hill town of Vézelay with its acclaimed Romanesque basilica should also offer the Résidence Hôtel le Pontot.　This is an unusual hotel, perhaps best summed up in the words of our host, Christian Abadie, "All is very simple here, nothing but the best!"　And when I commented that the residence was "like a museum" he immediately countered, "No, it *is* a museum!".　We learned that Monsieur Abadie does not exaggerate as we toured this medieval town house, a registered historical landmark whose oldest part dates from the eleventh century. The entry salon is Louis XVI and displays a parquet floor patterned after Versailles, surrounded by walls of wooden relief depicting the four seasons, love, the sciences and the arts, but their beauty is eclipsed by the salon's "piece de resistance" - its Baccarat crystal chandelier.　Upstairs, the bedrooms which date from the seventh century are all decorated with antique pieces, impeccable style and the finest linens.　A comfortable lounge is found in a part of the home that bridges the street below.　Breakfast is a rare treat, served on cobalt blue Limoges china encrusted with gold, flanked by silver pitchers and flatware.　On a summer morning, breakfast is served outdoors in the flower-filled garden.　The Résidence Hôtel le Pontot is for those who appreciate the fine taste and museum quality pieces exhibited. *Directions: Vézelay is located fifteen kilometers from Avallon. From Avallon take the D957 southwest in the direction of Vézelay.*

RÉSIDENCE HÔTEL LE PONTOT
Hôtelier: Christian Abadie
Place du Pontot, 89450 Vézelay
Tel: 86.33.24.40
10 Rooms - Dbl from 600F to 1000F
Open: Easter to 15 November
Credit cards: All major
No restaurant, boutique
Region: Burgundy

I was pleased to discover that the potential of this little inn has been realized under the direction of Monsieur Gounaud. In the sixteenth century the walls of L'Atelier sheltered fabric workshops. The front room has been converted into a lovely sitting room with tapestry chairs set on an Oriental rug before a large fireplace. A central stairway that led to the individual workshops in what was once an outdoor courtyard - exterior balconies remain as evidence on each of the floors - now climbs to the hotel's nineteen bedrooms. No two rooms are alike, but each is with private bath, charming and very reasonably priced. Old wooden ceiling beams have been re-exposed, walls are papered or freshly painted to contrast with supporting timbers, antiques contribute handsomely to the furnishings and a few rooms have a fireplace. One room is unique in that its top floor location and skylight window afford a view out over rooftops, across the river to the City of the Popes in Avignon. Sheltered in back is a delightful, quiet courtyard where one can enjoy a breakfast of croissants and "cafe au lait" and also two additional rooms of the hotel, each with a private terrace. Climb the old, exterior stone stairway off the courtyard to a peaceful terrace that overlooks the walls of the fort and village rooftops - a perfect spot to hide away with a book. *Directions: Villeneuve is across the river to the west from Avignon. Cross the Rhône and travel the three kilometers to Villeneuve les Avignon.*

L'ATELIER
Hôtelier: M Jean-Pierre Gounaud
5, rue de la Foire, 30400 Villeneuve les Avignon
Tel: 90.25.01.84 Fax: 90.25.80.06
19 Rooms - Dbl from 280F to 480F
Open: All year
Credit cards: All major
No restaurant
Region: Provence

Le Prieuré, constructed in 1322 on the orders of Cardinal Armand de Via, was purchased in 1943 by Roger Mille who transformed it into a small inviting hotel. At the heart of the lovely medieval village of Villeneuve les Avignon, Le Prieuré is charming. Ivy clings to its warm stone exterior, green shutters dress its windows and sun-baked tiles adorn its roof. The hotel has expanded and changed over the years. The Chapter House was completely remodelled, creating five pretty twin rooms with bathrooms and two lovely suites. The dining room was enlarged by moving the fireplace and adding large picture windows. Most recently, in 1987, the Milles renovated the last five "old" bathrooms in the original wing of the inn. Air conditioning has been incorporated throughout - a welcome luxury in the hot provencal summers. Le Prieuré is decorated with beautiful antiques add charm and beauty to the ambiance and setting. When blessed with the balmy weather of Provence, dine on the terrace surrounded by foliage and soft lighting in the subtle elegance of a summer night. Continuing in the tradition of her husband and in honor of his memory, Marie-France is your gracious hostess and her presence lends a personal and special touch to the very competent and professional service.
Directions: Villeneuve is across the river to the west from Avignon. Cross the Rhône and travel the three kilometers to Villeneuve les Avignon.

LE PRIEURÉ
Hôtelier: Mme Jacques Mille
7, Place de Chapître
30400 Villeneuve les Avignon
Tel: 90.25.18.20 Telex: 431042 Fax: 90.25.45.39
36 Rooms - Dbl from 670F to 1600F, Apt 1770F
Open: 10 March to 10 November
Credit cards: All major
Restaurant, pool, tennis, park
Region: Provence

This is a wonderful old home set amongst the vineyards just outside the village of Morgon. The cream wash stucco exterior, white painted windows and a red tile roof lend a Mediterranean flavor to the Domaine de la Javernière, home to the Roux family. Originally from Jura, Monsieur and Madame Roux settled here over eighteen years ago and just recently opened up their home to overnight guests. They offer delightful accommodations that reflect their warmth and graciousness. Uneven old stone steps lead to first floor rooms and wood steps and tile floors lead to second floor rooms tucked under beams. La Javernière's nine bedrooms open onto the Domaine's lovely and very private garden and look out over the surrounding walls to the valley and a mosaic of vineyards. Furnishings are comfortable and tasteful with family mementos and knick knacks. Public rooms also available to guests are a comfortable library with television and a salon warmed by a lovely fireplace. Gloriously warm days dictate that a leisurely breakfast be enjoyed at tables set in the garden. The Roux also offer evening meals with advance notice. *Directions: Travel twenty-two kilometers south from Mâcon or forty kilometers north from Lyon on the N6. At Belleville take the D37 to the right in the direction of Beaujeu. Five kilometers after Belleville in Cercie, turn right on the D68 in the direction of Villié-Morgon and travel four kilometers to Morgon. La Javernière is located on a small road that branches off the D68 halfway between Villié-Morgon and Morgon.*

LA JAVERNIÈRE
Hôteliers: Monsieur & Madame François Roux
Morgon, 69910 Villié-Morgon
Tel: 74.04.22.71 Fax: 74.69.14.44
9 Rooms - Dbl from 580F to 980F
Open: All year
Credit cards: AX, VS, MC
Table d'Hôte: 200F per person including drinks
Region: Rhône Valley

Deep in the Burgundy countryside, the elegant and highly comfortable Hôtel-Restaurant Georges Blanc offers gastronomical delights amidst luxurious surroundings. For three generations the Blanc family have been well known restauranteurs and innkeepers, a tradition now continued by the family's youngest son, Georges, a world-renowned chef. Sample his culinary skills in one of the two pretty riverside dining rooms, while seated in rosy-hued tapestry chairs at tables set elegantly with fine china, silver and glassware. Polished antique sideboards and chests display stunning flower arrangements and a beautiful tapestry covers the wall next to an expanse of windows. The extensive wine cellar is impressively displayed through its glass walls. Our welcome to the Georges Blanc was very professional and accommodating. Flower boxes spilling over with geraniums line the walkway to the back wing of the hotel where a good part of the rooms are located alongside the peaceful river. All of the fresh, clean bedrooms have private bath or shower and are tastefully furnished with antique reproductions and fine fabrics. The very large and luxurious suite with two floors and two smaller apartments are good options for those seeking more spacious accommodations as the standard rooms can be small. An inviting swimming pool, tennis court and even a helicopter landing pad are also found behind the hotel. *Directions: Located nineteen kilometers to the southeast from Mâcon. From Mâcon take the N79 to the turn off to the south to Vonnas.*

HÔTEL-RESTAURANT GEORGES BLANC
Hôtelier: Georges Blanc
01540 Vonnas
Tel: 74.50.00.10 Telex: 380776 Fax: 74.50.08.80
41 Rooms - Dbl from 760F, Suite to 3180F
Open: 8 February to 1 January
Credit cards: AX, VS, DC
Superb restaurant, pool, tennis
Region: Rhône Valley

Once a cisterian abbey, the Château de Gilly is surrounded by an expanse of grounds transected by a web of moats and has origins that trace back to the sixth century. Just north of Beaune, at the heart of Burgundy, the château guards a quiet location near Château de Vougeot, home to the Chevaliers de Tastevin. You can drive up over one arm of a moat to the entry of the Château de Gilly which was magnificently constructed to deceptively blend with two wings of the fortification that date back to the seventeenth century. Beautifully renovated, the interior of the château is rich in furnishings and comfort. Hung between dramatic beams, handsome tapestries drape the old stone walls. Lofty corridors, dramatic with vaulted ceiling, tile and stone floors lead to ground floor bedchambers and narrow, steep stairways wind up to rooms tucked under the heavy old eaves and beams. Quality fabrics and incredible fourteenth- and eighteenth-century paintings have been selected to decorate the spacious rooms, and bathrooms have been incorporated with thoughtful modern comforts. Descend to an underground passageway to the magnificent dining room. Dressed with deep red fabrics, candlelight, crystal, silver, and heavy tapestries the restaurant is elegant. *Directions: Travel twenty-two kilometers north of Beaune on the N74. Just before Vougeot, watch for a small road and sign on the right, directing you east to Gilly-lès-Citeaux and the Château.*

CHÂTEAU DE GILLY
Hôtelier: Jean Louis Bottigliero
Gilly les Citeaux, 21640 Vougeot
Tel: 80.62.89.98 Telex: 351467 Fax: 80.62.82.34
47 Rooms - Dbl from 740F, Suites to 2640F
Closed: February
Credit cards: VS, MC
Restaurant
Region: Burgundy

312

SAMPLE RESERVATION REQUEST LETTER

Hotel Name & Address

Messieurs, Mesdames:

Nous voudrions réserver pour _____ nuit(s),
We would like to reserve for *(number of)* *nights,*

du _____ au _____,
from *(date of arrival)* *to (date of departure),*

_____ une chambre à deux lits,
a room(s) with twin beds

_____ une chambre au grand lit
room(s) with double bed

_____ une chambre avec un lit supplémentaire,
room(s) with an extra bed

_____ avec salle de bains et toilette privée,
with a bathroom and private toilet

Nous sommes_____ personnes.
We have *(number)* *of persons in our party.*

Veuilliez confirmer la réservation en nous communicant le prix de la chambre, et le dépôt forfaitaire que vous exigez. Dans l'attente de vos nouvelles, nous vous prions d'agréer, Messieurs, Mesdames, l'expression de nos sentiments distingués.

Please advise availability, rate of room and deposit needed. We will be waiting for you confirmation and send our kindest regards.

Your Name & Address

Hotels with U.S. Representatives

The names of the following representatives and the hotels that they represent are provided for the convenience of those who would like to employ the services of a representative to assist with securing reservations. Please know, however, that representatives are in business, their services aren't free and to cover their cost of operation, the companies understandably charge for their services. Some companies quote an inflated room rate that incorporates their fee while others quote the actual room rate but add a fee for making the reservation. Fees and policies concerning charges and payment, and cancellations and penalties do vary, so it is strongly advised to check with the individual companies as to their charges and stipulations before making any reservation requests.

BEST WESTERN
P.O. Box 10203, Phoenix, Arizona 85064
Tel: 800 528-1234, Telex: 165743

TOWN	HOTEL	MAP	PAGE(S)
Paris (6th)	Left Bank Hôtel	II	131
Paris (8th)	Hôtel Lido	II	134
Mont St Michel	Hôtel La Mère Poulard	I	26 29 257

DMI TOURS

Didier Majoie, CTC, President
14340 Memorial Drive, Suite 117, Houston, Texas 77079
Tel: 713 558-9933, 800 553-5090, Fax: 713 497-6984

TOWN	HOTEL	MAP	PAGE(S)
Aubigny sur Nère	Château de la Verrerie	II	153
Bayeux	Le Castel	I	166
Bourgueil	Château des Réaux	I	177
Champigné	Château des Briottières	I	189
Chantelle	Château de Boussac	IV	191
Charny	Château de Prunoy	II	192
Crouttes	Le Prieuré Saint Michel	I	207
Fondettes (Tours)	Manoir du Grand Martigny	I	216
La Jaille-Yvon	Château du Plessis	I	230
Lacave	Château de la Treyne	IV	234
Marcigny	Château de la Fredière	III	245
Pleugueneuc	Château Motte Beaumanoir	I	31 266
St Amand-Montrond	Château de la Commanderie	II	271
Trévières	Manoir de l'Hormette	I	297
Villié-Morgon	La Javernière	III	309

JACQUES DE LARSAY, INC.

622 Broadway, New York, New York 10012
Tel: 212 477-1600 / 800 366-1510, Fax: 212 995-0286

TOWN	HOTEL	MAP	PAGE(S)	
Aix en Provence	Hôtel le Pigonnet	III	80	148
Arles	Hôtel d'Arlatan	III		150
Arles	Hôtel Jules César	III		151
Audrieu	Château d'Audrieu	I		154
Avallon	Le Moulin des Ruats	II		156
Avallon	Le Moulin des Templiers	II		157
Avallon	Château de Vault de Lugny	II	108	155
Avignon	Hôtel d'Europe	III	116	158
Baix	Cardinale & Residence	III		160
Barbizon	Hôst. du Bas-Bréau	II		161
Les Baux de Provence	L'Aub. de la Benvengudo	III		162
Les Baux de Provence	La Cabro D'Or	III		163
Les Baux de Provence	L'Oustau Baumanière	III	84	164
Bayeux	Hôtel d'Argouges	I	22	165
Beaumont (Chinon)	Château Hôtel de Danzay	I		168
Beaune	Hôtel le Cep	II		169
Beaune	Hôtel de la Poste	II		170
Billiers (Muzillac)	Domaine de Rochevilaine	I	36	173
Bourgueil	Château des Réaux	I		177
Brantôme	Hôst. Moulin de l'Abbaye	IV	53	179
Cagnes sur Mer	Le Cagnard	III	100	182
Carcassonne	Domaine d'Auriac	IV		183
Carcassonne	Hôtel de la Cité	IV		184
Chagny	Château de Bellecroix	II		186
Chaumontel	Château de Chaumontel	II		194
Chaumont sur Loire	Hôstellerie du Château	I		195

Hotels with U.S. Representatives

JACQUES DE LARSAY, INC., continued

TOWN	HOTEL	MAP	PAGE(S)
Chenonceaux	Bon Laboureur	I	197
Chissay	Château de Chissay	I	47 199
Conques	Hôtel Ste Foy	IV	66 203
Cordes	Hôtel du Grand Écuyer	IV	73 204
Courtils	Manoir de la Roche Torin	I	205
Dampierre-en-Yvelines	Abbaye des Vaux de Cernay	II	208
Les Eyzies de Tayac	Hôtel Cro Magnon	IV	212
Èze Village	Château de la Chèvre D'Or	III	102 213
Èze Village	Château Eza	III	214
Fère en Tardenois	Hôstellerie du Château	II	106 215
Fontvielle	La Régalido	III	217
Honfleur	L'Ecrin	I	21 227
Honfleur	La Ferme St Siméon	I	20 228
Hennebont	Château de Locguénolé	I	225
Luynes	Domaine de Beauvois	I	42 240
Lyon	Cour des Loges	III	241
La Malène (La Caze)	Château de la Caze	III	72 242
Marçay	Château de Marçay	I	244
Mercuès	Château de Mercuès	IV	61 247
Meyrargues	Château de Meyrargues	III	92 248
Meyreuis	Château d'Ayres	III	69 249
Millac	Relais la Metairie	IV	250
Moëlan sur Mer	Les Moulins du Duc	I	251
Montbazon	Château d'Artigny	I	253
Mont St Michel	Hôtel Mère Poulard	I	26 29 257
Mougins	Le Moulin de Mougins	III	98 258
Noizay	Château de Noizay	I	260
Onzain	Dom. des Hauts de la Loire	I	263

Hotels with U.S. Representatives

JACQUES DE LARSAY, INC., continued

TOWN	HOTEL	MAP	PAGE(S)
Paris (1st)	Hôtel Mayfair	II	123
Paris (1st)	Hôtel Vendôme	II	123
Paris (3rd)	Pavillon de la Reine	II	124
Paris (4th)	Hôtel de la Bretonnerie	II	125
Paris (4th)	Hôtel des Deux-Îles	II	126
Paris (4th)	Hôtel de Lutèce	II	126
Paris (4th)	Hôtel Jeu de Paume	II	127
Paris (5th)	Hôtel Colbert	II	128
Paris (6th)	Hôtel Abbaye St Germain	II	130
Paris (6th)	Relais Christine	II	132
Paris (7th)	Hôtel Duc de Saint Simon	II	133
Paris (8th)	Hôtel San Regis	II	135
Paris (16th)	Hôtel Alexander	II	137
Pérouges	Ost. du Vieux Pérouges	III	114 264
Rouffach	Château d'Isenbourg	II	119 270
St Émilion	Hôstellerie Plaisance	IV	275
St Jean de Luz	Hôtel de Chantaco	IV	276
St Paul de Vence	Hôtel La Colombe d'Or	III	278
St Paul de Vence	Les Orangers	III	280
St Paul de Vence	Hôtel Le Saint-Paul	III	281
St Père sous Vézelay	L'Espérance	II	109 282
St Rémy	Château des Alpilles	III	283
St Symphorien le Ch.	Château d'Esclimont	II	284
Les Sorinières (Nantes)	L'Abbaye de Villeneuve	I	289
Strasbourg	Hôtel des Rohan	II	290
Tailloires	L'Auberge du Père Bise	III	291
Tavers (Beaugency)	Hôstellerie de la Tonnellerie	I	292
Varetz	Château de Castel Novel	IV	57 301

Hotels with U.S. Representatives

JACQUES DE LARSAY, INC., continued

TOWN	HOTEL	MAP	PAGE(S)
Vézelay	Hôtel Poste et Lion d'Or	II	305
Vézelay	Résidence Hôtel le Pontot	II	306
Villeneuve les A.	Le Prieuré	III	83 308
Vonnas	Hôtel-Rest. Georges Blanc	III	310
Vougeot	Château de Gilly	II	112 311

RELAIS & CHATEAUX

2400 Lazy Hollow, Suite 152 D, Houston, Texas 77063
Tel: 713 783-8033 / 800 677-3524 (reserv) / 800 743-8033 (info) Fax: 713 783-0951

TOWN	HOTEL	MAP	PAGE(S)
Arles	Hôtel Jules César	III	151
Barbizon	Hôstellerie du Bas Bréau	II	161
Les Baux de Provence	La Cabro d'Or	III	163
Les Baux de Provence	L'Oustau Baumanière	III	84 164
Brantôme	Hôst. Moulin de l'Abbaye	IV	53 179
Cagnes sur Mer	Le Cagnard	III	100 182
Champillon	Royal Champagne	II	190
Châteaux Arnoux	La Bonne Étape	III	193
Chenehutte les T.	Le Prieuré	I	43 196
Èze Village	Château de la Chèvre d'Or	III	102 213
Fontvielle	La Régalido	III	217
Gramat	Château de Roumégouse	IV	56 224
Hennebont	Château de Locguénolé	I	225
Honfleur	La Ferme St Siméon	I	20 228
Lac de Brindos	Château de Brindos	IV	235

RELAIS & CHATEAUX, continued

TOWN	HOTEL	MAP	PAGE(S)
Levernois	Hôst. du Levernois	II	238
Luynes	Domaine de Beauvois	I	42 240
Marçay	Château de Marçay	I	244
Mercuès	Château de Mercuès	IV	61 247
Montbazon	Château d'Artigny	I	253
Noizay	Château de Noizay	I	260
Onzain	Dom. des Hauts de Loire	I	263
Rouffach	Château d'Isenbourg	II	119 270
St Martin du Fault	La Chapelle St Martin	IV	277
St Paul de Vence	Hôtel le Saint-Paul	III	281
St Père sous Vézelay	L'Espérance	II	109 282
St Symphorien le Ch.	Château d'Esclimont	II	284
Salon de Provence	L'Abbaye de Ste Croix	III	286
Segos	Domaine de Bassibé	IV	288
Tailloires	L'Auberge de Père Bise	III	291
Tourtour	La Bastide de Tourtour	III	90 293
Trémolat	Le Vieux Logis	IV	53 296
Trigance	Château de Trigance	III	90 298
Valençay	Hôtel d'Espagne	I	299
Valence	Hôtel-Restaurant Pic	III	300
Varetz	Château de Castel Novel	IV	57 301
Vence	Château St Martin	III	303
Villeneuve les A.	Le Prieuré	III	83 308
Vonnas	Hôtel Georges Blanc	III	310
Vougeot	Château de Gilly	II	112 311

ROMANTIK HOTELS RESERVATIONS

14180 Woodinville-Duvall Road, P.O. Box 1278, Woodinville, Wa. 98072
Tel: 206 486-9394 / 800 826-0015, Fax: 206 481-4079

TOWN	HOTEL	MAP	PAGE(S)
Courtils	Manoir de la Roche Torin	I	205
Meyrueis	Château d'Ayres	III	69 249
Paris (5th)	Hôtel Colbert	II	128
Tavers	Hôstellerie de la Tonnellerie	I	292
Trébeurden	Ti Al-Lannec	I	33 294

Index

Index Alphabetically by Hotel

HOTEL	TOWN	MAP#	page(s)
COLOMBE D'OR, Hôtel La	St Paul de Vence	III	278
COMMANDERIE, Château de la	St Amand-Montrond	II	271
COUR DES LOGES	Lyon	III	241
CRILLON LE BRAVE, Host. de	Crillon le Brave	III	80 206
CRO MAGNON, Hôtel	Les Eyzies de Tayac	IV	212
DANZAY, Château Hôtel de	Beaumont (Chinon)	I	168
DAUPHIN, Hôtel du	Honfleur	I	226
DEUX-ÎLES, Hôtel des	Paris (4th)	II	126
DIDEROT, Hôtel	Chinon	I	198
DOBERT, Château de	Noyen sur Sarthe	I	261
DUC, Les Moulins du	Moëlan sur Mer	I	251
ÉCRIN, Hôtel l'	Honfleur	I	21 227
ENCLOS, Domaine de l'	Gordes	III	221
ESCLIMONT, Château d'	St Symphorien-le-Château	II	284
ESPAGNE, Hôtel d'	Valençay	I	299
ESPÉRANCE, L'	St Père sous Vézelay	II	109 282
ESPLANADE, Hôtel de l'	Domme	IV	202
EUROPE, Hôtel d'	Avignon	III	116 158
EZA, Château	Èze Village	III	214
FERME DE LA HUPPE, La	Gordes	III	222
FERME ST SIMÉON, La	Honfleur	I	20 228
FREDIÈRE, Château de la	Marcigny	III	245
GALERIE DES ARCADES	Biot	III	174
GENTILHOMMIÈRE, La	Nuits St Georges	II	262
GEORGES BLANC, Hôtel-Rest.	Vonnas	III	310
GILLY, Château de	Vougeot	II	112 311
GORCE, Moulin de la	La Roche l'Abeille	IV	269
GRAND ÉCUYER, Hôtel du	Cordes	IV	73 204
GRAND MARTIGNY, Manoir du	Fondettes (Tours)	I	216
GRAND ST MICHEL, Hôtel du	Chambord	I	187
GRANDS HOMMES, Hôtel des	Paris (5th)	II	129

HOTEL	TOWN	MAP#		page(s)
GRIFFONS, Hôstellerie les	Bourdeilles	IV	53	176
HAMEAU, Hôtel le	St Paul de Vence	III	95	279
HAUTEGENTE, Manoir d'	Coly	IV		202
HAUTS DE LOIRE, Dom. des	Onzain	I		263
HORMETTE, Manoir de l'	Trévières	I		297
ISENBOURG, Château d'	Rouffach	II	119	270
JAVERNIÈRE, La	Villié-Morgon	III		309
JEU DE PAUME, Hôtel du	Paris (4th)	II		127
JULES CÉSAR, Hôtel	Arles	III		151
LEFT BANK HOTEL	Paris (6th)	II		131
LEVERNOIS, Hôstellerie du	Levernois (Beaune)	II		238
LEVÉZOU, Hôstellerie du	Salles Curan	IV		285
LIDO, Hôtel	Paris (8th)	II		134
LOCGUÉNOLÉ, Château de	Hennebont	I		225
LUTÈCE, Hôtel de	Paris (4th)	II		126
MAJESTIC, L'Hôtel	Paris (16th)	II		137
MARÇAY, Château de	Marçay	I		244
MAYANELLE, La	Gordes	III		223
MAYFAIR, Hôtel	Paris (1st)	II		123
MERCUÈS, Château de	Mercuès	IV	61	247
MÈRE POULARD, Hôtel	Mont St Michel	I	26 29	257
METAIRIE, Relais la	Millac (Mauzac)	IV		250
MEYRARGUES, Château de	Meyrargues	III	92	248
MONTESQUIOU, Manoir de	La Malène	III		243
MONTLÉDIER, Château de	Pont de Larn	IV	74	268
MORPHÉE, Le	Gacé	I		219
MOTTE BEAUMANOIR, Château	Pleugueneuc	I	31	266
MOUGINS, Le Moulin de	Mougins	III	98	258
NOIZAY, Château de	Noizay	I		260
NOYER, Auberge du	Le Bugue	IV		181
ORANGERS, Les	St Paul de Vence	III		280

HOTEL	TOWN	MAP#		page(s)
OUSTAU BAUMANIÈRE, L'	Les Baux de Provence	III	84	164
PANTHÉON, Résidence du	Paris (5th)	II		130
PARC, Hôtel le	Levernois (Beaune)	II		239
PAVILLON DE LA REINE	Paris (3rd)	II		124
PELISSARIA, Hôtel de la	St Cirq Lapopie	IV	63	273
PÈRE BISE, L'Auberge du	Talloires	III		291
PIC, Hôtel-Restaurant	Valence	III		300
PIGONNET, Hôtel le	Aix en Provence	III	80	148
PLAISANCE, Hôstellerie	St Émilion	IV		275
PLESSIS, Château du	La Jaille-Yvon	I		230
POITEVINIÈRE, Château de la	Avoine (Chinon)	I		159
PONTOT, Résidence Hôtel le	Vézelay	II		306
POSTE ET LION D'OR, Hôtel	Vézelay	II		305
POSTE, Hôtel de la	Beaune	II		170
PRIEURÉ, Auberge du	St André d'Hébertot	I		272
PRIEURÉ, Hôtel le	Ermenonville	II		211
PRIEURÉ, Le	Chenehutte les Tuffeaux	I	43	196
PRIEURÉ, Le	Villeneuve les Avignon	III	83	308
PRIEURÉ SAINT MICHEL, Le	Crouttes	I		207
PROCUREUR, Relais du	Lacoste	III		236
PRUNOY, Château de	Charny	II		192
RÉAUX, Château des	Bourgueil	I		177
RÉGALIDO, La	Fontvieille	III		217
RENAUDIÈRE, Château de la	Neuvy en Champagne	I		262
RÉSERVE, Hôtel la	Beaulieu sur Mer	III	100	167
RIVAGE, Hôtel du	Gien	II		220
ROC, Le Moulin du	Champagnac de Bélair	IV	52	188
ROCHECOURBE, Manoir de	Vezac	IV		304
ROCHE TORIN, Manoir de la	Courtils	I		205
ROCHEVILAINE, Domaine de	Billiers	I	36	173
ROHAN, Hôtel des	Strasbourg	II		290

HOTEL	TOWN	MAP#	page(s)
ROUMÉGOUSE, Château de	Gramat	IV	56 224
ROYAL CHAMPAGNE	Champillon Bellevue	II	190
RUATS, Le Moulin des	Avallon	II	156
SAINT GERMAIN, Le Relais	Paris (6th)	II	133
ST JAMES'S CLUB, The	Paris (16th)	II	138
ST MARTIN, Château	Vence	III	303
SAINT-PAUL, Hotel le	St Paul de Vence	III	281
SAINT SIMON, Hôtel Duc de	Paris (7th)	II	133
STE FOY, Hôtel	Conques	IV	66 203
SALLE, Château de la	Montpinchon	I	25 256
SAN REGIS, Hôtel	Paris (8th)	II	135
SEIGNEURS & LION D'OR	Vence	III	302
SOMBRAL, Auberge du	St Cirq Lapopie	IV	274
STANG, Le Manoir du	La Forêt Fouesnant	I	34 218
TEMPLIERS, Le Moulin des	Avallon	II	157
TI AL-LANNEC	Trébeurden	I	33 294
TONNELLERIE, Hôst. de la	Tavers-Beaugency	I	292
TORTINIÈRE, Dom. de la	Montbazon	I	45 254
TREYNE, Château de la	Lacave	IV	234
TRIGANCE, Château de	Trigance	III	90 298
URBILHAC, Château d'	Lamastre	III	237
VAULT DE LUGNY, Château de	Avallon	II	108 155
VAUX DE CERNAY, Abbaye des	Dampierre-en-Yvelines	II	208
VENDÔME, Hôtel	Paris (1st)	II	123
VERRERIE, Château de la	Aubigny sur Nère	II	153
VERTE CAMPAGNE, La	Trelly	I	295
VEY, Le Moulin du	Clécy le Vey	I	200
VIEUX CASTILLON, Le	Castillon du Gard	III	86 185
VIEUX LOGIS, Le	Trémolat	IV	53 296
VIEUX PÉROUGES, Ost. du	Pérouges	III	114 264

HOTEL	TOWN	MAP#	page(s)
VIEUX PUITS, L'Auberge du	Pont Audemer	I	19 267
VIGNE, Château de la	Pléaux	IV	265
VIGNY, Hotel de	Paris (8th)	II	136
VOÛTE, Château de la	Montoire	I	255

DISCOVERIES FROM OUR READERS

"Discoveries from Our Readers" features places to stay that sound excellent, but which we have not yet had an opportunity to visit. If you have a favorite hideaway that you would be willing to share with other readers, we would love to hear from you. The type of accommodations we feature are those with old world ambiance, special charm, and warmth of welcome. Please send the following information:

1. *Your name, address and telephone number.*

2. *Name, address and telephone number of your discovery.*

3. *Rate for a double room including tax, service and breakfast.*

4. *Brochure or picture (we cannot return material).*

5. *Permission to use an edited version of your description.*

6. *Would you want your name, city, and state included in the book?*

Please send to:

Karen Brown's Country Inn Guides, Post Office Box 70, San Mateo, CA 94401, USA
Telephone (415) 342-5591   Fax (415) 342-9153

Karen Brown's Country Inn Guides

The Most Reliable Series on Charming Places to Stay

KAREN BROWN'S
FRENCH
Country Inns & Itineraries

UPDATED AND REVISED • SIXTH EDITION

KAREN BROWN'S
CALIFORNIA
Country Inns & Itineraries

UPDATED AND REVISED • SECOND EDITION

KAREN BROWN'S
ITALIAN
Country Inns & Itineraries

UPDATED AND REVISED • FOURTH EDITION

KAREN BROWN'S
FRENCH
Country Bed & Breakfasts

UPDATED AND REVISED • SECOND EDITION

KAREN BROWN'S
ENGLISH
Country Bed & Breakfasts

UPDATED AND REVISED • SECOND EDITION

KAREN BROWN'S
GERMAN
Country Inns & Itineraries

UPDATED AND REVISED • THIRD EDITION

KAREN BROWN'S
ITALIAN
Country Bed & Breakfasts

NEW • FIRST EDITION

KAREN BROWN'S
ENGLISH, WELSH & SCOTTISH
Country Hotels & Itineraries

UPDATED AND REVISED • SIXTH EDITION

Order Form

KAREN BROWN'S COUNTRY INN GUIDES

Please ask in your local bookstore for KAREN BROWN'S COUNTRY INN guides.
If the books you want are unavailable, you may order directly from the publisher.

_____ *Austrian Country Inns & Castles (1988 edition) $6.00*
_____ *California Country Inns & Itineraries $14.95*
_____ *English Country Bed & Breakfasts $13.95*
_____ *English, Welsh & Scottish Country Hotels & Itineraries $14.95*
_____ *French Country Bed & Breakfasts $13.95*
_____ *French Country Inns & Itineraries $14.95*
_____ *German Country Inns & Itineraries $14.95*
_____ *Irish Country Inns (1988 edition) $6.00*
_____ *Italian Country Bed & Breakfasts $13.95*
_____ *Italian Country Inns & Itineraries $14.95*
_____ *Portuguese Country Inns & Pousadas $12.95*
_____ *Scandinavian Country Inns & Manors (1987 edition) $6.00*
_____ *Spanish Country Inns & Paradors $12.95*
_____ *Swiss Country Inns & Chalets (1989 edition) $6.00*

Name _____ Street _____
City _____ State _____ Zip _____ tel: _____
Credit Card (Mastercard or Visa) _____ Exp: _____

Add $3.50 for the first book and .50 for each additional book for postage & packing.
California residents add 8.25% sales tax.
Indicate number of copies of each title; send form with check or credit card information to:

KAREN BROWN'S COUNTRY INN GUIDES
Post Office Box 70, San Mateo, California, 94401, U.S.A.
Tel: (415) 342-9117   Fax: (415) 342-9153

Karen Brown's
French Country Bed & Breakfasts

The Choice of the Discriminating Traveller to France

Featuring The Most Charming Bed & Breakfasts

French Country Bed & Breakfasts is the perfect companion guide to Karen Brown's *French Country Inns & Itineraries*. Whereas *French Country Inns & Itineraries* features accommodations with great charm in small hotels and inns, *French Country Bed & Breakfasts* has a hand-picked selection of the choice places to stay in private homes. All the pertinent information is given: description of the accommodation, sketch, price, driving directions, meals served, owner's name, dates open, telephone and fax numbers.

KAREN BROWN'S
FRENCH
Country Bed & Breakfasts

UPDATED AND REVISED • SECOND EDITION

French Country Bed & Breakfasts does not replace *French Country Inns & Itineraries* - together they make the perfect pair for the traveller who wants to enjoy the comparitively low prices offered by travelling the bed & breakfast way. Both feature places to stay with charm, warmth of welcome and old world ambiance: *French Country Bed & Breakfasts* features places to stay in private homes; *French Country Inns & Itineraries* features small hotels and inns PLUS the added bonus of 11 itineraries, handy for use with the bed & breakfast guide. Each book uses the same maps so it is easy to choose a combination of places to stay from each, adding great variety for where to spend the night.

KAREN BROWN wrote her first travel guide on France in 1979. This original guide is now in its 6th edition plus 13 books have been added to the series which has become known as the most personalized, reliable reference library for the discriminating traveller. Although Karen's staff has expanded, she is still involved in the publication of her guide books. Karen, her husband, Rick, their daughter, Alexandra, and son, Richard, live on the coast south of San Francisco at their own country inn, Seal Cove Inn, in Moss Beach, California.

BARBARA TAPP, the talented artist responsible for all of the hotel sketches and delightful illustrations in this guide, was raised in Australia where she studied in Sydney at the School of Interior Design. Although Barbara continues with freelance projects, she devotes much of her time to illustrating Karen's Country Inn guides. Barbara lives in the San Francisco Bay area with her husband, Richard, their two sons, Jonothan and Alexander, and young daughter, Georgia.

JANN POLLARD, the artist responsible for the beautiful painting on the cover of this guide, has studied art since childhood, and is well-known for her outstanding impressionistic-style water colors which she has exhibited in numerous juried shows, winning many awards. Jann travels frequently to Europe (using Karen Brown's guides) where she loves to paint old world architecture. Jann lives in the San Francisco Bay area with her husband, Gene, and two daughters.

SEAL COVE INN - LOCATED IN THE SAN FRANCISCO AREA

Karen (Brown) Herbert is best known as a writer and publisher of the Karen Brown's Country Inn guides, favorites of travellers searching for the most charming country inns throughout Europe and California. Now Karen and her husband, Rick, have put sixteen years of experience into reality and opened their own superb hideaway, Seal Cove Inn. Spectacularly set amongst wildflowers and bordered by towering cypress trees, Seal Cove Inn looks out to the ocean over acres of county park: an oasis where you can enjoy secluded beaches, explore tide-pools, watch frolicking seals, and follow the tree-lined path tracing the windswept ocean bluffs. Country antiques, lovely original watercolors, flower-filled cradles, rich fabrics, and the gentle ticking of grandfather clocks create the perfect ambiance for a foggy day in front of the crackling log fire. Each bedroom is its own private haven with a comfortable sitting area before a wood-burning fireplace and doors opening onto a private patio with views to the distant ocean. Moss beach is a 30-minute drive south of San Francisco, 6 miles north of the picturesque town of Half Moon Bay, and a few minutes from Princeton harbor with its colorful fishing boats and restaurants. Seal Cove Inn makes a perfect base for whale-watching expeditions, salmon-fishing excursions, day trips to San Francisco, exploring the coast, or, best of all, just a romantic interlude by the sea - time to relax and be pampered. Karen and Rick are looking forward to meeting and welcoming you to their own inn.

Seal Cove Inn, 221 Cypress Avenue, Moss Beach, California, 94038, U.S.A.
telephone: (415) 728-7325   fax: (415) 728-4116